PRISONER
OF THE
TURNIP
HEADS

PRISONER
OF THE
TURNIP
HEADS

THE FALL OF HONG KONG AND
IMPRISONMENT BY THE JAPANESE

GEORGE WRIGHT-NOOTH
WITH MARK ADKIN

CASSELL

Cassell Military Paperbacks

Cassell
Wellington House, 125 Strand
London WC2R 0BB
www.cassell.co.uk

First published in Great Britain by Leo Cooper 1994
This paperback edition published in 1999

A CIP catalogue record for this book is available from the British Library

ISBN 0-304-35234-9

Printed by Guernsey Press Ltd.

TO MY DAUGHTER
DEBORAH-JANE

CONTENTS

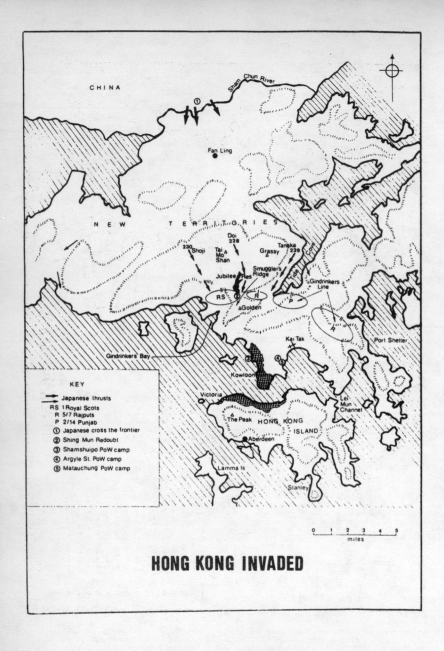

HONG KONG INVADED

HONG KONG ISLAND

KEY

1. Japanese landings
2. Main roads
3. Ammunition launch explodes
4. First Peace Mission rejected
5. Smythe and others recaptured
   Thompson and Priestwood escape
   on junk
6. Military party executed
7. Lt Corrigan kills Japanese officer
8. V-Nicoln attacked by plane
9. Adm Chan Chak's escape route
10. Dead bodies from HMS Thracian
11. W-Nicoln meets Sgt Bedward
12. Euclift massacre
13. Thompson and Priestwood's route
    Tooh: Begg's swim

0 1000 2000 3000
metres

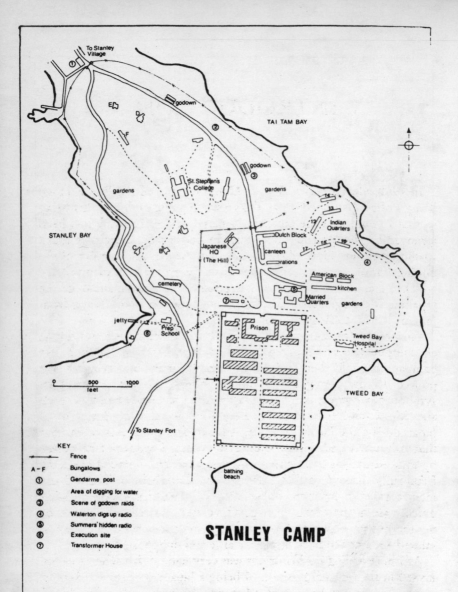

To Stanley Village

godown

TAI TAM BAY

E

F

godown

St. Stephen's College

gardens

gardens

14

13

12

Indian Quarters

STANLEY BAY

Dutch Block

A

Japanese HQ (The Hill)

canteen

15

16

12

18

American Block

rations

kitchen

B

4

cemetery

Married Quarters

gardens

jetty

Prep School

7

5

Prison

Tweed Bay Hospital

500   1000
feet

0

TWEED BAY

To Stanley Fort

bathing beach

KEY

Fence

A – F   Bungalows

① Gendarme post
② Area of digging for water
③ Scene of godown raids
④ Waterton digs up radio
⑤ Summers' hidden radio
⑥ Execution site
⑦ Transformer House

STANLEY CAMP

INTRODUCTION

In 1969 when I was a Deputy Commissioner of the Royal Hong Kong Police, I stopped off at Tokyo when going on leave, this being so that I could visit the Japanese Imperial Palace. The visit had been arranged by the Metropolitan Police in Tokyo with a promise that I would be shown more of the palace than the average member of the public. I took with me on that visit to the palace part of my diary which I had kept when I was a prisoner of the Japanese in the Japanese Military Internment Camp at Stanley in Hong Kong from January, 1942, to August, 1945.

The reason for taking this diary with me on that visit was not at all complicated. It simply gave me great satisfaction. What better companion could there have been than this diary into which I had poured all my thoughts and indeed hopes? My diary was then symbolically completed: it had been to the fountain-head of all those atrocities committed by the Japanese in the name of the Emperor of Japan during the Pacific War 1941–45. Its fruition is this book. But that visit nearly ended in disaster. That evening I was well entertained by some senior Japanese police officers and when I boarded the plane I suddenly discovered that I had left my diary behind. Then to my intense relief a Japanese police officer in uniform came padding quickly along the aisle. He stopped, saluted, bowed and handed to me the brown paper parcel containing my diary. He bowed again, saluted and padded back down the aisle and disappeared.

As I have feeling for history, it was very natural that when I found myself in the unusual position of being a Japanese prisoner I should instinctively want to record what was happening. It was also, I suppose, a psychological defiance of the Japanese. I hardly gave a thought as to what would happen to me if the diary was discovered but I was circumspect at times as to what I wrote in it, leaving it to innuendoes which were clear to me. I also tried to hide it but this was not easy in a very limited space and at the same time have it easily available for use. The best I could do was to hide it where it would not be easily discovered during a superficial search. My main concern was to find enough paper on which to write it. I ended up with a Police Arms and Ammunition Register, two school copy books and numerous pieces of paper of all shapes and sizes and quality. There were altogether 1050 pages not including various notes and also Camp notices and other memorabilia.

I kept this diary every day, with very few exceptions, from 13 February, 1942, until 30 August, 1945. Prior to that I had made notes, about events during the Japanese attack on Hong Kong and when we first became prisoners. It is on those notes and my diary that this book is mainly based. I was also able, because of my knowledge of the events and the names of those concerned, or indirectly concerned, to unearth from the Public Records Office and other sources supporting, and at times more detailed, accounts of those incidents recorded in my diary. It should be appreciated that the views expressed in my diary were those of a young man, but I would hasten to add that over the years I have had, with very few exceptions, no reason to change them. Again, in only very few cases have I changed any names and then only to avoid, if possible, unnecessary sorrow or embarrassment, and only provided that it did not detract from the veracity of this story.

I toyed for many years with writing this book, but, except for making notes and rough drafts, never really got down to it. Then I was lovingly bullied into it by my daughter, Deborah, who felt that what the Japanese did should not be allowed to be forgotten. This was reinforced by many of my young and not so young friends who invariably admitted their ignorance of how the Japanese behaved. "Nobody ever bothered to tell us this!" was the usual horrified comment and more so when they were told about the Japanese eating human flesh – American airmen – during the fighting in the South Pacific.

The story which I have to tell about the Japanese Military Internment Camp at Stanley, Hong Kong, does not pretend to compare with the hell which the Allied prisoners went through on the Siam Railway – "The Death Railway" – and in some of the other prison camps but it is a good example of how the normal Japanese behaved when in control. It also tells of how we coped with what was not exactly a pleasant situation. If it had not been for the members of the Hong Kong Police in that camp who were the backbone of the labour force it would have been in an even more dire state. The conditions in all the Japanese prison camps were appalling.

Here we should not forget the brutal and sadistic treatment handed out by the Japanese to the Chinese and also to those peoples of the South-East Asian countries they overran. So much to be said for the slogan with which the Japanese went to war – "Co-prosperity in Greater East Asia"!

The Chinese and the Japanese are traditional enemies. The Chinese not only hate the Japanese but also despise them. Their nickname for them in the Cantonese dialect is "Law Pak Tau" – Turnip Heads. Hence the title of this book.

George Wright-Nooth,
Hurlingham,
March, 1994

Acknowledgements

First of all I would like to thank Molly Chan, Christine Carter and Jill Bloomfield who at various times were my Secretaries for typing my diary in their spare time. It was, I am sure, no easy task deciphering my writing, particularly when it became minute because my eyesight was failing due to vitamin deficiencies. Fortunately, it fully recovered but not in time to make it easier for them!

I am very grateful to Mr Li Kwan-ha, CBE, QPM, CPM, Commissioner of the Royal Hong Kong Police, and his staff for all the assistance given to me in obtaining additional information required for this book and for some of the photographs which appear in it.

Furthermore, I am greatly indebted to Mike Humphries and Tony Boyd-Smith. They not only listened to my stories about the Japanese prison camp and my forty-one years in Hong Kong, but far more important obtained for me an introduction to Leo Cooper, the publisher.

Leo Cooper was throughout most helpful. This indeed is very much appreciated. I would also like to thank Tom Hartman for his editorial help.

My thanks are also due to Ingrid Hulse, Lois Watson and Alan Hoe for their assistance.

Finally, my partner in this venture, Mark Adkin, who had helped me to put this story together, would like to thank Martin Lewis, a senior Hong Kong civil servant, for his help in providing details of Stanley today.

The material held by the Public Record office is quoted by kind permission of the Controller of Her Majesty's Stationery Office.

CHRISTMAS DAY,
HONG KONG, 1941

"Their bodies were badly mutilated, their ears, tongues, noses and eyes had been cut away from their faces."
The Reverend James Barrett, in evidence at the Tokyo trial of the Japanese involved in the atrocities committed on 25 December, 1941, at St Stephen's College, Stanley.

Nowhere in Hong Kong has seen more blood spilled, more murder, more misery, more suffering and torture than the tiny Stanley Peninsula on the southern side of the island. Today almost every tourist brochure recommends at least a day trip to Stanley, not to see gruesome relics of its past, but rather to sample its natural beauty, bask on its beaches, or browse for bargains in its market. The shops in the narrow lanes offer designer denim, jazzy T-shirts, mohair sweaters, silk and leatherware, hand-painted porcelain and countless other oriental souvenirs.

The Tin Hau Temple, at the top end of Main Street, is dedicated to the Goddess of the Sea and comes alive every April as the centre of the Tin Hau Festival. Inside, an unusual ornament catches the eye – a somewhat moth-eaten-looking tiger skin from an animal shot nearby in 1942. The story of how it was hunted and killed is not recorded, but will feature in this book as one of the more bizarre anecdotes of life when Stanley was the Japanese internment camp for civilian prisoners during their occupation of the colony from 1942-1945.

Stanley is one of Hong Kong's oldest settlements, with its once picturesque fishing village nestling neatly on the sandbar and cliffs that make up the peninsula. A century ago it was notorious for its pirates and smuggling activities (one of the meanings of its name in the Hakka dialect is "Robber's Lair").

At the southern tip is a 500-foot conical hill on whose slopes is situated Fort Stanley. It is off-limits to the casual holidaymaker as it is still occupied by the military – normally one of the British garrison battalions. During the Second World War Japanese Army units were stationed at the Fort and to this day several sightings of a ghost have been claimed in the officers' mess. At rare but regular intervals a Japanese officer, complete with samurai sword, is said to walk slowly down the stairs. The hill itself is a superb spot – breezy, cool and with fine views in all directions. The soldiers' families who are fortunate enough to have quarters there always speak in glowing terms of the location.

But it is the central area, a thin strip of land only some 800 metres in length, bounded in the north by the village and in the south by the Fort, that is the scene for much of this book. This is the place where most of the dreadful events of 1941–1945 occurred. It was the site of desperate close-quarter combat, mass murder, rape, sickening torture and the most brutal multiple excution by beheading perpetrated by the Japanese in the Colony. Three prominent buildings, two of which are still in use for their original purposes, merit a special mention.

The first is Stanley prison. From the outside it looks much as it did fifty years ago, the same imposing high white walls, the same grim gates set back into the wall, and the same peep-hole through which the guard scrutinizes visitors. Now it is Hong Kong's largest maximum security jail housing prisoners under sentence of death (invariably commuted to life imprisonment), long-term inmates, men from the Triads, drug dealers and violent criminals.

The second building, located near the beach less than 200 metres from the prison's NW corner, is now a much happier place. The former Stanley Preparatory School is a thriving community hall operated by the Stanley Sports Association, whose activities take place only a few metres from where thirty-three men knelt pitifully on the sand awaiting the downward swing of the sword that removed (in most cases) their heads from their shoulders.

The last building is St Stephen's College, a private school for the sons and daughters of some of the more affluent Chinese. It has well over a thousand pupils. In late December, 1941, it had been

2

commandeered by the British to use as a hospital during the last few days of resistance to the Japanese assault.

To die violently on the anniversary of Christ's birth seems to many, and certainly to me, to be utterly tragic. When those deaths are the sadistic, mindless murder of helpless men and women who have sought sanctuary in a hospital the perpetrators surely epitomize all that is evil in man's character. God may forgive; I cannot. Nor can I forget.

One of my eventual companions as an internee at Stanley was a soldier. This was unusual as after the British surrender all servicemen were segregated from civilians and imprisoned in Kowloon on the mainland. Stuart "Tooti" Begg was a pre-war businessman who had joined the Hong Kong Volunteer Defence Corps (HKVDC) and risen to the rank of warrant officer. He was to become one of the few survivors of the St Stephen's College atrocity, owing his life to the courage and quick wittedness of his wife. Tragically, she did not live through the ordeal.

On 23 December, 1941, Begg was the senior of a handful of men from his company crouched in a cave at the foot of the cliffs close to Eucliff, a millionaire's mansion a short distance west of the Repulse Bay Hotel. The group was all that was left of the company that had been scattered by the Japanese 229th Regiment under Colonel Tanaka as it thrust south over the spur on the west side of Violet Hill. Several of his men were wounded, and the cave was already occupied by a small party of Canadians from the Royal Rifles of Canada (RRC).

Begg's objective was to rejoin that part of the British forces that he assumed to be falling back towards Stanley – but how? The road route was long, three or four miles, totally exposed, and passing in front of the Repulse Bay Hotel that he suspected was already in Japanese hands. The enemy swarmed over the hills, at least as far as Stanley Mound. An overland route courted disaster. The other option was to swim, to await darkness then strike out across Repulse Bay, possibly rounding the headland on the far side that would give access to West Bay and the Chung Hom Kok peninsula. Surely that would still be in friendly hands.

There was reluctance on the part of the poorer swimmers to follow Begg's suggestion. As they contemplated the next move a fusillade of rifle shots rang out above them, followed by the sound of crashing and thumping as though bodies were falling down the cliffs. They were. Begg and his comrades had just heard the finishing touches of the infamous Eucliff massacre. Then, as the light faded, a lone figure stumbled into the cave, his neck and face a mass of blood. It was Company Sergeant-Major Hanlon of the RRC.

After the war, at the trial of Colonel Tanaka, Hanlon told his story of how his captors had carried out the systematic execution of prisoners in that area. He, with three fellow Canadians, had surrendered near the Eucliff mansion. They were disarmed, beaten with rifle butts and had their hands bound behind their backs. Japanese bayonets prodded them forward to the edge of the cliff where they were forced to sit facing the sea. Hanlon was certain he had but seconds to live.

"We knew we were going to be shot because on top of the bank were pools of blood and at the bottom of the cliff, near the sea, were dozens of dead bodies. It was evident that they had been shot on the top of the cliff and had fallen down. . . . Owing to the fact that I turned my head to the left as I was being fired at, the bullet passed through my neck above the left shoulder and came out at my right cheek. I did not lose consciousness and the force of the bullet hitting me knocked me free of the others and I rolled down the cliff."[1]*

The three others fell on top of him, all dead. Afterwards a British officer compelled to collect the bodies counted fifty-three. At dusk Hanlon, who subsequently described himself as, "Looking like an underdone steak", moved cautiously into the nearby cave.

Most of the group now favoured the swimming option. As one of the Canadians put it, "I'd rather drown than get carved up by those monkeys." Precisely how many followed Begg into the sea will never be known, although the bulk of the uninjured did so. Among those who remained shivering and bleeding in the cave was Hanlon.[2]

As they waded into the water the phosphorescence betrayed them. Japanese above the bay swept the surface with machine-gun fire; some swimmers sank at once, others struggled on only to succumb later to cold and exhaustion. At around 5.00 pm on 24 December

* See Notes, p. 257

4

Begg, with two others, crawled ashore at Stanley after almost twenty-two hours in the water. They were in a state of collapse.[3]

Just to the NW of Stanley village, up on the slope of a hill overlooking the bay, is the Maryknoll Mission. It provided a religious retreat for the Maryknoll Fathers, American medical missionaries who worked throughout southern China. Here they rested and retrained after many months in the field. It was for them what we might today call an R and R centre. With Christmas the mission was crowded with priests, some of whom had but recently arrived from the US. Also among them were men of other denominations who had returned for medical or dental treatment. As the Japanese advance pushed south, so the fighting engulfed the mission. Christmas Eve had seen intense and prolonged firing all around as the remnants of Brigadier Wallis's East Brigade withdrew to the village. For a while the building was a part of the front line.

Shortly after dawn some Japanese broke into the building, ordering all the missionaries to assemble in the front hall. When more troops arrived they began to search for loot. During this period a number of British prisoners of war were brought in and tied up. At about 4.00 pm the priests, who had been herded together all day, were forced to remove their cassocks before being bound together in pairs with wire, and marched down towards the village with the British prisoners. There was still heavy fighting going on with bursts of machine-gun fire coming perilously close. After a short distance the entire group was told to take cover behind the bank of a sunken road. Many of the soldiers realized that their end was near. Within minutes a group of about fifteen of them was led away to be shot. They were the lucky ones.

Later the priests and remaining troops, still tied together, were locked in a garage, where they were to remain without food or water for three days. From time to time a Japanese would appear to taunt them by pouring the contents of his water bottle on the floor. It was while in the garage that the soldiers were singled out for the most sickening tortures. One officer was tied up in such a way that he slowly throttled himself. It was a relief to all when his gasping and gurgling finally ceased. Another man had his tongue cut out, others were blinded.

I recall one of the Fathers who was later interned with us recounting with deep emotion how those wretched men suffered. A favourite game was to untie a soldier, take him outside and surround him with a circle of bayonets before ordering him to run for it. Whether he did or not made no difference – he was speedily and agonizingly impaled. By some quirk of character, or respect for a faith they did not understand, their tormentors allowed the soldiers to kneel before a priest to seek a last blessing; many also blurted out the names and addresses of their families they knew they would never see again. To my knowledge not a single soldier of this party survived, although the missionaries, who felt sure they too were doomed, remained unharmed to tell the tale.

On arrival at Stanley Begg, along with his two companions, were admitted to St Stephen's College, now functioning as a hospital with a large Red Cross flag flapping above the roof. They were given beds in the main ward. The great majority of patients were battle casualties, amputees with bloodied stumps, men with shrapnel and bullet wounds in chests and stomachs, some with faces missing, some with splintered bones and broken heads. Few could leave their beds. Over a hundred wounded from almost every unit that was defending Hong Kong lined the walls. So confused and chaotic had been the fighting on the island that men from Canada, England, Scotland, Rajputana, the Punjab and Hong Kong lay side by side. Infantrymen, engineers, gunners, even prison warders were under treatment in the College that Christmas morning.

The staff consisted of two Royal Army Medical Corps (RAMC) doctors, one British nursing sister and six nurses, all from the Voluntary Aid Detachment (VAD), four Chinese nurses from St John Ambulance Brigade, several Chinese medical orderlies and stretcher-bearers, plus the Canadian padre James Barrett. The commanding officer was Lieutenant-Colonel Black, RAMC, a man in his late sixties who had been a prominent figure in prewar Hong Kong. Doctor Black, a senior member of one of the leading medical partnerships in town, knew most of the influential government officials and businessmen socially as well as professionally. He was not, however, a soldier. His present rank and appointment was due to the exigencies of war. His number two was Captain Whitney, a regular RAMC officer with five years service. By a curious coincidence one of the nurses was Mrs Begg.

As the Japanese pushed south the British defensive positions consolidated across the northern neck of the Stanley peninsula. At its narrowest this was barely 300 metres wide. For the British this was advantageous in that it required fewer men to hold the line, but disadvantageous as it meant enemy fire was concentrated into a small area. By 24 December St Stephen's College hospital, located on rising ground south of the neck, was under fire. Inevitably some defensive positions had to be sited nearby, so, despite the flag, the double-storey college blocks were a tempting target for the Japanese gunners. As Padre Barrett said, "It was not a healthy place, with broken glass and the odd bullet flying around."

Barrett had been unable to sleep on Christmas Eve so before it was light he dressed and went into the main ward:

> "This ward was lit up with two or three hurricane lamps. There was a great deal of confusion. All the sisters were there. Everyone was restless and wondering what was going to happen. Between 5 and 6 am I was preparing to hold Christmas communion when the Japanese entered the hospital by both the north and side entrances. As they came in I saw them bayonet wounded soldiers in bed."[4]

Barrett's calm, courtroom prose fails to convey the true horror of those first few minutes. The elderly Dr Black dashed forward the moment the leading Japanese came in, shouting, "Stop! Stop! This is a hospital; this is a hospital." He was closely followed by Captain Whitney, both determined to protect their patients. They were instantly gunned down at a range of a few feet. As they fell to the floor their bodies were mutilated by multiple bayonet thrusts. The enemy soldiers, some of whom appeared drunk, started on a murderous rampage up and down the ward, rushing to each bed and plunging their bayonets into the bodies of the helpless wounded. The scene almost beggars description. Nevertheless, the shrieks and screams of the dying, the demented yelling of the Japanese, interspersed with violent explosions as some victim was finished off with a rifle shot, failed to bemuse Mrs Begg.

Dragging her husband from his bed she pushed him underneath, crawled in with him and, clinging together they prayed that the holocaust would pass them by. It did; although for Mrs Begg the respite would be fleeting. Suddenly there was a soldier above them; they saw the filthy scuffed boots, sensed the raised rifle, heard the hysterical shout, saw the long blade as it pierced blankets, mattress and springs. Twice it it was jerked free only to come crashing through again as they cringed just beyond its reach. The Japanese moved on to the next bed, but over fifty died in five minutes.

When the frenzy of killing seemed to have abated the Beggs crept out from their hiding place. The Japanese were rounding up survivors. Initially all were packed into a store room where they were searched for money or other valuables. Padre Barrett had his prayer book taken as well. Next, the women were segregated from the men who, numbering about forty, were crammed into an even smaller room. Here there was scarcely space for the wounded to lie down. A second trawl for rings and watches took place, while one Japanese gave out cigarettes, yet another threw a fistful of bullets in their faces. The oriental mind was proving difficult for some of the prisoners to understand.

A short while later things seemed to revert to normal. The door was flung open and two soldiers appeared; they dragged out the nearest man who happened to be a Canadian. From outside a chilling scream was heard; the Japanese returned for another prisoner who, judging from the noise, met a similar fate. When they tried for a third time, however, the door was slammed in their faces so they gave up. Barrett has described what happened next:

"At the request of the men I told the Christmas story and said some prayers. We all thought it was our last Christmas day. Suddenly, the door was thrust open and a Japanese entered and through sign language gave us to understand that Hong Kong had surrendered. He said we were now friends and let us move to a larger room. They also gave us some water."[5]

For Mrs Begg, Mrs Buxton and Mrs Smith the changed attitude came too late. They, with the other British and Chinese nurses, had been handed over to the Japanese soldiery to do with as they pleased. Unspeakable things were done to those terrified women that Christmas morning. One recounted how she had been forced to lie on top of two dead bodies while she was raped by a succession of soldiers. Three of the British nurses died.

On 26 December Begg asked to see his wife. A Japanese officer called him outside where he saw a pile on the ground covered with a coat he recognized as belonging to her. On pulling it off he saw the crumpled, blood-soaked remains of the missing nurses, one of whom had her head practically severed from her body. Sergeant-Major Begg fainted.

That morning Padre Barrett started to organize burial parties, but the Japanese forced him to heap the corpses in one huge pile for a mass cremation. "I cremated one hundred and seventy bodies. Some came from the hospital itself, and the others from the fields surrounding it."[6]

Fifty years on, their remains lie buried in a communal grave in the tiny Stanley military cemetery. A simple headstone fashioned by one of the internees, a self-appointed stonemason, reads:

> "Met their death at St Stephen's on 25 December, 1941
> Col. G.D.R. Black, R.A.M.C.
> Capt. T.N. Whitney, R.A.M.C.
> Mrs. S.D. Begg, V.A.D.
> Mrs. H.D. Buxton, V.A.D.
> Mrs. W.J. Smith, V.A.D.
> and
> many unknown Chinese, Indian, Canadian and British ranks
> of various Units."

CHAPTER ONE

EARLY DAYS

"Commuting daily was not for me. It is soul-destroying."

As the SS *Stratheden* of the P&O Line nosed out of the Suez Canal into the Gulf of Suez I recognized that smell which told me that the Orient was just over the horizon. Behind, the small, whitewashed town of Suez glistened in the searing heat of the sun. Falling away on our port side was the barren Sinai Peninsular and desert where thousands of year before Moses and the children of Israel had wandered for forty years.

The smell is very nearly impossible to describe. It encompasses people, places and exotic foods overlaid with the smell of spices and in China that from the burning of joss sticks. Some people claim that the often not too sophisticated sewage systems to be found there play their part but I am not sure that this is so. All I am sure about is that it is a distinctive and pleasant smell.

The first time that I had actually smelt it was when I was about three years old. I was then on my way to England with my parents from Kenya where I was born in 1917. There my father, an officer in the Royal Engineers and attached to the King's African Rifles, had won a Military Cross. This was in the East African Campaign during the Great War 1914–18. He had been wounded when attempting to blow up a bridge over a river. The other soldier in the small boat with him was killed.

We had now left behind the German U-Boat packs hunting in the Atlantic and also the "Gullie Gullie" men in their dishdosha or jellabiah – long robe – and red tarboosh who had come on board at Port Said. The latter were magicians relying solely on sleight of hand. With the constant cry of "Gullie, Gullie!" they would produce baby chicks from everywhere, anywhere and nowhere, particularly from every orifice of the body, available and not readily available. When it was the latter this would be done with the sly, salacious smile which comes only too easily to the street Arab. Their sideline was "filthy pictures". So was it for every Arab urchin and male between the ship and the then famous Simon Artz's, a fourth rate Harrods and tourist trap. There was the constant whispered, "You want filthy picture?" or "You like . . . my sister? She nice girl", followed by a vivid and lewd description in broken English of her capabilities.

On board were three other police officers, all probationary Assistant Superintendents in the Colonial Police Service but going to the Malayan Police and not, like myself, to the Hong Kong Police. They had not been trained as I had been for one year at the Metropolitan Police College, Hendon – "Lord Trenchard's Young Gentlemen" as those who were there were called in the music halls. The Police College was the first and only genuine attempt to form an officer class or cadre in the British Police Forces. The other attempts since have been compromises. It was abolished in that form by the Labour Government after the Second World War with the result that can be seen today. The Malayan Police trained their own officers. Sadly, only one of those three officers survived the Japanese attack on Malaya and the subsequent occupation.

I stayed at the Gazetted Police Officers' Mess in Singapore for a few days and then took the SS *Conte Verde*, an Italian ship of the Lloyd Trestino Line to Hong Kong. It was there in Singapore that I made my first contact as an adult with the colonial way of life and liked it. It was what I had expected. I had spent part of my youth in Kenya, Antigua and the then British Guiana before being left at school in England. I was right. Commuting was not for me. It *is* soul-destroying.

It was on the afternoon before we reached Hong Kong that I knew that we were nearly there. We started to sail through vast fleets of sailing junks, most of them trawling. It was an awe-inspiring sight of a livelihood at sea spanning thousands of years. It will never be seen again in this modern era. I could not understand why, as we were cautiously moving through the fleets, some of junks went out of their way to cross our bow as near as was possible. This I was told was because they were using the ship to cut off any devil which might be following. I had come across Chinese superstition for the first time. They are, as I was soon to learn, a very superstitious people.

My first sight of Hong Kong after the green of England was a bit of a shock. From the distance it appeared to be barren hills badly scarred with brown earth roads. Later, I discovered that what I thought were roads were fire breaks. The Chinese had a practice of setting fire to the hillsides to get ash to fertilize their paddy fields lying in the valleys below. Nearer, I saw that the hills which were Hong Kong Island and part of the mainland were covered, but not completely, in small trees, shrubs and bushes. The trees had originally been hand-planted. The only big trees were those around the temples and villages – the "fung shui" trees of Chinese superstition – and in private and public gardens or lining the streets.

I was then, on that day in January, 1940, a Probationary Assistant Superintendent of Police and nearly twenty-three years of age. Europe was in the middle of what came to be called the "phoney" war. Although Hitler had already swallowed up the Rhineland, Austria, the Sudetenland, Czechoslovakia and Poland, the Allied forces, in other words the British and French, had scarcely fired a shot. They were content to remain dug in or sheltered in the concrete of the Maginot Line along Germany's western frontiers. There they waited events which, in the summer of 1940, saw the the British Expeditionary Force's desperate scramble for safety from the beaches of Dunkirk, and France brought to her knees with Hitler's armies goose-stepping through Paris.

The war had hit me personally and tragically with the death of my father. My family had been returning to St Lucia in the British West Indies where my father was a senior government official, a retirement post, when the SS *Simon Bolivar*, a neutral Dutch ship on which they were travelling, was struck by a magnetic mine off Felixstowe and sunk. She was the first ship to be hit by a magnetic mine in the war. My father, who was fifty-five, was very badly injured and spent about four hours in mid-November clinging to wreckage in the bitterly cold North Sea. With him was a Chinese doctor friend who did his utmost to help and encourage him in those terrifying circumstances. They were eventually rescued, as were my mother, sister Daphne, and younger brother Peter, but my father never really recovered from his ordeal and injuries. He died some seven months later. It was he who told me of the Chinese doctor's gallantry. It was a sad but promising introduction to the Chinese people who, I was to learn over the years, if they liked you there could be no better friend. They could also be devious enemies. I had left England extremely anxious about my family.

The war had not touched Hong Kong. However, it gave some of the self-important European matrons an excuse to organize frequent balls to collect money for the "Bomber Fund". I think that we donated one or two bombers! The war would not touch Hong Kong for almost another two years, by which time German tanks were on the outskirts of Moscow and most of Europe was occupied. It was only then that the Japanese launched their Pacific offensive to establish their vaunted "Greater East Asia Co-Prosperity Sphere". During all this time Hong Kong continued its peacetime life style but was increasingly concerned with what was happening in China. The Japanese, who had been at war with China since 1931, were becoming more and more belligerent towards the Europeans living there and particularly towards the Americans and English. After all, this was on the doorstep of Hong Kong and not half the world away. The Chinese naturally were even more concerned; their families and native villages in China were involved.

There were a few outward signs of this concern. In 1940/41 most of the British women and children were repatriated, mostly to Australia. Only those women who could prove that they were in essential services were allowed to remain. The result was that this was exploited by those with influence: those who remained later regretted it. This then led to protest meetings being held regularly in one of the larger hotels by the less fortunate husbands. It was also an excuse for a good drink. It was amazing how many of those husbands suddenly discovered that they had "adopted daughters" between eighteen and thirty and even older! "Let me introduce you to my adopted daughter," some middle-aged man would solemnly say, producing a Chinese girl who had obviously come straight out of Wanchai, the well known "red light" district on Hong Kong Island or Temple Street in Kowloon on the mainland. I think that some of them really believed it!

Other signs were the hurried building of pill-box and machine-gun emplacements all around the colony. It was again the good old Maginot Line principle. Anyhow there were far too many to be fully manned by the existing troops. You did not require any military training to realize that many were badly positioned. Large-scale corruption was involved both by government officials and military personnel. When it came to the fighting many of these fortifications proved to be as effective as *papier mâché* against bullets and bombs.

Then there was the frantic rush to build air raid tunnels and other shelters which was followed by the inevitable corruption. The organization responsible for this was the hastily formed Air Raid Precaution Department (A.R.P.). The main protagonist in the enquiry which followed was a retired RAF officer, Wing-Commander Steele-Perkins, who was the Head of the Department. "Mimi" Lau, a Chinese woman, was one of many witnesses. She was anxious to move in the Chinese and European upper social circles and was to become famous locally because of the concrete blocks which were used to build the shelters. These were square with a large hole in the centre and were referred to, and still are, as "Mimi Laus"!

Waiting on the wharf to meet me were Henry Heath, Lance Searle and Colin Luscombe, all Assistant Superintendents who will become part of this story. Very nearly the first thing they asked me was whether I would play for the Police Rugby XV that Saturday. I had been the Captain of the Bedford School 1st XV 1935/36 which was unbeaten by any school that year. I had also played for the English Public Schools XV against the Scottish Public Schools XV and then for the Nottingham 1st XV, so naturally I was delighted. Then I was told that I would be sharing a house with them at No.1 La Salle Road, Kowloon, and that Sgt Riddle would deal with my luggage. He was the square figure going to fat who had been hovering in the background. I was soon to learn that he was one of the founder members of the rugby team which had been recently started in the Police. He and Sir Atholl MacGregor, the Chief Justice, who was irreverently referred to as Sir "Alcohol", were, despite the vast difference in their social and official positions, good friends, their mutual interest being rugby and drinking, maybe in that order. As for living in Kowloon, in those days there was a saying, "Are you married or do you live in Kowloon?"

I barely had time to dump my bags before I was dragged off to start my introduction to Hong Kong's bachelor life. First of all I was taken to the Hong Kong Hotel which I suppose in those days just had an edge on the Peninsula Hotel as to which was the most fashionable in the colony. The Peninsula was in Kowloon! The Hong Kong Hotel was commonly known as the "Grips" but I have never been able to discover why. Certainly it had the best men's bar in town known as Bessy's Bar. It was named after a famous Chinese barman who had run the bar for many years. Having introduced me to one of the centres of social activity in Hong Kong, they then decided to show me another side of it which only a few Europeans ever saw. They were going to take me to the Toi Chung at West Point on Hong Kong Island. The Toi Chung was one of several Chinese millionaire clubs in that area. Not all of the members were millionaires but they were wealthy and certainly important among the Chinese community. These clubs were not open to Europeans. They only went there on invitation and only a privileged few ever got inside. West Point or Western District, known in Cantonese as Sai Ying Poon – Western soldiers camp – was the area where the British landed in Hong Kong when they occupied it in 1841. It was a traditionally Chinese area and has remained so to this day, but few, if any of the wealthy Chinese lived there.

We climbed a narrow, dimly lit stairway to a well lit, garishly painted door. The bell was rung, the peep-door opened a crack and something said in a language which I could not understand. We were let in and immediately given a hot towel with which to clean our hands. Around a table in a room furnished with lovely, blackwood furniture sat a number of Chinese playing poker. Some wore long Chinese gowns, others European clothes. Behind most of them stood fairly good looking but skinny Chinese girls with just the hint of breasts – the custom of binding breasts had only ceased in recent years. They were there to serve drinks to "their man", brandy being usually the favourite. They were there to serve all his needs! When he won he would usually give her a share of the winnings.

These girls were some of the "West Point girls", high class call-girls for wealthy Chinese who were finished if they ever consorted with Europeans. They were dressed in a "cheongsam" – the dress usually then worn by the Chinese middle and upper class women. It is a long, straight, closely clinging dress, its cut being judged solely by the way the high-standing collar had been made. The style only varied with the length of the slit at the side of the dress. It is a dress which only the Chinese women with their flat bottoms can wear: it can look elegant on a Chinese woman and ridiculous and ugly on a European woman. I knew then that if this was all that could be produced for the very wealthy Chinese, then Chinese women would never physically attract me.

Other Chinese men were watching the game of poker. The room was full of cigarette and cigar smoke. Every now and again there was an outburst of suppressed excitement. The so-called inscrutable Chinese was enjoying himself: he is, after all, human. The Chinese are, in fact, as emotional and excitable as any other race. Their physiognomy is such that they do not instinctively show their feelings, often expressed through their eyes. Among those watching was Tso Tsun-on, known to all as "T.O". His father was the first Hong Kong Chinese to be educated at an English Public School – Cheltenham. Later, as well as being a well known solicitor, he founded the Police Reserve of which he was the Commandant. During the war "T.O" was a captain in the army in India. He was to follow his father and much later become the Commandant of the Police Reserve, later the Auxiliary Police. I am sure that it was "T.O" who had invited us to his club. Many years later I often used to meet "Honky" Kwan there, the father of the actress Nancy Kwan of *The Life of Suzy Wong*. He too had been educated at Cheltenham. He was more British than the British. Yet, despite this he never wore European clothes, favouring a Chinese gown.

Later we sat down to an excellent Chinese meal. This had been a good introduction to the Chinese. There is nothing like starting at the top.

We were back home early because I had to meet the Commissioner of Police the next morning. The Commissioner, in short CP, was Thomas Henry King, known to all as "Thomas Henry". At the entrance to his office was a large mounted head of a tiger which had been shot by the police some time earlier in the century after killing several villagers and an Indian constable. The office had been built in the grand and spacious style of the Victorian colonial era. Everything in it shone: the large nearly empty desk; the two brass blades of the motionless fan suspended from the high ceiling above it and the constantly polished dark-stained teakwood floor. In the corner were a pair of long, black fireman's boots and a brass fireman's helmet. They too were shining.

"Thomas Henry" was tall and thin and looked more like a

missionary than a police officer. His passion in life was not the Bible but cricket. His other passion was being the Chief of the Fire Services. Sensibly, he was the last police officer to hold that position. Unfortunately, I had not been warned about his obsession with cricket. He looked me over in silence for a few moments and then said, "Well, Wright-Nooth do you play cricket?" Innocently, I replied, "Yes, Sir, but I'm not very good at it. I only played in the school 2nd XI". Then I jumped into it with two feet. "Rugby is my game, Sir. I'm far more interested in it and I would like to play it here." His interest in me completely evaporated and I was quickly passed back to his personal assistant. The fact that I had been the first Hong Kong police officer to be trained at the Metropolitan Police College at Hendon instead of by the Royal Ulster Constabulary for only three months, and that it had cost the Hong Kong Government several thousand pounds, was of no consequence. What was more important was that rugby and cricket are played in the same season in Hong Kong and I had chosen the wrong game.

This had obviously not been a good start to my career and a few days later I was not to improve on it. To my surprise, I received an invitation to tennis at the Commissioner's residence on "The Peak" and looked forward to it. "Thomas Henry" had two daughters, one being fairly attractive. I thought that it had been a pleasant afternoon and that it had gone off well, that was until the next day when I received a parcel, delivered by hand, from "Thomas Henry's" wife. It contained a curt note and a pair of washed and ironed underpants. They were a pair which I had changed out of and left behind after playing tennis. To me it had been merely a careless gaffe of little importance but it did teach me to be wary of the Hong Kong social matron. Maybe, it was just as well that a few months later "Thomas Henry" went on retirement. The better looking of the daughters later married an army officer.

The Personal Assistant to whom "Thomas Henry" handed me over was a Superintendent of Police. I had hoped that after my dismal "sports meeting" with the Commissioner I would now be given a comprehensive professional briefing and that, at least, some interest would be shown about my training at the Metropolitan Police College. I was to be disappointed. It was certainly a briefing but on how to behave. I was to learn there and then that he was an inveterate snob and soon afterwards that he was a real "Walter

Mitty". His first priority, as if his life depended on it, was to ensure that I called on all the right people.

Looking at me like a predatory eagle with his long beaky nose, Smythe said,

"You have to sign the Visitors' Books and leave your card." I smiled, already knowing the form as I had often heard my parents talk about it. Smythe, however, must have thought that I looked perplexed so he continued.

"The Governor, the Colonial Secretary, the Chief Justice and the GOC British Forces. They are your top priority. They all have books which must be signed within the next few days. The Governor's must, of course, be signed today."

Puzzled, I asked,

"Where are they?"

Only too eager to feel important, he replied,

"Don't worry. I'll give you a list of the names and addresses and a car will take you to GH, you know, Government House. You'll have to find you own way to the others."

The list seemed ludicrously long. The majority were senior government officials on whom I was expected to leave my card so that I would eventually appear on their guest list to be invited to tea, lunch or dinner to be vetted, particularly if they had a young daughter on the marriage market. Tea I knew from previous experience was sheer purgatory and to be avoided.

I had already had my embossed visiting cards printed before arriving in Hong Kong and had brought the plate with me. There was nothing which he could teach me on that subject. I am sure that he would have loved to have said, "My dear Wright-Nooth, you cannot leave cards with unembossed lettering." This was not the first time I had left cards so I was careful to avoid meeting anyone when I arrived at the house. Fortunately, there was usually a post box at the gate.

Then having explained what he thought were my social duties, he launched into a long lecture on the dangers of sex with Chinese and other non-European women. He pointed out the danger of having a Chinese girlfriend, often referred to when learning Chinese as a "sleeping dictionary" and repeatedly emphasized that, in my position, if ever I was foolish enough to marry a Chinese, I would be called on to resign. He also warned me about being seen out on my own with a Chinese girl. This would be a black mark and lessen my opportunities of going out with the European girls who were much in demand. I did not bother to point out that from what I had seen so far of Chinese women this would be highly unlikely. I was later to meet many charming, intelligent and good-looking Chinese women who could grace any situation, but my basic feelings about them did not change. They simply did not attract me physically. What Smythe had said was sense. Take on a Chinese girl and you take on her family. They would always be around asking for favours; Chinese families can be very large. It was a situation of which Government were alway very conscious. The long-established businesses and banks were maybe not quite so inflexible but did not like it.

Racialism, which was rampant in those days, played a large part in that attitude. Even then, with any thought, it was hard where the Chinese were concerned to reconcile this posture with the fact that when we British were running around painted with woad and living in caves, the Chinese were already steeped in culture.

The European matrons and their daughters also played their part in fostering this attitude. They were strongly opposed to any such liaison: the former had to keep the marriage market as wide open as possible for their daughters; while the latter preferred not to knowingly have husbands who were orientally shop-soiled. The matrons were also very conscious of the strong competition from the "fishing fleet". They were girls sent from England to stay with friends and relatives to broaden their minds with travel but primarily to find husbands. The course which the "fishing fleet" charted was Egypt for the Guards officers and the Sudan Civil Service; India for the armed services, the Indian Civil Service and police and maybe the odd European merchant – then in India called by the armed services "box wallahs" – or tea planter; and finally Malaya and Hong Kong with the same catch in mind. By the time the fleet had crossed the various oceans, a very battleworn group arrived in Hong Kong. What icing there was at the outset had already been removed from the cake, but it was still cake and competition.

The upper class and wealthy Chinese were just as protective and fussy about their daughters. If they mixed with European men on their own, their chances of making a good Chinese marriage were negligible.

The result of all this: European men were seldom seen out with Chinese women unless accompanied by other Chinese. If they had Chinese girlfriends, they were invariably from the lower-class Chinese. They were also kept out of sight in some small apartment, usually in Kowloon and only visited at night. Whatever was the arrangement, they were kept well away from the European women. As I have already mentioned, this changed when the European women and children were evacuated from the Colony.

I was to learn most of this later. Smythe's lecture was based on, "It's just not done, old boy, to have a Chinese woman". Then, as if he had suddenly remembered, he started to make arrangements for my two years' study of the Cantonese dialect. There would be an examination every six months upon which my confirmation and promotion would depend.

As I left, Smythe reminded me of the importance of signing the Visitors' Books as soon as possible. He then most likely returned to designing himself a new uniform. He had a private pilot's licence and felt that he should be allowed to wear wings on his uniform tunic and, because he was a staff officer, black field boots. He got nowhere with it. I left Police Headquarters not very impressed.

The house which I shared with Henry Heath, Lance Searle, Colin Luscombe and Charles Drage in Kowloon on the mainland opposite Hong Kong Island was very modern, yet had the high ceilings of the older type of house. It is still there today, not looking at all out of place among the high-rise buildings.

We lived in complete luxury, surrounded by a bevy of servants. There was the No.1 boy, Fu King, who had been a steward in the Royal Navy. He was to re-join the navy after he escaped from Hong Kong during the Japanese Occupation. He was to prove absolutely loyal to the British and also to us personally in the dangerous days ahead. Then there was a No.2 boy, a cook boy, a wash amah and her "makee learn" to assist her, and the "Fa Wong" – "the king of the flowers" or in other words the gardener. We hardly lifted a finger. Their total monthly wages were less than £6 in the then sterling rate. We also often gave them a sack of rice of 240 lbs which cost just a little over £1. There was also what I considered the real height of luxury. One could employ a barber on a monthly basis for about £1 which included one hair cut a month and a shave every morning in bed whether asleep or awake. Being new and suspicious,

I decided not to avail myself of this offer. He used a "cut-throat" razor.

Later when Henry went on long leave prior to going to India to learn Urdu, we were joined by "Wu" Huston. He was an officer in the Administrative Service – the service from which governors were usually chosen – and a "Senior Wrangler" at Cambridge. "Wu" was a brilliant, erratic Irishman who was probably wasted on the Hong Kong Government. At the time he was serving as a magistrate in Kowloon. He was later to die of malnutrition in the Japanese prison camp at Shamshuipo.

Charles Drage was not a policeman. Officially he was the commercial adviser to the government and had offices in the Head Office of the HongKong and Shanghai Bank. But many of us knew that he was the head of MI6 in South China. He was, believe it or not, responsible to a man called Steptoe in Shanghai. Charles Drage had been a midshipman at the infamous Gallipoli landings in the Dardanelles in World War I. He was a man in his early forties who had retired from the Royal Navy as a commander. After World War 2 he wrote several books about famous personalities in China, some of whom will feature briefly in this book.

I vividly recall the ritual when Charles Drage had his first gin in the evening. After a bath and a change of clothes he would slump down in the most comfortable of our armchairs. Then his personal "boy", who looked more like a pirate, would enter with a tray on which was a bottle of Plymouth Gin, several squashed fresh limes, a silver bucket full of ice and, most prominent of all, a pint glass. The "Pirate" would fill a third of the glass with gin, followed by fresh lime and topped to the brim with ice, which he would stir gently. Charles would then take a large swig and settle down to his homework. This entailed reading the newspapers and snipping out articles of interest. These, we were convinced, formed the basis of his intelligence reports to the government. Whatever his sources, he anticipated by a few months the Japanese attack on Hong Kong. When he said goodbye to us before leaving hurriedly on a cruiser for Singapore we were more concerned that he settled his household bills before he left.

Charles Drage's boy, the "Pirate" as he soon came to be called, was a Cantonese, as against our boys who were from the Province of Shantung in North China. They were bigger men who spoke a completely different dialect and whose staple diet was wheat and not rice. They are more open and direct and less devious than the Cantonese who are intelligent, quick-witted, and hard-working, shrewd traders and excellent businessmen. The majority of Chinese one sees overseas are Cantonese. Our boys wore white jackets buttoned up to the neck and black trousers over Chinese black slippers. The "Pirate", being a Cantonese wore a long white gown over white socks in Chinese black slippers. Despite all those differences, they appeared to get on well.

During my first year in Hong Kong I did not wear uniform and did not do any police duties. This was because I was a full time student of Chinese learning the Cantonese dialect and to write Chinese. Cantonese is spoken in Hong Kong and in the adjacent Province of Kwangtung where about 40 million Chinese spoke it. Mandarin is the official language of China but then and now it is not spoken throughout China. It is the national language only in name. Basically each province has its own dialect. The only language which is understood in the whole of China is the written language, the characters, but the problem is that not all can read and write it.

Until 1938, when the Japanese captured Canton, Administrative Service Officers and police officers from Malaya and Singapore as well as Hong Kong were sent to study Cantonese in that city. Canton is the capital of the Province of Kwangtung and one of the largest cities in the world. Just before the Japanese entered Canton these language students, who were known as government cadets, left for Macau, the small Portuguese colony only forty miles from Hong Kong. With them also went a few of the Chinese girls on their payroll!

Macau was the oldest European settlement in the Far East, the Portuguese taking possession of it in the sixteenth century soon after the *Mayflower* arrived in America. It is only a few miles long and wide and was then a quiet, dopey place where the only real activity was legalized gambling. This was like a magnet to the Chinese in Hong Kong who flooded there in their thousands every weekend. The population consisted mainly of Chinese and Mecanese, a corruption of Macau/Chinese, who were a mixture of Portuguese and Chinese. There were very few pure Portuguese. There was also a small community of Indians who were shopkeepers and supplied the local watchmen. The Portuguese and Mecanese women were on the whole better looking than the Chinese but ran to seed at an early age. Most of them were heavily chaperoned, usually by highly suspicious brothers, as the cadets were soon to learn.

The untrammelled freedom of the government language cadets was to end soon after the outbreak of the war in Europe. No longer could those who wished to do so openly keep Chinese girls in their quarters without comment. One night a fight broke out in the bar of the select Macau Club between the cadets and some Germans who had moved from Hong Kong to Macau to avoid internment. The Portuguese, our "oldest allies" but then neutral, were embarrassed and so was the Hong Kong Government. The cadets were hastily moved back to Hong Kong. This was shortly before I appeared on the scene.

There the cadets settled in the ex-German Consul-General's house, he by then being back in Germany with his staff. It was an old style house with high ceilings. The verandahs and the exterior wall were semi-faced with green porcelain tiles. The balustrade of the ground floor verandah was supported by green bamboo-shaped porcelain pillars. Years later my wife Frances and I used the same idea for our retirement house in Italy. The house faced south looking over Lamma Island to the South China Sea. It was there that I went every day to learn Chinese. Often between lessons I used to swim from the rocks below the house. That idyllic scene did not always remain so. During the Japanese Occupation Starlight Villa, as the house was called, was the scene of murder, torture and other atrocities by the Japanese. It was said to be haunted and lay derelict for over forty years.

Chinese, whatever the dialect, is probably one of the most difficult languages in the world to learn. Not only is it tonal but it is monosyllabic and lacks grammar, there being only a few basic rules. If you are tone deaf you will never be able to speak Chinese even passably well. We had to speak, read and write it, at least to the standard of being able to understand articles in a basic vernacular newspaper. On an average we needed to do six hours of study daily. The first hurdle was to learn the tones – nine in Cantonese. This involved incredibly monotonous repetition, hour after hour, day after day for several weeks. This method, which was the one used in the Chinese schools at the time, has fortunately now been refined. There were no formal classes, each cadet being instructed on a one to one basis. We could also, within reason, choose when we wished to study. Some of the cadets did not like getting up early!

I well remember the first day I arrived at Starlight Villa to learn Chinese. It was not very much removed from being in the last year at school. The senior cadets decided what teachers you would have and usually the best were grabbed by the more senior. Here I was fortunate in being allocated Tsui Chi-ming and "Young" Lau, whose father was also a teacher. I cannot recall whether it was Bob Thompson, later Sir Robert, one of the world's leading experts on subversive warfare, or Eddie Teesdale, an Oxford athletic Blue and English International miler and half-miler who later won the Military Cross and became the Colonial Secretary, Hong Kong, or Ronnie Holmes, later Sir Ronald, another Colonial Secretary in Hong Kong and holder of the Military Cross, who allocated the teachers, but it was fair.

Tsui Chi-ming was my first teacher. He was an ascetic looking man, slim with a thin face; he always wore a long silk gown with Chinese black slippers. He invariably carried a fan which he used vigorously in the hot weather. He was a wonderful, old-world Chinese gentleman who looked as if he had stepped straight from a child's story book of ancient China. I did not know whether to shake hands or what to do. I shook hands which was correct and ever since I have been shaking hands. It is very much a Chinese custom. He said something which I knew must be Cantonese, closed his fan, sat down and pointed with it at an open book on the table. Then began the agonizing several weeks of learning tones. It was a relief when now and again he pointed, again with his fan, at some picture with Chinese characters and made a noise which I had to repeat. He was a truly courteous Chinese of the old school with whom I never spoke one word of English during the many years I knew him. I never did know if he could speak English.

"Young" Lau was one of the new style of teachers. He wore European clothes and spoke English well but only when it was necessary. English was not encouraged. It was Tsui who drove the tones into me and Lau who disentangled my difficulties. They were complementary to each other, a good team.

There are many amusing stories told over the years about those cadets who had Chinese, let's call them girlfriends. The wise ones did not get involved. It was treated as a matter of temporary expediency. There was "Poo" who lost touch with her boyfriend when he left Canton. Then one day when in Hong Kong she happened to recognize his pyjamas hanging on a washing line. Fortunately, the quick thinking of his "boy" prevented a confrontation with the officer's new wife. Another officer paid his ex-girlfriend maintenance for months to support what he thought was their child only to discover subsequently that she had hired the baby. And so it went on.

The cadets, when they returned from learning Chinese in Canton or Macau, were regarded with suspicion by the European mothers and their daughters. They had heard vivid stories about their disgusting behaviour; VD must surely be around the corner. As I had not been to either place, I suppose that I was in the clear. On my side the field was limited and the competition great but I was not desperate. A party was not considered a failure because the girl one was after had not leapt into bed with one. We were not yet in the grip of the psychologists. As far as we knew we were normal young men. We took it as we found it. There was, anyhow, always Rosalie Lewis' place or some other such place.

Prior to 1931 there were both European and Chinese licensed brothels in Hong Kong. Then at midnight on 31 December, 1931, they were abolished. This was the result of the efforts of the then famous Lady Astor, MP. When she had visited the colony earlier she had discovered to her amazement that it was full of licensed brothels and was encouraged to take action against them by Lady Clementi, the Governor's wife. Lady Clementi had already, with other Chinese and European women, been clamouring for their closure. It is said that Clementi, a brilliant Chinese scholar, used to leave Government House late at night dressed in Chinese clothes to visit his favourite Chinese brothel. Shortly after the European brothels had been closed down advertisements began appearing in the English newspapers. They stated that a black pussy cat had been lost and if the finder would return it to such and such an address the finder would be suitably rewarded. It was signed by some of the girls. They were back in business. There were smiles in the Hong Kong Club, Navy wardrooms and army officers' messes. Rosalie Lewis was one of those girls. She was still running an unofficial European brothel when I arrived in Hong Kong.

It was the custom in the Far East in those days and even now where possible to sign "chits" rather than pay cash. The bills would be settled at the end of the month. When a person, say in a club, regularly avoided paying his round of drinks he was said to be "pencil shy". On this hangs a story.

Ethel Morrison was, before 1931, the "madam" of the largest brothel in Lyndhurst Terrace which was reserved for licensed European brothels. She was an American who had worked her way by various contortions to Hong Kong, via Honolulu and Shanghai. Now well into her forties, a well preserved and good looking woman, she was the most famous "madam" on the China Coast. Ethel liked to regard herself as the playing manager of a team.

The European brothels were run in a very civilised manner. There was nothing crude or bawdy about them. There was a lounge with a bar where you could buy drinks – expensive – and mix with the girls. They could be a mixture of Americans, British, French, White Russians, Hungarians and Italians and so on – a willing United Nations! You did not have to take any of them to bed. You could just call in for a drink. If you did take any of the girls to bed there was a very definite procedure. Each girl had a register in which you had to record your name and the date. It did not have to be your correct name. Julius Caesar, Hitler or Mussolini were good enough so long as you remembered the name. The reason was simple. If you caught VD, then the girl could be traced and removed from the brothel should this be necessary.

Then there was the payment. This was governed by convention rather than rules. Cash was considered vulgar and if you paid by cheque you were just a fool. You were expected to sign a chit, I suppose for "services rendered". Then at the end of each month a sleazy looking Chinese would slide furtively into your office and present you with an envelope. It would contain your chits which you were expected to settle there and then. The Chinese staff knew exactly where the man came from and so he was not questioned. If you had no office the transaction was a bit more awkward. One thing our Chinese friend never did was to go to your house.

There was a young man – a "junior" he would be called – working in one of the old, well established business houses or "Hongs", whom I will call Fortesque. He was a frequent and regular visitor to Ethel's and the girls liked him. He also without hesitation signed the

27

chits and with equal readiness failed to settle them each month. This did not please Ethel who warned him, pointing out that it was a debt of honour. Fortesque continued. Then one night Ethel gave him a final warning with, "I'll fix you if you don't pay". Confidently, Fortesque ignored her.

Ethel attended the morning service at St John's Cathedral every Sunday much to the consternation of many of her clients. They lived in fear that she would catch their eye or, even more dreadful, openly acknowledge that she knew them. She always sat in the same pew which was assiduously avoided by the others. Then one morning the day of reckoning came. When the offering plate – a nice piece of silver presented by one of the "Hongs" – was passed to her, she made the most of rummaging in her handbag to draw attention. Then she fished from it, to the utter horror of some of her clients, a large bundle of chits which with much show she placed on the plate. They were Fortesque's chits. In the vestry the bishop, dean and verger had no difficulty in indentifying them. They were delivered next day to Fortesque's "Taipan". Fortesque settled at once and was on the next boat to the Philippines.

When I arrived in Hong Kong in those early days of January,1940, it was a beautiful backwater on the coast of South China, far removed from the pulsating concrete jungle of today. It was only really known for its magnificent landlocked harbour, one of the largest in the world. Its main business was an entrepôt trade with China. Some four days' sailing further north up the coast was Shanghai, a famous cosmopolitan city and port. Both the Chinese and Europeans living there considered Hong Kong very suburban. When the Communists entered Shanghai after the war the European and Chinese industrialists moved to Hong Kong, playing a large part in the writing of the success story of the modern Hong Kong.

Like Gaul, Hong Kong is divided into three parts. Hong Kong, a mere eleven miles long by two to five wide, was occupied by the British in 1841. Within twenty years it had added the second part, a tiny peninsula across the water to the north of the island. These two are owned outright by Britain and theoretically do not have to be handed back to China in 1997 with the third part – the New Territories. This is an area of hinterland stretching back some twenty miles to the present Anglo-Chinese border. It was leased to Britain under the Treaty of Peking in 1898 for one hundred years. Although they are the commercial heart and head of the colony, Kowloon and the island cannot survive without the body – the New Territories. Fresh water is but one example of this dependency.

Hong Kong, before it was occupied by the British, was inhabited by a small fishing population. It was also a favourite haunt for pirates. Its magnificent natural harbour was first used by the British navy during the Opium War of 1839–42 and as a base for troops. It was then that its commercial and strategic importance was recognized, resulting in it being permanently occupied. This ownership was confirmed by the Treaty of Nanking in 1842. It is interesting to note that it was opium that first brought the British to the island and that for virtually a hundred years the Hong Kong Government had a monopoly of the sale of opium for use in the Colony. Up to the time I arrived it used to be sold from various centres in small silver tubes like oil paint tubes. It was only legal to buy the drug for personal use. If two or more gathered together to smoke it, then the place became an opium divan and illegal. This hypocrisy ended only a few months before the Japanese attacked the Colony.

In 1940 about 700,000 of the 1.7 million in Hong Kong lived on the island. Of these 14,000 were Europeans which included a sizeable minority of Portuguese, the only Europeans who were really indigenous to Hong Kong. There were also some 7500 Indians of various sects. The remainder were Chinese. The total population today is about 7 million. Then virtually all the top positions in government, banking, business and commerce were filled by Europeans. There was a strict observance of status and seniority; the Colony was layered deep in snobbery. The Chinese were also acutely class conscious. There was an almost unbridgeable gap between the upper and lower social levels, all based on position. From what I had experienced this was probably typical of most of the colonies, but in Hong Kong there was one agreeable difference: the Europeans did mix more with the Chinese.

A fairly high percentage of the British community were the Scots and the Irish. The former were particularly prevalent amongst the first seamen and traders of the China coast and many of them had red hair. Hence one of the Cantonese words for a European is "Hung Kwai" – red devil. The other is "Fan Kwai" – foreign devil – and the most common is the slang "Kwai Lo" – old devil or devil which has derogatory implications.

The Scots provided many of the foremen in the two large dock-yards – the largest in the Far East – and also in similar positions in other organizations. In the social clime of Hong Kong it was not unusual to hear them being referred to as "Scotch coolies", a term commonly used for any Scot who was not liked. On the other hand at the top end of the business echelon and in the accountancy world, there were many very shrewd and competent Scotsmen who were very much in control. Jardines is a good example. The Irish were everywhere and predominant in the Colonial Legal Service which was often called the "Irish Legal Service".

The Peak, 1200 feet or so above sea level on the island, was where most people aspired to live, not only because it was cooler but also because it was the "right" place to live. Then it was reserved exclusively for Europeans. No Chinese were allowed to live there unless working as a servant or even visit there other than delivering goods or having been invited. But there was one exception. He was Sir Robert Ho Tung who was said to be the illegitimate son of a Jardine "Taipan", his mother being an amah in the household. It is also said that in his dotage he was breast fed. Whatever the exact truth, he had dined with most of the Crowned Heads in Europe. I personally found from experience that The Peak was a much over-rated place. It was covered in mist for three months of the year and in the days before air-conditioning everything became damp and mildew was a great enemy. Often one had to telephone one's office down below to find out what the weather was like.

The big five of Hong Kong in the thirties remain but now have innumerable rivals for power and prestige. There was naturally the government, then the Hongkong and Shanghai Bank whose chairman had reputedly as much authority and influence as the governor on the Colony's prosperity, Jardine and Matheson which thought that they were Hong Kong, Butterfield and Swire which was much respected by the Chinese, and the Royal Hong Kong Jockey Club which the Chinese, being inveterate gamblers, were sure was Hong Kong.

The Hongkong and Shanghai Bank is not a government bank but does most of its business and issues its own bank notes. Its building in those days was regarded with great awe. Outside stand two huge bronze lions which the Chinese rub as they go past for luck or wealth. The Japanese took over this building as their headquarters during the occupation. Today, the new building looks as if it has been built with a Meccano set. The two bronze lions still stand there.

Jardines is one of the oldest trading companies in the Colony, having been started somewhere near the beginning of the last century by a doctor and an officer, both lowland Scots, on an East India Company ship trading between India and the China coast. In the early days it prospered on trading in opium. As it grew it assumed a pretentious aura of superiority, many of its staff really believing that they were the cream of the commercial society. This attitude still lingers on. There actually was, and maybe still is, a member of staff employed specifically to watch the image of the company. The correct letter headings, the doormen and messengers smart and in the appropriate uniform and the "juniors" properly dressed when coming to office were some of his tasks. The Cross of St Andrew forms part of its house flag. It is probably best known for the "noonday gun" of Noel Coward's "Mad dogs and Englishmen. . . .". Sometime in the last century when the Jardine's "Taipan" was returning from leave he was greeted with a twenty-one gun salute, to which only the governor was entitled. As a penalty Jardines, from then on, had to fire their gun at midday. On New Year's Eve they fire it at midnight, this being an excuse for an enormous party. To be invited to it is regarded by many as nearly as important as attending a Royal Garden Party.

Butterfield and Swire was also an old trading company which was far less ostentatious than Jardines. In addition it went in for shipping. Now, known simply as Butterfield, it is the owner of the Cathay Pacific Airline. It was always well liked by the Chinese.

The Royal Hong Kong Jockey Club had the monopoly of horse racing and now also of off-course betting. It pays a percentage of its takings to the government and also by law must donate to charity. Its donations far exceed that laid down by law. It is popular with the Chinese. Like racing everywhere the trainers and the jockeys play it very close to the chest. A waiter – or "foki" as they are called – in a Chinese teahouse is more likely to know what might win. He is probably a friend of one of the "mafoos" – stable hands. I worked for the Club for some years after I retired from the Police and until then never knew that I had so many Chinese friends.

Other old establishments, not perhaps in the same league as those five but still very much part of Hong Kong life, were the big hotels such as the Hong Kong, Peninsula and the Repulse Bay – the last to be the scene of fierce fighting and close to the start of "Tooti" Begg's adventure already described. When I arrived, if a whisky was ordered or, for that matter, a gin, a full bottle would be placed on the table and later you would be charged in accordance with what you had drunk. There were also strict rules about dress. I remember on one occasion when in uniform going with two other officers to the Hong Kong Hotel for lunch. As we were wearing shorts which was part of our uniform, rather than turn us away we were placed discreetly in a corner and a screen placed around us. Those were the days when managers and assistant managers and head chefs were Europeans but not necessarily British. They could be French or Italians or White Russians. Those were also the days when not everyone had cars and taxis were not easily available; when public transport was predominantly dependent on trams and buses and rickshaws and even sedan chairs, particularly where there were only paths. Things are vastly different now and in many ways vastly better but selfishly not always in that subtle quality of life. We were spoilt.

Having given the reader something of the flavour of Hong Kong when I arrived, and the sort of reception I received, I believe it would make for a better understanding of wartime events in the Colony in which I was involved if I devoted the second part to the lead up to the Japanese invasion. I will cover briefly the Japanese attack on China, the composition of the Hong Kong Police and the last-minute preparations made once it was apparent that the attack was inevitable.

It should first of all be appreciated that the Chinese and the Japanese are traditional enemies. The Chinese not only hate the Japanese but also despise them and, being masters at giving nicknames, it is not surprising that they call the Japanese "turnip heads" – *law pak tau* in the Cantonese dialect. The Japanese head does remind one of a turnip. There was fighting between them for years before I arrived in Hong Kong and, of course, the Japanese invasion only increased this animosity.

By 1940 Japan had had troops in China for ten years and for much of that time they had been in action. Since Japan's victory in the Russo-Japanese War of 1904–05 she had maintained economic rights in Manchuria which were enforced by a strong military presence. In 1931 friction in that area turned into open conflict. The Japanese Kwangtung Army captured Mukden with its arsenal, before rapidly extending its occupation to all of Manchuria. Some fighting even broke out in the huge international metropolis of Shanghai, with further clashes following in the north in 1932–33. Japan, whose economic development was now deliberately designed for war purposes, was only waiting for an opportunity to initiate a full-scale attempt to overrun the whole of China.

It came in July, 1937, at the Marco Polo bridge a few miles outside Peking. There was an accidental confrontation involving casualties on both sides between a Chinese patrol and Japanese soldiers on manoeuvres. Japan launched an all-out offensive and, in December, swept into China's capital city, Nanking. The result was the infamous "Rape of Nanking", during which at least 150,000 soldiers and civilians were executed as a backdrop to an orgy of rape and pillage. Men of the 16th "Black" Division under Lieutenant-General Nakajima were particularly enthusiastic. The Chinese would never forget this harrowing atrocity. On 7 December, 1937, the *Japan Advertiser* carried an account of a friendly competition between Sub-Lieutenants Toshiaki Mukai and Takeshi Noda as to who would be the first to kill 100 Chinese with his sword. The score was given as Mukai 89 and Noda 78. Then the referees got confused so the goal was adjusted to the first to kill 150. Mukai later explained that his blade had been damaged by cutting one man in half – helmet and all. This was the worst of many Japanese atrocities. From 1940–45 Nanking was the seat of the Chinese puppet government, nominally under President Wang Ching Wei, who had been appointed by the Japanese in 1937. It was from the followers of this puppet régime that the Japanese recruited Chinese agents and saboteurs to operate before and during their attack on the Colony.

By the end of 1937 the Japanese had spread out across Northern China, occupying the main towns and principal railway lines north of the Yellow River. Opposition took the form of large-scale guerrilla activities. The Chinese Nationalist administration had moved 600 miles up the Yangtze River to Hankow. The Japanese fought their way up the valley towards the city and, in October, 1938, after a surprise landing at Bias Bay, also stormed into Canton – the event that triggered the retreat of our language students. Hankow also fell a few days later. The capture of Canton put Japanese troops just over the border from the New Territories.

Chang Kai-shek's Nationalist government retreated yet further up the Yangtze to Chungking, west of the Yangtze gorges, at the centre of the "rice bowl" of China. There it was to remain until well after the Second World War, despite heavy bombing coupled with strenuous efforts by Japanese ground forces to reach it. The vast size of China, combined with the mountainous character of some of the interior provinces, and the paucity of railways or good roads, made the problem of total occupation virtually insoluble. Japan was in possession of seven of China's largest cities – Peking, Tientsin, Tsingtao, Nanking, Hankow, Shanghai and Canton – plus all her major ports, but a position of stalemate had been reached by 1940. By that date Japan had deployed some 36 divisions from Manchuria in the extreme north to Canton and the Hong Kong border in the south. When one considers that Japan launched her simultaneous attacks on Malaya, the Philippines, and Hong Kong with a total of only seven divisions, none of which came from China, the scale of Japan's Chinese adventure is brought sharply into focus.

Like all armies of occupation in countries of such size the Japanese could not be strong, could not even maintain a presence, everywhere. Nationalist forces infiltrated back into some regions no longer held in strength, while communist guerrillas established themselves in areas abandoned by the Japanese and Nationalists. It is important to realize that the struggle inside China developed to some extent into a three way war. The Japanese fought both the Nationalists and the communists, while the latter two sometimes cooperated against a common enemy and sometimes fought each other. One area in which the communists predominated was around Mirs Bay to the NE of Hong Kong. This was to be of considerable significance later for escapees from the Colony.

After about a year the wartime pressures on the police resulted in my being recalled from full-time study to take over as the second-in-command of half of Hong Kong island, based at the Central Police Station. This entailed a move across the water from Kowloon to a flat in Victoria which I shared with Colin Luscombe and Brian Fay, another ASP. Needless to say I was expected to continue learning Cantonese in my spare time.

In those days the Hong Kong Police Force numbered about 1500 compared to 27,199 today, plus aproximately 5000 civilian staff. A new commissioner had recently arrived from Malaya. This was Pennefather-Evans, a small, dapper man with fair hair, who was less than popular with the senior officers, who regarded his appointment from outside as a blow to their promotion prospects. Although a strongly religious man who belonged to the Oxford (Christian) Group, straightforward, and a gentleman, he was probably not tough enough to handle the rougher, more rebellious element among the lower ranks of the Europeans. He was certainly misunderstood, being regarded as something of an oddity by many.[2] His acting deputy was Walter Scott, whose substantive post was head of Special Branch (SB), commanded in his absence by "Mui" Major, a superintendent. He had married an American woman who had run an antique shop in Peking and was a thoroughly professional policeman who had had experience as an officer in the Black and Tans during the earlier troubles in Ireland. He could be woundingly sarcastic to his subordinates, and had a reputation as a womanizer. Under these two there were about a dozen European gazetted officers divided between the New Territories/Kowloon and the island. There were no Chinese officers of this grade.

The composition of the Force is relevant to the story. To me it seemed an odd mixture at first, although I soon appreciated that the principle of divide and rule predominated in recruiting policy. Below gazetted rank there were Europeans, two categories of Indian, White Russians, and Chinese from two widely differing regions of China – a cocktail of three races and five languages.

The Europeans, other than gazetted officers, joined as constables and then, after a year, became sergeants, followed, where suitable, by the rank of inspector. They were appointed by the Hong Kong government, while the gazetted officers were appointed by the Colonial Office.[3]

About a third of our numbers were Indians. They were recruited in India for a full career in Hong Kong (Singapore and Malaya had similar arrangements). They had their families with them, and wore their distinctive, colourful puggaris or turbans with their uniform.

They looked extremely smart and, in most cases, towered above their Chinese comrades. They all spoke Urdu (and some English), although they were expected to learn colloquial Cantonese. Some European officers went on Urdu courses at the Indian Police Training Depot in the Punjab. The Indians were divided roughly equally between Sikhs and Punjabi Muslims. It was to be my experience during the Japanese occupation that most of the Sikhs, except for the older men, were disloyal and took an active part in humiliating and beating Europeans. Not only did they do this, they also turned on the Punjabi Muslims in a most vicious way. The Punjabi Muslims generally were very loyal.

We also had about fifty White Russians. Their parents had fled east into Manchuria after the 1917 revolution. The majority settled in Mukden, but a sizeable number came south to Shanghai. These families were renowned for their beautiful women. Those that we recruited were largely kept together, employed on large passenger or cargo ships in an anti-piracy role. They were not harbour police, rather a temporary addition to the vessel's complement, much in the same way that a detachment of marines might sail on a warship to defend the crew.

Well over half our members were Chinese, but even with them there were big differences. With the Chinese some 70 percent were Cantonese, recruited in Hong Kong. The other 30 percent were Wei Hai Wei men. Wei Hai Wei was a former naval and coaling station in NE China, near the tip of the Shangtung peninsula which juts out into the Yellow Sea 500 miles north of Shanghai. With the tiny island of Liu Kung, the harbour, and the ten-mile belt of mainland, all of which were leased to Britain in 1898, it was virtually a replica of Hong Kong in miniature. It served as a base for the RN squadron on the China station during the summer months until 1930. On the signing of the lease it was handed over to Britain by Japan, who had seized it in 1895. They reoccupied it in 1938. The British had formed the 1st Chinese Regiment (commonly called the Wei Hai Wei Regiment) for local protection, but it only existed for eight years from 1899–1906, although it had fought valiantly in the Boxer rebellion. These people were quite different from the Cantonese. Not only did they speak a different dialect, but they were larger, taller men – wheat eaters as distinct from rice eaters. As I mentioned earlier my cook boy, Fu King, was from Shangtung.

Within a short space of time I was to witness religious difficulties in my division, and later on a larger scale within the Indian units (two Indian Army battalions and one gunner regiment) in the army in the Colony. Both instances involved the Sikhs. The first was a minor matter. A Sikh constable was discovered having his beard shaved off in the bathroom by a Punjabi Muslim. For some reason he had requested this, which, although not an offence under police regulations, was flouting his religious rules. Both were brought up in front of me with the senior NCO of the Sikhs making an enormous fuss. Being inexperienced I was at a loss as to how best to handle it until somebody suggested that, as the offender had transgressed a religious code, his religious authorities should deal with him. I had the Sikh sergeant-major take him down to the temple where he was fined a hefty sum.

The time the Sikhs gave real cause for concern was during the run-up to the Japanese invasion; strong reports began circulating that the Sikhs in the Army were plotting a mutiny. Encouraged by Japanese propaganda many Sikhs were claiming their religious beliefs were being ignored by the British Authorities. An example was their being compelled to wear steel helmets. The matter was treated with the utmost seriousness (perhaps somebody remembered the Indian Mutiny of 84 years earlier). Three officers were sent from Delhi to investigate. Bill Robinson, a superintendent from the Indian Intelligence Bureau at Delhi, and also a Major Goring, and a Sikh superintendent carried out a widespread, covert inquiry. They had also been empowered to act because suddenly a large number of Sikhs disappeared from Hong Kong. They seemed, literally, to have been spirited away in the night from their barrack rooms, even from their units on exercise. I personally took no part in these arrests, although both the police and Army authorities were involved. All potential mutineers, together with their families, had been shipped back to India where the sheep were sorted from the goats. They never returned. It was this incident, coupled with the behaviour of many Sikhs during the Japanese invasion and occupation, that resulted in Hong Kong never recruiting them again after the war.

I was, of course, aware during 1941 that the likelihood of a Japanese attack was growing but I do not recall it having much effect on the everyday life of the Colony. The social round and the weekly race meetings continued, as did my rugby games. With the news and rumours of the Japanese activities in China there was apprehension as to what would happen next, but not fear. There was much indignation, much huffing and puffing by Europeans in the clubs as each new outrage was reported. Few of us understood the reality of the situation of Hong Kong in the context of the war as a whole and we had little inkling of the problems under which the military planners laboured.

The RAF contingent had three obsolete Vildebeeste torpedo bombers plus two Walrus amphibians whose primary task was target towing. The RN presence was not reassuring either, especially when everybody seemed to think any invasion would come from the sea. Based in Hong Kong were the destroyer HMS *Thracian*, eight Motor Torpedo Boats (MTBs), four gunboats and a few armed patrol boats. The Army too lacked adequate manpower and firepower. Until November, 1941, when two Canadian garrison battalions arrived (the Winnipeg Grenadiers and the Royal Rifles of Canada) there were just four regular infantry battalions in the Colony. They were the 2nd Royal Scots (2RS), the 1st Middlesex, the 5/7 Rajputs and the 2/14 Punjab. To these must be added the locally raised Volunteers – the Hong Kong Volunteer Defence Corps (HKVDC). For infantry to give of their best they need adequate artillery support; here was another serious deficiency. First, there was an acute shortage of anti-aircraft guns. The only mobile artillery was composed of two mountain batteries with 3.7 and 4.5 inch howitzers, and three medium batteries with 6 inch howitzers, all belonging to the Hong Kong and Singapore Royal Artillery (HKSRA). This unit had a mixture of British and Indian officers and senior NCOs, with Indian other ranks. Because it was much below strength a number of Chinese had to be enlisted. Finally, there were the 8th and 12th Coastal Artillery Regiments whose 29 guns were scattered around the coast pointing out to sea.

As a police officer I had no real conception of what all this meant in terms of our chances of defeating the Japanese should they come. I was, however, conscious that our potential enemy would not have a hard task in collecting accurate intelligence as to what was happening in the Colony, what precautions were being taken, or even on the actual defences or troop dispositions. Security was lax, a good example being the supposedly top secret fact that the Colony's garrison was to be reinforced by two Canadian battalions. Two weeks prior to their arrival Chinese contractors were going to Fortress HQ to bid for contracts to supply them. Japanese consular staff were in their consulate building overlooking the naval dockyard, Japanese nationals continued to work and there was unrestricted movement of Cantonese from China into Hong Kong which facilitated the task of enemy agents. Basically, Britain had her hands full with Germany with no time or resources to spare for a minute pimple on the coast of China that could not be saved if attacked in strength.

It did not help that all the top decision-makers of government and the military were new to their jobs. Pennefather-Evans was the longest serving senior commander, having been in Hong Kong for just over a year. The GOC, Major-General Maltby, had arrived in July, and the governor, Sir Mark Young, not until September. The real latecomer was the Colonial Secretary, Franklin Gimson, a man who will feature frequently in the story. The story is that he stepped ashore from Ceylon on the day of the attack, and had to find his own way to the Colonial Secretariat.

Some obvious preparations were made, such as the storage of water on the island, which was where the main defensive battle was planned to take place, and the stocking of food supplies in godowns (warehouses). Then there was the digging of a few tunnels as air raid shelters and the repatriation of British women and children which I have already mentioned. This was wise and generally acceptable until it became obvious that many people with power and influence were being allowed to keep their families and, as we have seen, this led to an outcry. Nevertheless, some 1646 service families and over 1800 wives and children of European civilians were sent away. Those who remained were not averse to taking a Chinese girl to comfort them, even resorting to the ridiculously transparent subterfuge of introducing them as their adopted daughters. As a bachelor I was unaffected by all this commotion.

At about the same time Geoffrey Wilson, (another ASP) and I were asked to join Z-Force by a tough, expansive man who was to command it, Mike Kendall. It was to be a secret, stay-behind unit of about twenty Europeans who would allow themselves to be overrun by the Japanese, and then undertake demolition and other guerrilla type operations behind enemy lines. We were told that Generalissimo Chang Kai-shek would issue us with special passes to facilitate our eventual escape through China to India. We both agreed to join. We started with weapon training and then progressed to hiding stocks of ammunition and food in secret dumps in the New Territories. One of the main dumps was in the disused Ling Ma Hang mine. We had to conceal these supplies by night, usually on a weekend, and using the mules of an Indian Army mule transport company – hardly conducive to security. The Indian Muleteers were inordinately fond of their animals, and on one occasion when a mule injured itself falling down a deep gully and had to be shot we all had to form up to salaam (salute) the dead beast.

After some weeks we received a confidential document setting out our police duties in an internal security situation. These conflicted with our tasks as members of Z-Force, bringing home to us that if push came to shove we could not do both jobs. Wilson went to see Pennefather-Evans. Our membership of Z-Force ceased abruptly.[4]

As November, 1941, gave way to December, there were increased indications of a Japanese build-up around Canton and refugees began pouring into the Colony from China. The British intelligence interpretation of what was happening was optimistic to the point of being foolhardy. So much so that 24 hours before the invasion the GOC signalled London that, "in his opinion reports that ten to twenty thousand troops were expected to arrive [on the frontier] for an attack on the Colony were certainly exaggerated". Nevertheless, certain obvious precautionary measures had been implemented. The harbour was closed at night, the Lei Mun Strait was blocked off by booms, British and Allied ocean-going ships were diverted to Singapore where possible, vital points had armed guards and all troops were on immediate stand-by to move to battle stations.

But life in the city seemed absurdly normal. On Saturday, 7 December Happy Valley race track had a capacity crowd for the day's events. The Royal Scots band arrived from their barracks at Shamshuipo to play on the course. The Middlesex Regiment played Rugby at the Cricket Club, followed by a party at the Hong Kong Hotel. That evening a charity ball was held at the Peninsula Hotel. It was called the "Tin Hat Ball" as its purpose was to raise money towards the cost of buying bombers, which the people of the Colony were to present to the British government. Sir Mark Young and General Maltby, along with much of Hong Kong's high society, were present.

However, to those in the know all was not well. On that Saturday afternoon the more senior officers in the police had been called to the Commissioner's office where he told them that Japanese troop transports escorted by naval craft were moving across the Bay of Siam to Kota Bharu on the north coast of Malaya. He emphasized that an invasion of the colony was probable.

I spent that night dealing with several attempts of sabotage in my police area by Japanese agents, probably followers of Wang Ching Wei, the Japanese puppet President of China. It was not until nearly dawn that I returned to my flat. This was just before the first Japanese air raid on the colony. The invasion of Hong Kong by the Japanese had already started.

CHAPTER TWO

INVASION

"I was mesmerized by my police sergeant, who calmly produced a penknife and proceeded to pare the soles of his feet and clean his toe nails with studied deliberation."

The "Gindrinkers Line" was the name given to the main British defensive position in the New Territories. Not much of a name to inspire confidence. The Japanese, had they known it, might have felt it appropriate, but it was not in fact a disparaging illusion to the troops deployed in it. The name was taken from Gindrinkers Bay at the western end of the nine miles of defensive positions that were strung out eastwards as far as the hills overlooking Port Shelter. The Bay was so called because of the quantities of empty gin, and other bottles, deposited there by tides and currents.[1] The line followed a gentle curve along the Shing Mun River to the range of hills just north of Kowloon and Kai Tak airport. It was 10–12 miles from the frontier over which any enemy assault might be expected. Three of the six regular infantry battalions available for the defence of the Colony were destined for the Gindrinkers Line, the remainder being deployed on the island. Only demolitions and one company would delay the attackers forward of this line.

The problem with this line was simple. It was far too long for the troops available to hold it. Once it was breached Kowloon and the airport were doomed as there was no fall-back position. If the Japanese penetrated anywhere the whole line must pull back to begin the scramble for ferries and boats across to the island. This was always the intention eventually, as it was the island that had to be held indefinitely if possible. Companies were given areas up to one and a half miles in length, positions that entire battalions would have found hard to hold. Of the twelve companies available all except two were in the front line; the exceptions being one from the Second Royal Scots (2 RS) in reserve, and one from 2/14 Punjab pushed forward as the covering force. Gaps between companies and platoons were wide and numerous, there was no depth, artillery support was inadequate, air cover was zero.

This forward (mainland) brigade was commanded by Brigadier Wallis, an Indian Army officer whose black patch over one eye gave him a fierce, almost piratical look. He had 2 RS on the left, 2/14 Punjab in the centre, and 5/7 Rajputs on the right. His task was to delay any enemy advance as long as possible, but always to keep in mind that the main battle was to be fought out on the island, and that his brigade must be kept intact for that job as well.

The critical part of the line was the left. If the Japanese advanced overland they would strike the Royal Scots at the bottleneck between Gindrinkers Bay in the west and the Tide Cove in the east. The key to opening this door was the Shing Mun Redoubt. This was a fortified area of underground bunkers, tunnels, trenches and barbed wire on the NW end of Smuggler's Ridge, immediately south of Jubilee Reservoir. It was later alleged that the Japanese had a mock-up of this redoubt constructed at Canton on which they rehearsed assaults. Its size cried out for a company to defend it, but only a platoon could be spared. This belonged to 2nd Lieutenant Thomson of A Company, Royal Scots. His company commander was Captain 'Potato' Jones, an officer well known for his social attributes but as yet untested as a soldier.[2] He sited his headquarters alongside an artillery OP (observation post) at the rear of the redoubt. The CO, (commanding officer) Lieutenant-Colonel Simon White, who had only recently taken over the battalion, had three companies in the front line, with the fourth held back in reserve on the forward (northern) slope of Golden Hill.

As dawn broke, just before 7.00 am on 8 December, 1941, Japanese troop movements were spotted along the Sham Chun River which formed the frontier with China. Demolition charges were fired under road and rail bridges. Enemy engineers started work; their infantry advanced. The invasion of Hong Kong had begun. Deliberately, to encourage divine approval, the Japanese attacked under a rising sun, the sacred emblem on their flag. It was not only Hong Kong that faced Japanese bayonets and bombs that morning. Simultaneous assaults were also taking place in Thailand, Malaya, the Philippines and at Pearl Harbor. It was the start of the Emperor's grandiose plan for a 'Greater East Asia Co-Prosperity Sphere'.

The commander of the Japanese 23rd Army, Lieutenant-General Sakai, had only allocated one reinforced division to take Hong Kong. The infantry element of the 38th Division, under Major-General Ito, had three regiments each of three battalions, and was sustained by an abundance of artillery and mortar units. After crossing the border the divisional plan envisaged a concurrent advance by two wings on the Grassy – Tai Mo Shan feature. From there a concerted assault on the left end of the Gindrinkers Line was intended. The right wing consisted of the 230th Regiment (Colonel Shoji) together with the 228th Regiment (Colonel Doi), while the left had the 229th Regiment (Colonel Tanaka). In this first phase Shoji and Doi would advance via Shui Tau and thence up onto the south-western slopes of Tai Mo Shan. Tanaka would take the Tai Po road before moving on Tai Mo Shan and Grassy Hill. A detachment was to cross Tide Cove to make contact with the eastern part of the British line. Despite delays by demolitions and the small covering force, by the afternoon of the 9th the leading battalions were closing up to the positions held by the Royal Scots. Colonel Doi's men had forged ahead and at the same time veered to the east thus putting them in Tanaka's area of operations. At 3.00 pm Doi was on Grassy Hill gazing through his binoculars at the Royal Scots' positions.

He was not impressed with what he saw. "Although no enemy was to be seen, a good view of the defensive positions was obtained, and a sighting of something like white clothes being dried gave a clue to the presence of enemy troops. My impression was that the enemy was still inactive."[3] Doi, who was out of touch with his superiors, resolved to launch a night attack on his own initiative on what he perceived as a key position. His 3rd Battalion would lead the assault at 11.00 pm. He later recorded:

"The companies leading the attack assaulted the eastern position [Shing Mun Redoubt]. First a small number of troops threw hand grenades into the air ventilation chimneys of the connecting tunnels and engaged in fierce close-quarter fighting. In the meantime each tunnel exit was blocked by several men. Although the hand-to-hand fighting was continued for more than an hour, a small number of enemy remnants continued to offer stubborn resistance."[4]

Well before dawn Doi had the Shing Mun Redoubt. The Gindrinkers Line had been breached, but there was no counter-attack. Having achieved this remarkable success Doi was astounded to be ordered to withdraw. Staff at divisional HQ demanded, "Who authorized this attack? Why is your regiment in Colonel Tanaka's area? You are to withdraw immediately." Twice Doi ignored this order. It nearly cost him his command as the chief-of-staff came forward later to investigate the colonel's temerity. Only with difficulty were his actions accepted by his superiors.

There seems little doubt that the Shing Mun Redoubt garrison had been caught napping, with the majority of the platoon down inside the bunkers and tunnels. Command had devolved on the platoon sergeant, Rob, as Thomson was away at company HQ with Captain Jones and Lieutenant Willcocks, the gunner observation officer. No immediate, pre-arranged local counter-attack had been planned or rehearsed as was the normal tactical procedure, and to scrape together an ad hoc force for the purpose proved impossible in the confusion and darkness.

The capture of such a critical position, which it was hoped could have held out for a week, within 48 hours, caused consternation to the British high command. In the words of a staff officer present at the time this loss "really caused chaos in Fortress HQ. I have never seen General Maltby more shocked or angry."[5] The brigade commander, Wallis, urged Lieutenant-Colonel White to retake the redoubt at first light, promising him a Rajput company, most of the mainland guns and some island artillery in support. White declined to try. Wallis reported back to Maltby that, "It seemed useless to force a battalion commander to execute a plan in which he had no confidence."[6]

Worse was to follow on the 11th. Colonel Shoji's 230th Regiment drove back the Royal Scots from their new positions astride the Kowloon road and, after a bitter battle, forced D Company off Golden Hill. Maltby had no option but to begin the retreat to the island far earlier than planned. This was successfully carried out during the next two days.

I was not personally involved in any of these dramatic events and I did not learn the details until much later. Nevertheless, I was profoundly shocked to hear of the rapid enemy advance and the speed with which the Royal Scots had been pushed back. Inevitably a number of derogatory reports and rumours circulated about their performance. One was that the battalion second-in-command, Major Stanford Burn, who had gone forward to try to sort out the mess, was shot by his own men. A more charitable version was that he shot himself when he realized he could do nothing to stop the rot. It is certainly true that for long afterwards the Royal Scots, who pride themselves on being the "First of Foot", were known by many as the "Fleet of Foot". In fairness it must be said that they did much to redeem their reputation on the island.

For me war came with an air raid warning. I had been on duty all night investigating bomb explosions, and had returned to my flat for a bath and breakfast. I was having breakfast as the sirens started their banshee wailing and within a few moments Fu King rushed up in a state of some agitation, pulling on his white jacket, as he shouted, "Master! Master! Japanese planes". Ah Ying, the wash amah, joined us pointing at the aircraft, quite beside herself with excitement, and shrieking in her squeaky voice, "Law pak tau! Law pak tau!" – 'Turnip Heads', the Chinese nickname for Japanese. She followed up with a series of "Ah yahs", while from Fu King came a flow of Chinese expletives as to what should be done sexually to the pilots' mothers and grandmothers. A typical Chinese reaction to the event.

The planes flew lazily along the length of the harbour chased by white puffs of exploding anti-aircraft (AA) shells. Kai Tak was strafed and bombed, destroying our handful of antiquated aircraft on the ground in a matter of minutes. Fu King grabbed my arm, "Master! Master! They're shooting the flying boat." Then another torrent of abuse. "Its on fire." He was right. The Pan Am Clipper, a passenger flying boat lying at anchor on the Kowloon side of the harbour, having arrived the day before from San Francisco via Honolulu and the Philippines, was ablaze. Having emptied their bomb racks the planes flew slowly out of sight back to China, leaving behind a stunned and confused British Colony.

I left at once for my office, little realizing that I would never live in that flat again. A day or so later it received a shell through the roof which, although it failed to explode, opened it up to looters. In the meantime I had not gone back as I was posted as second-in-command of Central and Western Divisions with an office in Upper

Levels Police Station in Caine Road. From there I was to fight my brief war, on duty 24 hours a day, snatching cat-naps when I could.

On the top floor of the station were four flats, intended mainly as living accommodation for inspectorate officers, one of which had been vacated by "Our Frankie" Shaftain who was a Superintendent. He had retained the flat after his promotion and his White Russian wife had been evacuated to Australia. Shaftain, a man in his mid-forties, had always seemed to me as head of CID a self-important, though efficient officer. When exhaustion overcame me I risked his wrath and moved into his spare bedroom. I remember one night lying on his bed, my mind in turmoil thinking of the war and my family and quite unable to sleep. My eye caught his bookcase; perhaps I should try reading. The books were an uninspiring collection put there to fill space rather than to read, but I noticed a paperback with an odd title – *The Autobiography of a Flea*. One page was sufficient to show that it was pure, hard-hitting porn. The flea lived in the pubic hairs of a virile, oversexed man and shared all his erotic adventures with him. Sleep still eluded me. At that moment, however, "Our Frankie" had more important things on his mind than his bed or fleas.

As head of CID Shaftain had responsiblity, with the small Special Branch section, for dealing with subversion, the 'internal enemy' as he called it. Hong Kong had been very much an open city in the years preceding the invasion; any Chinese who could prove he was from Kwangtung Province on the other side of the border could, by treaty, enter Hong Kong without a permit. As early as 1932, for example, Formosans (Taiwanese), whose country had been occupied by Japan for 45 years, were infiltrated into the Colony as sleepers, posing as businessmen, farmers or fishermen. Now, with their masters advancing, these, and other agents became active. Using long-hidden wireless sets they began transmitting the locations of British units or guns. A number were caught sending messages. When this happened, as Shaftain later wrote in his report, "I took upon myself the responsibility of having them shot."

A key element in this confusion of clandestine activities were the secret Triad societies. Prior to the attack on Hong Kong the local Triads had split into three camps. One was prepared, in the event of invasion, to work for the Nationalists against the Japanese. They had been persuaded to do so by Admiral Chan Chak, who was Chang Kai-shek's colourful intelligence chief. Another group had decided to assist the Japanese, while the third proposed to sit on the fence to see who came out on top. All this was known to the police, so a few months before the invasion over a hundred members of the Wo Shing Wo group of Triads were arrested when attending a meeting to decide how best to support the Japanese.

After war broke out Shaftain relied heavily on outside assistance in finding these agents as his Chinese detectives had become "very shaky". He was in close touch with a Colonel S. K. Yee (from the Nationalist Chinese Secret Service) who was chief-of-staff to Admiral Chan Chak. The admiral, who had lost a leg in a naval action on the Yangtze River, had only arrived in the Colony on 7 December. His task was to coordinate the activities of the Nationalist agents, many of whom were northern Triad members, in winkling out Japanese sympathizers. Some Lam Yi Dui (Chiang Kai-shek's secret police) wore a blue armband with the white Chinese sun emblem on it for identification purposes, although just as many did not bother. They were a merciless bunch of thugs. When arrested, suspects as often as not ended up in the narrow, dead-end lane between the Gloucester Hotel and Lane Crawford's store. There, I believe, they were made to kneel before being given the coup-de-grace – a revolver shot in the back of the neck – by a police NCO who had volunteered for the job, although the first time a batch of these saboteurs was executed it merited a proper police firing party. The lane was nicknamed "Blood Alley".

Early on 11 December Shaftain received a startling report from a paid agent in a Hong Kong Triad to the effect that local members of these secret societies, who numbered some 60,000, had agreed to slaughter all Europeans on the 13th. In other words they would attempt to carry out a massacre on behalf of the Japanese, in order, so Shaftain was told, to help bring about a British defeat and thus save the Chinese population from prolonged bombardment. Shaftain was at first disbelieving. But, "from another source I received additional facts which satisfied me as to the authenticity of an apparently fantastic and improbable story."

Shaftain, who had set himself up on the eighth floor of the Gloucester Hotel, realized he needed to contact the main Hong Kong Triad bosses immediately, and also that money might be the key to changing minds. Within an hour of informing him Penne-father-Evans had produced $20,000, but his efforts to reach the Triad leaders were less successful. Then he got in touch with Colonel Yee. Yee contacted Chang Ji Lin, the head of the Shanghai underworld and a senior member of the northern Triads, who was then in Hong Kong. Within hours the five top Hong Kong leaders agreed to a meeting in Admiral Chan Chak's office. At this gathering, which was a polite affair with the massacre of Europeans being referred to as the "celebration on the 13th", all that could be agreed was another meeting in the commissioner's office that night.

At 9.00 pm the conference convened at Police HQ. Present were Pennefather-Evans, Shaftain, Yee, Chang Ji Lin and the five leaders who insisted on being called "mediators". This time there was more acrimony, talk of murder and massacre seemed to shock the "gentle, priestly looking cut-throats ... who were merely threatening to bump off the Fan Kwai (foreign devils) and thereby save the lives of hundreds if not thousands of Chinese."[7] After a lengthy impasse the Europeans withdrew, leaving Yee and Chang Ji Lin to try to force an agreement. This tactic worked. Buses were requisitioned to gather over 200 junior Triad chiefs at the Cecil Hotel, where the manager later complained that a large amount of silver had disappeared.

This final meeting on the 12th produced results, or rather cooper-ation – at a price. Yee intimated that the $20,000 was not enough, a much larger sum was needed to secure the cancellation of the "celebration" planned for the following day. Government was being blackmailed by the Triads. It was then that Chang Ji Lin came to the rescue. He undertook to deal with the funding shortfall personally, on the verbal understanding that the matter would be settled after the war. The Triads kept faith in so far as no Europeans were killed, they furnished valuable information up until the British surrender, and many members worked against the Japanese throughout the occupation. At the end of the war Shaftain was only prepared to say that, "Our debt to Mr X [Chang Ji Lin] was discussed and settled."

The seventeen days it took the Japanese to capture Hong Kong were frenetic. I did not keep a proper diary until I was interned in Stanley so in some instances my recollections as to precise dates or timings of events before then may be imperfect, but I have never forgotten details of events I witnessed. Virtually all my time was spent dealing with the Chinese civil population, 90 percent of it involving the maintenance of law and order, guarding vital points, the prevention of looting or related activities. Over a million people required feeding and controlling. The densely packed urban and commercial areas of Kowloon and Victoria were at the mercy of enemy aircraft and artillery, with the Japanese being generous in the use of both. Tens of thousands of refugees fled into these already overcrowded and dangerous areas in search of shelter or food as the enemy advance swept south. Within four days the Japanese were in Kowloon, with a flood of desperate people trying to cross to the island in front of them.

From the moment Japanese troops set foot in the New Territories and for the next three and a half years the Chinese (and everybody else) had but one priority, and that was securing the next meal. The great bulk of people did not take sides, they merely went about the business of surviving with the stoical fatalism that has been one of their characteristics for thousands of years. A tiny majority went out of their way to please their new masters. Some actively helped Japanese military operations by informing on British locations, or with acts of minor sabotage such as filling fire buckets with kerosine, putting sand in rice bags or signalling gun positions with mirrors. At the other extreme were those who remained totally loyal to the British, fought alongside them and later gave every assistance, including their lives, to alleviate the sufferings of prisoners. We even had occasional help from Rosalie Lewis and her girls who passed on information about Japanese movements they had seen.

Rice became worth its weight in gold. This was almost literally true after several years of occupation and even at the start, on the black market, its price soared like a rocket. It was officially rationed from the outset of hostilities and issued from various depots, one of which was at the Central Market in Victoria. Huge queues formed, and I remember watching the reaction of the people in one queue as a Japanese plane flew in over the roof-tops, machine guns blazing. I expected the queue to dissolve as everybody scattered for cover, but not a soul moved for fear of losing his place. The pilot fired directly into the queue cutting down dozens of people – still no reaction, other than the survivors stepping over the dead or injured to get nearer the front.

As conditions worsened most of my time was spent deploying

men to deal with looting. At one stage two rice godowns near the waterfront were shelled, breaking them open and starting a serious fire. This led the Chinese to begin what I can only describe as a looting frenzy. Nothing I tried stopped them, and they were completely oblivious of the shells and the fire. I saw one man pinned under several 200 pound bags. His head was showing and his hands protruded from underneath the sacks, waving feebly. His muffled yells could barely be heard and he was certainly near to suffocation. All around looters were grabbing and scrambling for bags but none for the ones crushing him. He was totally ignored – one less competitor I suppose. My police pulled him out. By now I was desperate to stop it all. Shots were fired – no reaction. If I opened up indiscriminately and massacred them that would surely put an end to it, but for me that was not an option. As a last try I ordered my armed Indian police I had with me to fix bayonets. They advanced, jabbing at the Chinese. Within seconds they had gone. Cold steel had been the answer. It was unbelievable.

Looting became progressively more rampant as people abandoned their houses in the face of the Japanese advance. To the Chinese looters it did not matter a wit whether or not they were within Japanese lines. The opportunity to grab was there and they took it in their thousands. Nothing would be left in a house; it would be stripped to the bare bricks. Countless millions of ants could not have picked it cleaner. Years later, after the reoccupation, residents often found items of their own property on sale in the "Thieves Market". Many houses had a double dose. The first was during the Japanese attack with the second coming in the period between their surrender and the British resuming control. Even the smallest piece of wood missed on the earlier visit was removed. The BBC was to call Hong Kong the most looted place on earth.

An event which sticks in my mind clearly was the first Japanese "peace mission". It occurred on the morning of 14 December, when Kowloon had been lost, and the last part of the mainland brigade was being pulled back to the island, from the Devil's Peak area, across the Lei Mun channel. I was moving along the waterfront with a party of police, keeping under cover from firing across the harbour, when I saw it. A launch was heading for Queen's Pier from Kowloon and strung across its bows was a white sheet with the words "Peace

Mission" written on it. I headed for the pier, arriving a few minutes before the British reception party under Major Boxer, an intelligence officer on Maltby's staff who was a fluent Japanese speaker.

Three Japanese officers, trailing long swords, one carrying a pole with a white flag, came swaggering onto the pier. The senior was Colonel Tada, of Military Information, the second was Lieutenant Mizuno and the third, a darker, thickset man clutching a briefcase, was a Mr Othsu Dak – at the time I did not know their names. But it was their companions that seemed so absurdly out of place. One was a highly pregnant European lady, who I now know was a Mrs Macdonald; the other was Mrs Lee, wife of the secretary to the governor, with her two fat little dachshund dogs, appropriately named Otto and Mitzi. Mrs Macdonald was handed over to us. Mrs Lee was the hostage who would have to return with the delegation to Kowloon.

It transpired that the previous evening the Japanese had accosted Mrs Lee in her hotel and asked her if she would consent to be the hostage. She agreed on two conditions – first, that her friend Mrs Macdonald could be brought across to the island to have her baby delivered by the British, and secondly if she could bring her dogs. The Japanese had readily agreed. The departure the next morning was delayed in Kowloon as frequent rehearsals were necessary to ensure sufficient photographic coverage of this historic event. It had all the makings of comic opera.

Before Major Boxer's party arrived there appeared to be an air of uncertainty about what to do or where to go as the only people around were ourselves and two American reporters, Gwen Dew and Van Miserling, who busied themselves taking photographs or talking to Mrs Lee. When Major Boxer arrived he was immediately involved in a sort of saluting and bowing competition in response to the Japanese, who interspersed theirs with extraordinary hissing noises. As this was going on one of my NCOs, Sergeant Sullivan, said, "Sir, see that bugger holding the pole with the white flag. He used to run a sports shop in Wanchai." He was referring to a stocky, bespectacled young man, now a lieutenant in the Japanese Army – Mizuno.

My police cordoned off the pier while Major Boxer departed with the surrender terms to the governor. They were categorically rejected. Boxer was driven back to the pier with the written rebuff.

There was hand shaking, more salutes, more bows before a somewhat deflated delegation departed with Mrs Lee and her dogs.

That night, while out on patrol, we suddenly heard several bursts of firing which caused us to pause. Then, after a few seconds, we were momentarily stunned and deafened by a monstrous explosion that seemed to shake the whole of Victoria. The sky was immediately illuminated as if by a gigantic firework display. Burning fragments fell all around us punctuated by subsidiary blasts. "It can't be shelling!" said someone near me. "What do you think it is sir?" I had no idea. Nor did Willie Sparrow, a Senior Superintendent, who appeared round a corner with a Browning automatic in his fist. In his slow, broad Irish brogue he calmly told me, "You go this way and I'll go that way," pointing in opposite directions. So saying he disappeared into the shadows.

The answer was a tragedy, of precisely the sort that so often happens in war. Lying a few hundred metres off the western end of Hong Kong island waterfront is Green Island, barely bigger than a football pitch. It was used as an explosives store for some ten tons of dynamite for demolition work. It was needed for use by the units defending the island. The job of shifting it was given to the Harbour Department with the help of volunteers to do the humping. During the afternoon the police had helped carry some 4000 boxes of dynamite, detonators and fuses to the loading point on Green Island. The plan was for it to be loaded onto the steam launch *Jeannette* and brought to the Star Ferry terminal during darkness. It was supposed to leave Green Island at midnight. All defensive posts along the waterfront were warned. Unfortunately, as they finished loading early they left two hours ahead of schedule, and were approaching the wrong landing point (the vehicular ferry) when a Middlesex NCO manning the nearest pillbox gave the order to fire. Long bursts of machine-gun fire ripped into the barge with catastrophic results. The detonation broke nearly every window within half a mile, and caused a spate of wild shooting as many thought it was a prelude to the anticipated enemy landings. Sub-Inspector Hudson and Police Sergeant Donahue were among the many dead.

After the withdrawal of the British forces to the island there was a period of several days while we waited and wondered where the Japanese would strike next. Whilst there was a respite from ground attack there was no let up from the air. We were bombed by aircraft, and blasted by shell and mortar fire at an unprecedented level. This never-ending bombardment was supplemented by propaganda appeals for surrender. The former took the form of pamphlets thrown from aircraft. My favourite was the drawing of a nude Chinese girl (very daring in those days) sitting on the lap of a fat John Bull, complete with Union Jack. The caption read, "This is what the British Imperialists have been doing to your women for years." One was inclined to say, "So what?"

The other attempt to subvert us took the form of a nightly concert. A launch would ply up and down between Kowloon and the island broadcasting supposedly nostalgic songs such as "Home Sweet Home". These would be interspersed by a distorted, high-pitched voice saying, "British Tommy [soldier], British Tar [sailor], think of your wives and families. Surrender and you can go home". Hardly subtle. Just in case we had not got the message these appeals were usually followed by a string of abuse and threats. Often the proceedings would be in Urdu for the benefit of our Indian allies.

Police HQ came in for considerable punishment despite the efforts of Smythe at camouflage. His method was the generous application of large blobs of green, brown and black paint to the compound. On 15 December it was struck by a stick of bombs that destroyed the basement and ground floor offices, killing Inspector Hopkins and wounding Thompson, a Superintendent, and Inspector Saunders. The next day it was hit again. Camouflage or no camouflage the commissioner decided to move to the Gloucester Hotel and Pedder Street buildings. There was no escape from the pounding, however. On one occasion, when I happened to be nearby, I witnessed the removal of an unexploded 8 inch shell, fired from a Japanese naval vessel, which had penetrated the hotel earlier on. In one of the shopping arcades I saw two coolies shuffling along with this huge shell suspended from a bamboo carrying pole. Clearly marked on it were the words, "Woolwich Arsenal 1918". They took it down the street to dump it in the harbour – an elementary form of bomb disposal!

Being bombed, shelled or mortared is an extremely frightening experience. You have absolutely no control over the situation. Nothing seems to offer adequate protection; the awful explosions, the unbelievable noise, the violent shock waves and the sickening apprehension as to where the next one will land, can combine to produce terror and inertia in all but the most courageous individuals. A part of a possible solution lies in activity, preferably physical. This lesson was demonstrated to me by an old Chinese police sergeant when my station came under heavy mortar fire. We had taken cover in the basement with the bombs raining down just outside. The noise was terrifying, the ceiling shook and I felt trapped. My policemen were huddled on the floor, their frightened eyes flitting from me to the stairs. One slight signal and they would have bolted, probably never to return.

I then registered what my sergeant was doing. He had removed his boots and socks, soaked his feet in a bowl of water before carefully drying them with a towel. I was mesmerized when he calmly produced a penknife and proceeded to pare the soles of his feet and clean his toe nails with studied deliberation. I watched him. My men watched me. It was a fine example of steadiness and courage that I have never forgotten.

A few abbreviated extracts from the Police War Diary, that was compiled later in Stanley, will perhaps give more insight into the everyday occurrences of this period.

"15 December
    – Wright-Nooth reports heliograph from Lugard Road. Two Chinese arrested.
16 December
    – The Peak wireless station abandonded by the Wei Hai Wei police who report to Wright-Nooth.
    – Saukiwan Station shelled. All Sikhs deserted.
18 December
    – 1930 hrs ex-sergeant Jessop, watchman at the Tai Koo docks, reported Japanese landings.
19 December
    – Sergeant Morrison captured after repelling a bayonet charge.
22 December
    – Heavy shelling of Upper Levels Station at 1100 hrs [This was when I watched the feet paring incident].
    – CP instructs Wright-Nooth and 5 European NCO volunteers to collect 1,000 grenades from the Shouson Hill magazine."

The above illustrates how elements of both the Chinese and Indian junior ranks were becoming jittery and unreliable. Important or risky tasks were being given to the Europeans.

My trip on the afternoon of 22 December took me to the front line of the fighting along the road east of Aberdeen. The idea was that if we could secure a thousand grenades from the military magazine at Shouson Hill, which at that stage was still thought to be in our hands, they could be distributed to the Lam Yi Dui. They would use them in guerrilla attacks on Japanese headquarters behind the lines. Somebody had visions of these ruffians and Triad members dashing around in civilian clothes tossing grenades everywhere. No thought had been given to the likely reprisals that would surely follow for the ordinary Chinese population. It was not my place to argue the merits of the plan, just to get the grenades.

I asked for European volunteers and got five reliable men (Sub-Inspector Taylor, Sergeants Appleton, Haynes, Michie and Mac-Donald). Armed with revolvers and rifles we set off in an unarmoured truck with myself in the cab with the driver. Our route was south from Victoria, out on the Aberdeen road. We passed through the village. As we approached the left-hand turn-off to the magazine signs of war were apparent, including the dead bodies of a group of naval ratings from HMS *Thracian* who must have been ambushed on their way forward to fight as infantry. At the turn-off I stopped the truck as there was a pillbox close to the road manned by men from the Middlesex Regiment. They belonged to C Company, and the NCO I met was Sergeant Bedward who was then in command in that area as his platoon commander had been wounded. I told Bedward my mission and, after asking if I had a spare cigarette, he proceeded to advise against going further, certainly in daylight, as the approach road to the magazine was as narrow and winding as an English country lane. My truck could not turn in a hurry – a perfect setting for an ambush.

The Japanese had taken the critical Wong Nei Chong gap which meant that the British east–west line along the hills of the island was breached. The gap was less than a mile from the magazine. While I was there Bedward opened up with his twin Vickers guns on enemy infantry on the eastern slope of Mount Cameron. I took his advice and returned empty-handed. Poor Bedward was to die soon afterwards manning his machine guns. Two subsequent attempts to grab grenades failed as the Japanese overran the magazine well before our final surrender.

It was about this time I had an offer to join an escape bid to get out of Hong Kong at the eleventh hour, which we could all see was fast approaching. At the highest level it had been decided that certain individuals should not be allowed to fall into Japanese hands. The British had promised to do their utmost to get Admiral Chan Chak and Colonel Yee out. They were key Chang Kai-shek men who had given us every assistance in clandestine operations and would be a fat catch for the enemy. Similarly, men like the Canadian Kendall who led Z-Force, and Bill Robinson, the Superintendent, from the Indian Intelligence Bureau who had come to sort out the Sikhs, knew too much. Under prolonged torture most men have a breaking point.

The quickest way of getting these men to China (Mirs Bay) was by sea on the MTBs. Plans were made to have them taken on board from the Aberdeen area. It was Robinson, the fellow policeman whom I had got to know quite well, who offered me a passage on one of the boats. It was an alluring offer. I went so far as to borrow (from Robinson) and hide quite a substantial amount of cash to facilitate the journey. But my main concern was leaving my men. As a soldier I would have a duty to escape after capture, but as a police officer the position was not so clear cut. In some circumstances under the Hague Convention police could be expected to carry out their duties under the orders of an occupying power. Certainly I felt I would need the consent of my commissioner. I baulked at just disappearing without his say so. I resolved to speak to him at the first opportunity. The chance never came as life became so chaotic in the run up to the surrender that our paths never crossed. In the event the boats left without me. They all reached safety after some hair-raising adventures getting out of Hong Kong waters, and I have often wondered how I would have spent the war had I gone with them.

As I will recount shortly I was, by coincidence, in the Aberdeen area as the escapees were desperately trying to find the boats. The five MTBs had assembled on the afternoon of Christmas Day to the west of Aberdeen Island to keep out of sight of the Japanese gunners around Brick Hill. They were ready for their dash to freedom. Kendall was on board with the boats' CO, Lieutenant-Commander Gandy, but not so Chan Chak, Yee or Robinson whose whereabouts were unknown. The admiral and his party knew they had to rendezvous at Aberdeen but nothing more. Meanwhile Naval HQ was becoming agitated as time ticked by. Twice Gandy was given orders to leave without them. Twice he deliberately delayed, heeding Kendall's pleading to wait.

At 5.30 pm Chan Chak and Yee were driving along the Aberdeen coast road in an old Austin car frantically looking for the MTBs. They actually drove through several enemy road blocks east of the village with one of the admiral's staff yelling in Japanese, "Banzai! Long live the Emperor!" Eventually, after returning to the harbour, where they joined up with Robinson and about a dozen other personnel, the decision was made to commandeer a small motor boat and go it alone. They chugged slowly out to sea down the Aberdeen Channel, straight into view of the Japanese guns which, firing at close range, killed several men and started an engine fire. The gallant admiral unstrapped his wooden leg, which he had stuffed with money, gave his life jacket to a Chinese who could not swim, and leapt into the sea along with eleven others. Bullets chopped up the water around them and Chan Chak was hit in the wrist. Nevertheless, one good arm and one leg were enough to propel him to the beach on Ap Lei Chau Island, now under shellfire.

The survivors, who included Yee, tottered across the island to be greeted at last by the wondrous sight of a single, solitary MTB, moored not far from shore.[8] Furious shirt waving followed. The response was several bursts of machine-gun fire and the boat moving further out to sea, as the crew had no way of knowing who they were. More swimming seemed the only answer, and several men did eventually struggle out to the MTB led by an RNVR cadet, Holger Christiansen. Unfortunately, Chan Chak had been unable to face another swim so was still on the island, sheltering in a cave. A skiff sent to fetch him returned after dark to report that he was no longer in the cave. Robinson and Lieutenant-Commander Yorath volunteered for a last try. After crashing around in the dark for some time they found him. As Yorath later wrote: "The Admiral was practically at the top [of the hill] although it was a difficult climb. I think he must have gone up there to die – Chinese like having their graves on hillsides. We lugged him down and got him in the boat. He must have suffered agonies. As we rowed back, he sat facing me in the stern and crossed himself which rather surprised me."⁹ The rest of the journey was plain sailing by comparison.

The day before, our police station at Aberdeen had been shelled and hit five times, forcing all personnel to take shelter in a nearby air-raid tunnel. The situation merited my taking a party of police, mostly Punjabi Muslims, down to bolster the force there and assess whether we could continue to operate from Aberdeen.

We set off in our truck, past the Hong Kong University where Dr Sun Yat Sen, the founder and first president of the Republic of China, had taken his medical degree. Leaving Queen Mary Hospital on our left we started the long, narrow twisting road to Aberdeen. As we approached the village the way ahead became decidedly dangerous with shells bursting on or near the road. Knowing that much would depend on Sergeant Matthews, who was driving, I asked, "Have you been to Aberdeen recently?" "No sir." Trying to appear calm I said, "Well, before you get to the last bend before the village pull in to the side of the road. Keep as close as you can to the hillside. If I'm right that corner is under mortar fire so I want to judge the intervals of fire before we dash through." At that moment I caught a glimpse from the corner of my eye of a Japanese plane turning to dive on us. It roared at us, guns crackling from each wing. I did not have to say anything. Within seconds everybody leapt out in a mad scramble to take futile cover between the vehicle and the hillside. Luckily Matthews had already pulled into a cutting so that the pilot did not get a straight run over us. He banked violently at the last moment and pulled away, machine guns still firing. We were untouched. Immediately afterwards we successfully ran the gauntlet of mortar bombs into Aberdeen.

Aberdeen was then no more than a large fishing village tucked in a natural harbour in beautiful surroundings. Once it had been a pirate stronghold. Now the stink of cordite had taken over from the scent of sandalwood, joss sticks and the pungent smell of small fish spread out to dry. In the days before the British settled in Hong Kong the clipper sailing ships of the old East India Company would call at Aberdeen for fresh water from a nearby waterfall, before sailing up the Pearl River to trade with the Manchus. Now, out in the harbour gun boats were being scuttled while the village was under continuous bombardment. The Japanese were a mere half a mile down the road to the east, having advanced well beyond the place at which I had halted three days earlier. I wondered briefly how Sergeant Bedward was getting on.

Confusion reigned. The only semblance of order that I saw was a long chain of Service personnel stretching from the naval godown to the water's edge. Along this motley line were passing a never-ending stream of liquor bottles – gin, whiskey, brandy, the lot. At the seaward end they were being systematically smashed and tossed into the harbour. I turned to the naval petty officer in charge and asked, "What the hell's going on?" "They're just up the road, the little buggers," he replied. "If they get hold of this lot God knows what will happen." We were not to know that such diligent attention to detail was in no way to lessen the horrors ahead.

After leaving my reinforcements in Aberdeen (which never actually fell to assault) I returned to Upper Levels. Lance Searle, my Commanding Officer, was waiting outside the station. Standing there, face strained and grim, he announced, "We have surrendered, George. All arms must be put in the arms cage. These are the CP's orders." "You're fooling?" I replied. Never had he been more serious.

Although the military details of the battle for the island are not the subject of this book I feel that something of the nature of the ferocity of the fighting should be included at this stage, together with a brief look at the struggle for Stanley which has been alluded to in the Prologue, as an important part of the background to my years as a prisoner there.

Maltby had divided the island with an imaginary line running north–south through the centre. The garrison was split into two brigades. East Brigade, under Wallis, had the 5/7 Rajputs on the north shore, the RRC on the south shore, and about half of the Middlesex battalion manning pillboxes around its entire coastal perimeter. Two companies of the HKVDC were in reserve. West Brigade, under the Canadian Brigadier Lawson, had the 2/14 Punjab along the north shore waterfront (my area), the Winnipeg Grenadiers guarding the southern part of the area, while the Royal Scots were the GOC's reserve near Wanchai Gap. Four companies of the HKVDC garrisoned the Peak and, as with the East Brigade, half the Middlesex were in pillboxes overlooking the shoreline. In other words the defenders were strung out all round the island. The thinking at Fortress HQ was that landings on the south of the island were the most likely.

The assault came on the night of 18/19 December. Six Japanese battalions, two from each regiment, in two waves hit the north shore under cover of concentrated artillery fire. On the right, landing at North Point, was Shoji's 230th, in the centre at Braemar Point was Doi's 228th, and on the left across the Lei Mun strait came Tanaka's 229th. This frontage of 3500 metres was held by the 5/7 Rajputs, one of whose Indian company commanders, Captain Ansari, I knew well from before the war. The story of how he was later awarded the posthumous George Cross is one of the heroic highlights of this book. By dawn on the 19th the enemy were as far inland as Jardine's Lookout, Mount Butler and Mount Parker – over 3,500 metres in some places. A remarkably successful night attack.

On that day (19th) a serious tactical error was made by the British. Instead of East Brigade withdrawing SW towards Violet Hill and thus maintaining contact with West Brigade, Maltby allowed himself to be persuaded by Wallis that his brigade should retire south towards Stanley Mound. As a result, by the 20th the Japanese under Tanaka had themselves taken Violet Hill and split the defences in two, virtually unopposed. From then on each British brigade fought its own battle.

The final five days saw infantry combat at its most vicious, at short range and often hand-to-hand. The experience of Lieutenant Corrigan of the Winnipeg Grenadiers on the morning of Christmas Eve is a uniquely gripping example.

"By this time they were too close to permit the firing of my rifle, and I had to grasp it by the barrel and wield it club fashion. I had foolishly neglected to put a bayonet on it. I was able to knock the rifle and bayonet out of the hands of one of the Japanese and with his weapon I managed to run through another of the enemy, but unfortunately I had difficulty withdrawing the blade and while trying to do so I caught the flash of a sword being raised to strike me.

"Quite subconsciously I jumped for my assailant, grasped his blade in my right hand and, circling his neck with my left arm, forced his head against my chest. Locked together in this fashion we struggled, each reluctant to let go of the sword. We both lost our footing and rolled down a slope. I tried to turn his head to deliver a knockout blow. Unfortunately I had forced his steel helmet down over his face and the net result of a terrific undercut was a sprained thumb for me. At this stage my opponent gave two shrill cries to get help from his men. Glancing up I noticed a figure nearby. I had completely forgotten that I carried a pistol, and in something of a frenzy I tried to reach it. After inserting my forefinger in the trigger guard, I found that the cut I had received when I first grabbed the sword had deprived it of the strength to squeeze the trigger. I tried to withdraw my finger and found that the flesh, acting much the same as a barb on a fish hook, prevented it. However, at last I managed to fire the pistol and end the weary struggle."[10]

At the same time that Corrigan was locked in his deadly embrace Tanaka's troops had converged on the Stanley peninsula. That morning had seen the Maryknoll Mission in the front line, and by the afternoon St Stephen's College south of the village was taking hits from direct fire weapons. The RRC had been withdrawn to the Fort to try to recuperate from the bloody repulse of its counter-attack on Stanley Mound the day before. The actual firing line across the neck of the peninsula was manned by an extraordinary hotch-potch of defenders. They included B Company, plus other stragglers, from the Middlesex, some Canadians, Volunteers, gunners, engineers, drivers, clerks, policemen and prison warders.

The handful of European prison staff at Stanley jail had been incorporated into the HKVDC and thus formed up to fight in military uniform. When it was over they quickly changed back into prison uniform and were eventually interned at Stanley as civilians with us. A remarkable revolving door situation – warder, soldier, warder, prisoner all within a few weeks. Even more bizarre was the situation of their unofficial commander during the fighting, ex-Captain "Crumb" Chattey, who was serving a two year sentence at the time of the invasion.

Chattey had formerly been adjutant of the Middlesex in Hong Kong. I recollect meeting him on a number of occasions in the US Recreation Club, and listening with considerable amusement to the fund of stories he told of soldiering with the Aden Levies. His family had served for generations in the Regiment and his brother was later to command the 1st battalion. Some time before the war with Japan, however, it was the disagreeable duty of my friend Lance Searle to investigate the case, which resulted in his being charged with homosexual offences with a Chinese "boy". In those days this was a criminal matter, regarded with absolute horror within the Army. A court case, disgrace, dismissal and imprisonment followed as swiftly and as inevitably as night follows day. But with the desperate need for trained soldiers in the run up to the surrender the governor agreed to release Chattey to fight.

He took charge of his former jailers, together with various "odds and sods", including the Colony hangman who had exchanged his rope for a rifle, and displayed outstanding courage and leadership in the battle for Stanley. He was always in the thick of the action, several witnesses feeling that he might be trying to get himself killed by sheer recklessness. He came through unscathed, however, to change back into prison garb to continue his sentence, subsequently joining us as an internee. Had he still been officially serving I am sure he would have been decorated. After the war I believe he became a successful farmer in Gloucestershire.

There was a bitter battle for Stanley Police Station. It was defended by Sergeants Simpson and Whitley, with a mixture of Chinese and Indian policemen armed with a Lewis gun and grenades in addition to their rifles and revolvers. Alongside them was a section from the Middlesex with four Vickers machine guns. For several hours this massive fire power was sufficient to keep the Japanese at bay, but as casualties mounted, ammunition dwindled, and two Vickers were destroyed the enemy got to within 50 metres of the building. At this point the Chinese and Indians bolted. Simpson and Whitley, with the remaining Middlesex men withdrew down the Wong Ma Kok road under cover of the machine guns.

The last shots in the defence of Hong Kong were fired at Stanley. On the evening of Christmas Day in the Peninsula Hotel Sir Mark Young formally surrendered unconditionally to Lieutenant-General Sakai. At Stanley, however, despite the arrival of two staff officers at 10.00 pm with verbal orders for him to do so, Wallis refused to give in without written authority. In his view a surrender was "unwarranted by the local situation". Intermittent clashes continued into the next morning. Only when his brigade major returned with written confirmation did he allow the white flag to be raised. At 2.30 am on 26 December, 1941, Wallis walked across to the Japanese lines.

CHAPTER THREE

A CHANGE OF LIFESTYLE

"The Japanese general pointed the revolver at my friend Searle and slowly and deliberately pulled the trigger. There was a click, followed by an hysterical, hyena-like laugh from the general who, giving Searle a knowing look placed the revolver back on his desk."

Colonel Eguchi has been described as "a short man of about forty-two. He had a Hitler type moustache and wore a uniform weighed down with decorations, neat white gloves and a huge, unwieldy sword." As the chief medical officer of the occupying forces Eguchi naturally put the comforts of his troops first. He summoned Doctor Li Shu-fan, who was a senior Chinese surgeon, and came straight to the point. "I want five hundred girls. Where can I get them?" To the victor go the spoils of war. Although on nothing like the same scale, Hong Kong experienced a taste of Nanking at St Stephen's College and at the temporary Jockey Club hospital at Happy Valley where rape and murder were perpetrated by troops during the fighting. The new director of medical services was also a man who set great store by having his meals on time, as his Chinese cook was to discover. An Italian priest who later escaped to Macao related how on one occasion, "Eguchi was annoyed because the dinner was late and so bullied the cook before cutting off his head with his sword. A Portuguese lady who saw the whole performance had to go to bed for a week."[1]

Eguchi's problem of satisfying the long-term licentiousness of his soldiery was solved by allowing them free reign in the Wanchai and Happy Valley areas, which were in effect declared colossal brothels, and profusely decorated with patriotic Japanese flags and bunting. However, even this was insufficient for the 15,000 troops and 3,000 Japanese civilians who were to garrison the Colony. Importation of prostitutes from the ports on the China coast was also arranged on a generous scale. Such actions were the norm throughout the Japanese occupied territories.

It is of interest to record that now, over fifty years on, some of the unfortunate girls who were forced to become "comfort women" as the Japanese liked to call them, are claiming financial compensation in Tokyo. As recently as December, 1992, it was reported that a South Korean woman, Kang Soon Ae, said that she serviced up to 35 men a day. "It hurt so much I cried out in pain but if I did they beat me. If comfort women cried in pain they could have their nipples cut off with Japanese swords."[2] In 1991 the Japanese government finally acknowledged that its imperial army had run a network of front line brothels, but is still "considering" whether to recompense the thousands of women still alive.

After the surrender I remained at my station where I had over two hundred European, Chinese and Indian police under my command. The European wives and daughters in the married quarters at the station were a particular worry. Reports of the rapes and killings going on were common knowledge. I had also heard it rumoured that in one instance this fate had been avoided if the women had, or pretended to have, their periods. It might be worth a try, so I called my senior inspector, a portly married man, for advice as I was dubious as to how to broach this delicate subject. Remember I was 24, unmarried, and living in an age when these matters were never discussed openly, so my diffidence was much greater than my knowledge. What I said was:

"Inspector, I'm worried about the married women and their daughters should Japanese troops come here. You know what happened at Happy Valley?"

"Yes sir! The wives are all talking about it."

"Well," I continued hesitantly, "wouldn't it be a good idea if they all pretended they had their periods, the curse, or whatever you call it? I can't very well suggest this to their husbands. Maybe you could deal with it if you think it's a good idea."

He was a married man nearly twice my age.

"Don't worry sir," he replied with a smile, "I'll fix it."

Unbeknown to me at the time another method of protecting women was being tried at St John's Cathedral – marriage. About a dozen of the European NCOs who had been living with Chinese girls had a sudden rush of conscience, feeling that if they did the right thing and married them it would give them the protection of British nationality. Wishful thinking of course, but they went ahead anyway. Colin Luscombe, an ASP, officially gave away the girls at a multiple marriage hastily convened on Boxing Day. It was the last religious service held in the cathedral for a long time. The Japanese initially turned it into a stables for the Army's horses and later into a social club.

I noted in my diary that the first few days after the surrender were "soon a general reign of terror". While the Japanese troops were indulging in their own excesses and moving into areas as yet unoccupied, the opportunity was taken by hundreds of Chinese criminals and thugs to come out of the shadows to openly pillage and murder. They were armed with weapons that had been abandoned or picked up from the battlefield – revolvers, daggers and even grenades being popular.

In theory at least we were supposed to do something about this lawlessness. The police were still responsible for the maintenance of order. Under the Hague Convention we were, subject to certain conditions, liable to continue working for the occupying power. There was much confusion about this at the time and many of us could, I believe, have escaped if we had had definite guidance from the commissioner. There was no clear lead, so most of us, for a while at any rate, continued to try to do our duties as police officers. This rapidly became a virtual impossibility, not so much because of the surge of anarchy as the plummeting discipline and morale among the Asiatic members of the Force.

In the event the Chinese and Indians were given permission to work for the Japanese, although most of the former opted to disappear to their villages, mostly in China. This option was not available to the Indians so a large proportion continued to work in some capacity during the occupation. The Sikhs did so with varying degrees of enthusiasm, whereas the Muslims were usually much more reluctant. Both were subjected to continuous anti-British propaganda designed to subvert them from any remaining loyalty to their former wicked, white colonial masters. Some were persuaded to join the Indian National Army to fight against the Allies, while others did a variety of guard duties in Hong Kong under the control of the

Japanese Gendarmerie (military police). I found it impossible to maintain any proper discipline. The only way I could exercise control was through a series of empty threats and bluffs, the most effective being to stop their rations.

On 26 December, following instructions, I was attempting to go through the motions of policing my district. At 11.00 am I sent a patrol of Wei Hai Wei police under Sergeant Leslie to check looting in the area. Within fifteen minutes a constable dashed in to report that Leslie had been shot in Hospital Road. Together with several European and Indian police, all armed, I ran to the scene. Had we met Japanese troops we would surely have been involved in a gun battle. My diary records:

"There I found Sergeant Leslie lying on the pavement outside a Chinese tenement house with a bullet wound in his groin. Beside him on the pavement was a dead Chinese robber who had been shot by the patrol while trying to escape. We surrounded the block and at the back I found another Chinese who had apparently thrown himself out of the window in a panicky endeavour to get away. He was dead. He was probably not one of the robbers. Meanwhile Sergeant McHardy and myself searched the block but found no one but terrified Chinese females. The other robbers had seemingly escaped across the roof tops."

Leslie had gone up the narrow stairs to the second floor of No. 8 Hospital Road to investigate a robbery. He was accompanied by a constable but before he had a chance to enter the flat he had been shot through the letter-box on the door. The constable had then pulled him down the stairs to the pavement. We moved him as quickly as possible to the Queen Mary Hospital where he died in the presence of his sister, who by chance worked there as a Nursing Sister. His death was a sad blow to us all. I wrote later that it was a "great tragedy that this should have happened after he had got through the war [fighting in Hong Kong]. He was a good policeman and sportsman and this affair cast a bigger gloom than ever over us." After this Police HQ withdrew all patrols – the police had in effect ceased to function.

That afternoon two European sergeants brought Leslie's body back from the hospital in a motor cycle sidecar wrapped in a white sheet. With them was a request from his sister that he should not be buried in a communal grave but somewhere she could find him after the war. I decided the best place would be in the grounds of the station. Then the problems began. The first was my being unable to contact a priest; so I decided to conduct the service myself. Then we could not find a Church of England prayer book in the station or the married quarters. We did locate a Catholic one but, as Leslie was a Presbyterian and a Scot, this posed something of a dilemma. I chose what I thought was appropriate from the Catholic book and we said the Lord's Prayer. Afterwards Leslie's body, wrapped in the Union Jack, was lowered into the grave. It was the best we could do.

Easier to deal with was the request from the Wei Hai Wei men who had been with him to fire a volley of shots over the grave. Had I permitted this the Japanese would have been on to us in minutes. The grave was carefully smoothed over so as to leave no sign. All this worked. After the Japanese defeat in 1945 Leslie's remains were disinterred and reburied in the War Graves Cemetery.

A slight digression is in order here so that I can fully explain briefly what was in store for Hong Kong at that moment. I was fully aware of what was happening around me, of the fact that anarchy stalked the streets and that the air was polluted with the stench from excrement, raw sewage and rotting bodies. I could see the destruction of buildings, the wrecked cars and the sunken boats in the harbour. What I did not appreciate was the scale of things, or that we faced three and a half years of starvation, decay, disease, and death that would reduce the Colony to a shoddy shadow of its former self.

Within that space of time the population was to shrivel from 1.7 million to some 650,000. To the Japanese, the Chinese were useless mouths to feed. Within a matter of weeks after the British capitulation an official announcement was made to the effect that it was their intention to reduce the population to 500,000. They just fell short of the target, although not for want of trying. They needed some people for certain key jobs and to provide a free labour force (coolies got a handful of rice, not money, as their daily wage); the rest must be encouraged to disappear with various inducements. The easiest and most effective was to make life so wretched that most would welcome compulsory evacuation, or willingly flee, north into China. By early 1942 a mass exodus was under way. Day and night the Tai Po road to the border was jammed with a pathetic stream of refugees. This haemorrhage averaged almost a thousand a day throughout the occupation.

When the Japanese authorities felt people were not dying quickly enough of beri beri, or some other starvation related sickness, they were not averse to speeding up the process. Often this was done by rounding up people from the streets straight into junks, which were then towed out to sea, shot up, sunk or set alight. Charred or bloated bodies were a common find on beaches. I certainly witnessed the destruction of several junk loads from Stanley. Even the imposition of a curfew increased the death rate. The Japanese enforced it with dog patrols. Many Chinese were homeless and thus unable to keep off the streets at night so were mauled to death if the dogs found them.

Much military booty was collected from the battlefield and British depots for shipment to Japan or other theatres of war. Something like 1500 cars were lashed to the decks of vessels bound for Tokyo. It has been estimated that up to 2.5 million tons of looted freight were removed from the Colony during the occupation.

Businesses, shops, schools, government departments, industries, libraries closed down. Black marketeers, racketeers, gambling den and brothel owners thrived with the consent of the Japanese. A new currency was introduced instead of the Hong Kong dollar – the Japanese Military Yen (MY). Four dollars would get you one MY, which was worth about 12p of today's money. I noted in my diary in early 1944 that a pound of rice sweepings cost MY 7.50 ($30). Before the war such a sum would have bought several 240 pound sacks of top quality rice. Right from the start our lives revolved around how we would get the next meal. The economy stagnated, acute shortages developed, while the Japanese priority was to feed themselves. The situation worsened as the Allied blockade tightened into a noose around the Colony's shipping lanes. Almost every square inch of the New Territories was devoted to rice growing. Formosan rice was introduced to try to give a heavier crop but it attracted destructive insects, and the soil, like the people, was starved of nourishment.

From 27 December we were all confined to our stations awaiting a decision of the Japanese on how they were to organize the policing of Hong Kong. For all of us the paramount necessity was food. How did I arrange rations for my men when the Japanese had taken over the distribution depots, and special passes were required for both the food and travel? My friend Lance Searle, who was at No. 7 Police Station, had solved the problem with a display of considerable courage and coolness.

He suddenly appeared sitting in the side car of a motor cycle combination waving his pass. He triumphantly explained that not only did he have the documents for food and travel but also the use of a truck and a Japanese soldier to guard it. It seemed to me to be a minor miracle. It transpired that No. 7 (Western) Station had been taken over by the military under a high ranking officer who Lance was sure was a general. Using his powers of bluff and bluster he had been allowed in to see the general, who was fat and round with close-cropped hair. He had been seated at a desk encircled by a bevy of staff officers. But what was really alarming was the display on the desk. Neatly lined up were various types of revolver, barrels pointing at Lance. The general eyed him stonily and silently while Lance launched into his plea for a pass while trying, not entirely success-fully, to avoid glancing at the weaponry.

Lance explained that he had several hundred men under his command, many being Indians, for whom he had few rations. He stressed that feeding the Indians was particularly difficult as for religious reasons they were not permitted to eat certain sorts of food. The general listened for a while and then, without speaking, picked up a revolver and started to fiddle with it as though he did not understand how it worked. On impulse, and with more courage than sense, Lance leant forward and reached out to show him. Instantly the general pointed the revolver at Lance and slowly and deliberately pulled the trigger. There was a click, followed by an hysterical hyena-like laugh from the general who, giving Lance a knowing look, placed the revolver back on his desk.

"Do you know the Germans are now in Paris and France has surrendered?" the general asked, thinking perhaps that he was imparting some startling news. As these events had occurred six months previously Lance did not reply so the general tried again.

"You're a gentleman." It was a statement, not a question.

"Why do you think that?"

"Because you have wavy hair. Only English gentlemen have wavy hair." More squeaky laughter. Lance, sensing that things might be moving his way, again pressed the point on the need for passes.

Possibly because of his hair, the fact that he had not cringed when the empty revolver was fired at him, and because the Japanese professed to be the friends of Indians, the passes were issued, plus a truck and guard thrown in for good measure.

Having regaled me with this story with much laughter Lance suddenly said, "George, why don't we try to get a pass for you?" Why not indeed? I certainly had Indians to feed, although I lacked wavy hair so might not be regarded as a gentleman with whom a general could deal. We roared off through deserted streets, a European sergeant driving, Lance in the side car and myself riding pillion. Regretfully the general was not available, and no amount of persuading could make him so. I did not get my pass, although I was able to scrounge some rations so the effort had been worthwhile.

The next day, the 28th, luck intervened on my side, although at the time I was certain the reverse was true. Two young Japanese soldiers each armed with rifle and fixed bayonet arrived at the station. One, who I later found out was a Private Sukoo, said:

"You officer in charge?" I nodded.

"Come, you wanted." He declined to elaborate, only repeating. "You come – now." It was not reassuring.

As I was marched along Caine Road to the university, about half a mile away, I was acutely conscious of the bayonets behind me. I had to do something to keep my confidence up so I lengthened my stride. It was the only way I could think of equalizing the situation, make them feel small having to scurry along on their bandy little legs to keep up. It worked, although not for long. Soon I felt a rap on the shoulder and turned to hear Sukoo say, "Ah! So sorry, you walk too fast. You big man, we small." I had made my point. Then around a bend came about two or three hundred British soldiers under heavy guard. Some waved at me, others cheered. I felt bucked, if only fleetingly, as I was under no illusions as to what might be waiting for me once we reached our destination. Being singled out to be marched away was not exactly a pleasant feeling.

Had I known we were heading for the headquarters of the Japanese Gendarmerie, and had I known their notorious reputation for ruthlessness, or the awe in which even Japanese senior officers held them, I would have been a decidedly worried man. As it was the significance of being paraded in front of a major in that organization did not perhaps hold the horrors it would have done a few months later. The officer, sitting behind what had once been a dining room table, chain smoked and wore a reasonably well fitting uniform with the chrysanthemum flower emblem on his collar. As I learned later this national flower of Japan was worn exclusively by Gendarmerie personnel of all ranks. It seemed a highly inappropriate badge for such a hated, all-powerful organization responsible to no one but the Emperor.

The major motioned me to sit down. With Sukoo interpreting he told me he was the, "officer in command of the Western Safety-Making Area". When he got up and moved towards a map in the corner of the room I saw he was wearing slippers instead of the usual field boots. The laces at the end of his breeches were dangling over his socks. It looked highly comical and most unmilitary, but I was not so foolish as to laugh. Afterwards I was to see this form of dress frequently, as it was a favourite way of relaxing – ill-fitting boots off at the first opportunity, or better still stripped to a "fan-douche" (jock strap).

He placed a map on the table and unrolled it. I saw that it was a cheaply produced replica of my Police Division. He then gabbled something at Sukoo which sounded like staccato bursts from a Bren gun. His hard face, covered in short stubble, was not unpleasant. All he needed was a good shave. I sensed Sukoo gripping his rifle for support as he said, "The major says you look this place?" I replied that I did. Whereupon the major pointed again at the map and, through Sukoo snapped, "Which place bad man?" I did not really have much of a choice so I gave the areas where the main opium divans and gambling dens were located. The major drew red rings on the map. Then came the awkward one. "You tell me name of bad men." I did not feel it would help the proceedings to say we have destroyed all important records so I made up a few half names and vague addresses hoping that I sounded convincing.

The questioning continued along these lines for a while. Then the major brought it to an end with: "Ah so! You like cigarette?" He offered me a tin of Gold Flake and I noticed another of Players on his desk. There were no signs of any Japanese brands. As he seemed in a mellow mood I resolved to try my luck on the question of a pass. I spun him the line of how difficult it was to feed my Chinese and Indian police, deliberately not mentioning the Europeans. There was no hesitation; he wrote something on a piece of paper and chopped (stamped) it. Translated the pass read: "This officer can go anywhere. Do not stop him." Short and decidedly sweet. With a Gendarmerie chop it was a passport nobody would query. I had gone one better than Lance.

From then on Sukoo visited the station every day until we moved. Why he did so I was not sure. He sat around for an hour or so and then left. I found him useful when making requests, and I was intrigued to learn that he had learnt his English from a Presbyterian missionary in Japan. He was as helpful as he could be in his rank, and one of only two Japanese I had dealings with who were basically decent men, not corrupted or brutalized. The other was an official interpreter at Stanley towards the end of our internment called Watanabe, of whom more later. He was a Lutheran minister.

I had hidden a motor cycle combination at the station before the Japanese arrived to seize our transport, and this is what I used to go about collecting rations. The Japanese had found a heavy duty Norton motor cycle which was a great fascination to them. They would sit on it, feel its weight and then get off. It was far too big and cumbersome for them to risk driving it, and for many their legs were just not long enough. It would have been a humiliating loss of face to have tried and crashed. It was several days before a somewhat taller and braver individual did ride it gingerly away. What was left of the other vehicles were towed away as they had either been damaged by mortar fire or deliberately sabotaged by our Chinese transport sergeant.

Sergeant Blackburn, usually known as "44 Blackburn" because of his police number, used to act as my driver for the combination. At frequent intervals we would be stopped at checkpoints or by sentries, but the pass always worked. They would examine it with infinite care, making a great show of how diligent they were being. Sometimes a soldier would be holding it upside down while going through the motions of checking its authenticity. Undoubtedly most could not read, but there was no mistaking the Gendarmerie chop. It never failed. On one trip when Lance was with me we were waved down by two young Japanese officers complete with swords. After much grunting and gesticulating on their part we realized that they wanted a lift. One got onto the pillion behind me, and as Lance remained glued to the seat in the sidecar the other perched on the front of it. Then, pointing down into the town they shouted, "Go!". Blackburn let in the clutch and accelerated hard. It nearly had the desired effect, but they managed to hang on. To the amazement of some Chinese onlookers we deposited them at their destination without mishap.

Soon afterwards I called in at Police HQ (Gloucester Hotel) to be told that I had just missed witnessing a sickening scene. Some of the Sikh police who had not already defected to the Japanese had got drunk and run amok. They had stripped off their uniform, then, in their ridiculous red underpants and with their long dank hair let down, except for the topknot with a silver dagger stuck through it, had gone on the rampage. They had rushed around swearing and spitting at European officers and civilians as well as cursing the British government.

During the days following the surrender a number of Sikhs took the opportunity to settle old scores with Punjabi Muslim Policemen as well, particularly with senior ranks with whom they had a grudge. The worst example I know of this was when they tied a Punjabi Muslim sergeant-major to a truck and dragged him along the road until he died. Although some of those who actively sided with the Japanese later became disillusioned we never recruited Sikhs again after the war. Those who did remain loyal, mostly the older men, were allowed to serve on to their pension.

By way of contrast I shall always remember on our way to the temporary Police Headquarters at the Gloucester Hotel, after being ordered to assemble there by the Japanese, passing an old government Punjabi Muslim watchman. He was standing quite alone, holding an ancient Lee Enfield rifle of World War I vintage, watching us approach. As we came level he shuffled to attention and presented arms, embarrassingly trying to look dignified. But the most touching moment was when my Punjabi Muslim sergeant-major, with tears in his eyes and swearing loyalty to the King, gave me a box of cigars as we said goodbye. I can see him clearly today, a tall thin man with finely chiselled features. I never saw him again.

On 29 December the Japanese held their Victory Parade. Over 2,000 men, with detachments representing all the units that had taken part in the conquest of Hong Kong, took part. They marched through the streets to Happy Valley from the Western District with Lieutenant-General Sakai, commander of the 23rd Army, on a white horse in the lead. They had every reason to celebrate. Not only had Hong Kong fallen quickly, but it was the first British territory to surrender, and it was the first time since their victory over the Russians in 1904 that they had defeated a European army. I described my glimpse of it in my diary:

"The afternoon of the 29 December found me on one of my visits to the Gloucester Hotel [Police HQ] and from there I saw part of the Japanese Victory Parade. Streets in the vicinity were cleared. No one was allowed to look out of the windows or doors overlooking the route. Everything had been done to ensure the safety of the high ranking military and naval dignitaries participating in this show of arms. This, however, did not prevent a careless soldier firing his rifle by mistake and killing one of his own officers. We heard about this later. As part of the route was along Des Voeux Road past the hotel we were able to take a sneaking look at the procession despite all precautions. Nowhere was there any rejoicing. Everywhere was quiet except for marching feet and occasional military commands. Overhead three flights of planes flew up and down the route several times. Then the parade came in sight headed by a bugle band, a large part of which appeared to be composed of officers. They were followed by the general and other high ranking naval and military officers, all of whom were mounted. Following them on foot came a large party of Japanese soldiers carrying little white boxes on their chests. These contained the ashes of those Japanese killed in action.[3] Their casualties had been high. It is no use expressing what I felt as what seemed a never-ending column of men filed past. Words are inadequate. I went back to my station a sad man."

It was on the same afternoon that the first Japanese representative arrived to take over my police station. I had expected a Japanese officer, perhaps from the Gendarmerie, so I was somewhat taken aback by the inoffensive little Chinese who appeared. He was wearing the blue uniform of the Japanese-controlled police in the neighbouring Chinese province of Kwangtung and was pathetically unsure of himself. I doubt if he had ever dealt with Europeans before, and we certainly did not make any effort to put him at his ease. I handed him the keys to the arms cage, and that was that. We studiously ignored him while he sat silently on the narrow bench in the charge room.

Sometime later the wretched Chinese was galvanized into action. He sprang up, saluted, bowed, saluted again and froze to attention, staring ahead like a mesmerized rabbit that suddenly realizes he has been trapped by a fox. The reason for his fright was the Japanese colonel standing in the charge room. He was small but broad, with stunted legs thrust into badly fitting field boots topped by baggy khaki riding breeches, and a jacket which barely covered his ample backside. His uniform cap covered a wide, but not unkind looking, peasant face. Dangling at his side, almost touching the ground, was that symbol of terror and suffering usually associated with Japanese officers or NCOs – a Samurai sword. He was escorted by two soldiers with rifles, plus an obsequious White Russian, with a nasty, smirking face, who acted as interpreter.

The colonel ambled slowly round the station showing no interest in anything until he spotted the arms cage. There he turned to the policeman from Canton and barked something in a language of which I knew nothing but would soon recognize anywhere. The Chinese police officer went through the saluting and bowing rigmarole once more before turning to me and saying in Cantonese, "The colonel says he would like to see the arms." In his agitated state he had forgotten that he had the keys. After the cage had been opened up the colonel moved forward to inspect the weapons. Huffing and puffing, interspersed with hissing noises and several "Ah Sos" he actually got down on his knees to examine the arms. I then realized why he was showing such an interest. His badly fitting tunic had ridden up over his broad bottom to reveal two revolvers stuck into an old belt around his waist. After carefully choosing two he added one to his collection and handed the other to the interpreter, who said with a smirk, "The colonel says that all Europeans must leave this station tomorrow and report to the Gloucester Hotel." Thus ended my visit from the newly appointed Japanese commissioner of police.

I managed to take a suitcase and one small bag containing what I thought were essential clothes. In the pockets of my uniform I put some family photographs together with my passport and a silver cigarette case. Except for the passport I still have all these today. We marched to the Gloucester Hotel the next morning having sent the women on ahead in a truck. Our stay there was, apart from being overcrowded, fairly comfortable compared with what was to follow in the months and years ahead.

It was at the hotel that our informal "mess" evolved. With only a few changes it was to last us over three and a half years. Looking back it was probably this banding together of a small group of young officers of similar interests and background that kept us alive. One of us was later to escape, but we all survived internment and subsequently continued to serve in the Colonial Police. Two became commissioners; three of us are still around at the time of writing. To begin with it was an unconscious decision to stick together which, after we were imprisoned at Stanley, developed into a lasting arrangement with agreed "rules". It became our guiding principle that everything we had except for sentimental possessions was shared. This was primarily to mean food, but also other things such as money, cigarettes, International Red Cross (IRC) parcels, soap and books. We also shared out any privileges, or proceeds from black-market sales, chores, cooking or camp duties. We ate as a mess, the same food, the same amount of food and at the same time. We became practical communists and in our case it worked.

To begin with there were six of us, including myself. The senior was W. P. Thompson or "W.P." as he was commonly known. He was a tough, forceful character who I certainly regarded with some awe. When I met him at the Gloucester Hotel he was looking even tougher than usual with his face badly scarred by bomb fragments, as he had been wounded when Police HQ was hit a few days earlier. Behind the hard exterior was a shrewd and artistic mind. Geoffrey Wilson, a senior ASP, was clever and a leader, with a touch of the cynic in his makeup. Puffing away at his pipe he was full of drive and, with the added maturity that marriage gives a man, he ran the mess after Thompson escaped. Henry Heath, another ASP, had been born in the West Indies where his family had lived for generations. I had briefly shared a house with him and others before he had gone to India to learn Urdu. An accomplished games player, he was tall, with fair hair. Colin Luscombe, another ASP, was the rough and rugged type bursting with energy, and the business man among us. At that time he was full of the story of how he had given away the girls at the "mass" wedding in the cathedral on Boxing Day. Lance Searle, a Cambridge Boxing Blue, He had also shared a house with me and I had worked with him in his district. He was one of the bravest men I have known. The most junior – myself.

At first we were able to leave the hotel for short walks and we made the most of this. After one such walk with Henry Heath I was later to record in my diary my impressions:

"The main streets had again become crowded, but it was a crowd without law and order, without aim or purpose. Most of the shops were shut but the hawkers were doing brisk business in, I suspect, looted foodstuffs. . . . The Chinese faces looked blanker than ever, they looked miserable, they looked lost. I suppose most of them were wondering where the next meal was coming from. Many of them had lost their jobs."

Japanese soldiers were out and about demanding valuables such as pens or watches off Europeans. It was not uncommon to see a soldier with up to four or five Rolex (always the favourite) watches on his arm. They were also collecting cap badges. I kept out of the way and my cap badge, which was solid silver, survived until my dining out night on retirement when one of my brother officers "borrowed" it. After all those years to lose it like that hurt.

It was during this time that Geoffrey, Henry, Colin and Lance decided they really must get one last decent meal. They decided to dine at the Parisien Grill, known to most as the "P.G.". It was a highly fashionable restaurant which was still open and run by Emile Landau, a Jew of indeterminate nationality, who was then claiming to be a French citizen and therefore neutral. In the circumstances nobody could blame him for juggling with his nationality. He was a typically suave, smooth operator.

Emile greeted them profusely, but, mindful of all possibilities, seated them at a table in a dingy corner furthest away from the entrance. Within a few minutes four or five Japanese officers came in and sat down at the opposite end of the restaurant. At first, with Emile fussing over them, they paid no attention to the four European officers hurrying through their meal, anxious to get out unnoticed but determined not to waste a mouthful. Then as the drinks slipped down the Japanese started to focus their attention on the Europeans in uniform in the corner. They stared. Plainly they did not believe what they saw. Then they started hissing like a cat when it sees a dog at close quarters and banging the table. As my friends told it afterwards: "When they started to fiddle with their swords we didn't wait. We went through the kitchen like a dose of salts and over the

back wall. Poor Emile, we didn't wait to pay the old bugger his bill."
Neither, I suspect, did the Japanese.

Emile remained a Frenchman until he found it helpful to become
a Turk, although in the end he caught up with us as a prisoner in
Stanley jail. His offence was connected with his failing to agree terms
for the sale of the Parisien Grill to the Japanese, whose Civil
Administration wanted to acquire it. He was, however, one of the
world's survivors. At Stanley he was given the job of looking after
the prison commandant's pigs. By drinking the pig swill, and
sneaking choice pieces of the pigs he slaughtered, he became positively plump. In the end he was by far the fattest man ever to
complete a sentence in Stanley jail. His younger brother Leo, who
had been helping his father run Jimmy's Kitchen (another restaurant),
was not so lucky. He fought with the Volunteers and spent nearly
four years in a prisoner of war camp.

On 4 January, 1942, the Gendarmerie issued a proclamation
ordering all Europeans, except third nationals and the police, to
assemble at the Murray Road parade ground. They were to bring
only what they could carry. They were divided into groups and
moved under guard into various waterfront hotels. The first stage
towards internment for them had started. I watched them go, and
later wrote:

"I saw them go past the Gloucester Hotel, herded together under their
guards. There were old men and women struggling with what they had
managed to save from the wreck. There were women with children in
their arms. Some carried blankets strapped across their backs with
suitcase in hand, others had packs, others still used Chinese carrying
poles or had bundles wrapped in blankets. The rich and the poor were
alike. It was a pathetic sight. Never in a hundred years had the Chinese
seen such a thing as these people struggling along to an uncertain
future. Some smirked, but most showed their normal inscrutable
expressions. It was no business of theirs. They had their own worries."

Soon it was to be our turn.

"Get out! Get out! You have half an hour." The two Gendarmerie
officers' yells were the signal that the days of comparative comfort
in the hotel were over. It was 6 January. I wrapped up my blankets
and a few clothes in my valise which I strapped to my back; other

belongings I thrust in a suitcase. In a haversack I put some tinned food, and in my free hand I carried a lamp. My companions were equally burdened. Japanese soldiers formed us up in Des Voeux Road, and eventually we moved off with Fu King and Geoffrey's "boys" faithfully following at a distance to see where we were going. It was to the Luk Hoi Tung Hotel.

The Luk Hoi Tung was nothing like the Gloucester; rather it was a seedy, fourth rate establishment near the waterfront catering for travelling traders or seamen. It was one of many similar hotels in the area which were the hangouts of pimps and prostitutes. Very much a "one night stand" joint, called in those days "sly brothels". About 250 of us were packed into its forty odd rooms (meant for two each) which opened onto narrow verandahs along each of the two floors. Once everybody had been pushed in the iron grill door at its dingy entrance was slammed shut and locked. A solitary sentry sat on a stool outside, leaving us none the wiser as to our ultimate fate, or our immediate problem of food.

The six of us commandeered a room and settled down to wait. This was much to the annoyance of the Chinese representative, Mr Wu, a miserable little man who was in effect now our jailer. The Japanese had specified a minimum of seven people per room, so he was terrified of the consequences to himself of there being one less in ours. Only with prolonged persuasion and veiled threats could Wu be induced to overlook our transgression.

It was a small, dark room with plywood walls, the only ventilation being the half-size swing door that opened onto the verandah. Taking up most of the room were two small, Chinese-style double beds with wooden bed boards and straw mats over them. Rolled up at the end of each bed was a filthy "mintoi", Chinese quilt. The pillows were two oblong porcelain bricks. In one corner was a hideous Victorian china wash basin and jug. Taking up yet more space was a chest of drawers plus a cupboard. Two of us slept on each bed, the rest of us on the floor. I preferred the verandah despite the constant stream of visitors to the three stinking lavatories at the end of it. I found them less offensive than the rats running around the room or the cock-roaches dropping from the ceiling.

Food, together with extreme boredom coupled with lack of exercise, was our main preoccupation while at the Luk Hoi Tung. There was also endless speculation as to what the Japanese had in store for us. Two meals a day of a bowl of rice with a few chicken's feet or three or four lumps of rotten meat was all we got. In the coming months we were to look back on the size of these meals with hungry relish.

We were able to supplement our meals by bribery or, if not, food was for sale by hawkers through the grill door at the front entrance when the Indian guards (mostly ex-police) allowed it. Nevertheless, it was to our "boys" that we looked for our main supply. Every day one of them appeared outside the hotel to receive our requests. These were shouted from the verandah and we then threw down the money. Later in the day the "boy" would return and, guard willing, hand us his purchases through the grill. If the guard was difficult we lowered a basket from the verandah when the moment was right. No praise is high enough for Fu King and the others for what they did at considerable risk to themselves. They had nothing to gain by helping us and everything to lose and yet they continued until we were interned at Stanley.

It was at the Luk Hoi Tung that I had the best rice pudding I have ever eaten. Several tins of Carnation milk and a handful of raisins and sultanas went into it, although we later regretted our extravagance. This was Henry's and Geoffrey's first serious effort at cooking, although listening to them one would have thought they were gourmet chefs whereas I doubt if either had ever done more than boil an egg. Our lack of fuel for the primus was solved by the daring initiative of Lance and Colin who had discovered a way out of the hotel. This was by way of a crude dumb waiter into the kitchen, and thence out the back door. Easy once you knew. They went back to the Gloucester Hotel and returned with two cans of kerosene – hence our pudding was not only delicious but demonstrated commendable "mess" enterprise. I was the only one who had not really contributed.

We spent much of the day on the verandah watching passers-by and those who stopped to gawk at us. The boredom was relieved every now and then by the beating of gongs accompanied by shouts of "Ta Kip" (robbery) or "Kau Meng" (save life). The latter would get us dashing to the verandah, if we were not already there, to try to get a glimpse of any excitement below. At night the silence was frequently broken by shots, cries and the inevitable gong beating followed by running feet, more shots and more cries.

Several days beforehand we were made aware that we were to be moved again. The first intimation was a copy of a Japanese document written in quaint, barely understandable English which we read with much amusement. Paragraph one stated:

"1. The Head Quarter of the Internists Quarters of the Foreign Division of Political in Charge Department (Gyoseika) will be established in Hong Kong. . . ."

The gist of what followed was clear in that the British, American and Dutch nationals were to be interned, and living quarters would be divided up by nationality and sex. There was more about ration scales, behaviour expected, and prohibited possessions – ". . . internists are not permitted to keep with them any corresponding apparition, Camera, Books, Maps, and other prohibited belongings." The section on treatment of internees is of interest in the light of what was to actually happen – "The treatment towards American, British, and Dutch will be based on the treatment which are going to Nipponese by the Government of the relative countries dealing in the way of gentleman-like."

We actually moved on 23 January, although for a couple of days prior to this we had seen many Europeans under guard from other hotels struggling past the Luk Hoi Tung with their belongings. The rumour was we were heading for Stanley, which seemed to make sense in so far as the main prison of the Colony was located there.

When our turn came we marched about 400 metres to the quay where two old ferry steamers were lying alongside. Despite the short distance we found it something of a struggle humping all our gear, due, I suppose, to the meagre food and lack of exercise over the past weeks. Before boarding an interpreter asked: "You gun?" I only understood what he was talking about when he added radios, cameras, and field glasses. "No," I replied. Unsmilingly he said, "OK, go". Surprisingly there was no attempt to search anybody or their baggage, which was perhaps just as well for "W.P.", as he still had a revolver in his possession.

The sea was smooth and the weather glorious. We sailed out of the harbour, turned west, and then south and south-east past Aberdeen headed for the Stanley peninsula, followed by the second ferry boat. It was good to talk to old friends, and it made a change from the monotony of the last three weeks. For me the most depressing thing was to see so many young mothers with their children, mothers who had either lost their husbands in the fighting or who were now prisoners of war. Some had absolutely no idea whether their menfolk were alive or not. I think it was when I saw HMS *Thracian* beached on a small island off Repulse Bay, with the Japanese flag flying from her mainmast, that the stark reality of what had happened hit home. I was a prisoner, subject to the every whim of my captors. Now it was a question of survival. It was late January, 1942, and I thank God that none of us had the power of foreseeing events to come, or the fact that it would not be until August, 1945, that we would be free again.

CHAPTER FOUR

INTERNMENT

"I am learning lots of things in this camp about human nature and people's characters which in normal times would have taken me years to learn. Above all I have learned that people should be happy if they enjoy good health, a good bed and three square meals a day."

Diary, 12 April, 1942.

Colonel Tokunaga Isao was nicknamed the "Fat Pig" as it best described his behaviour and appearance. He was a 54-year-old Japanese Army officer who had spent some 30 years in uniform. He lived in a palatial residence in Kowloon with a Chinese mistress where he supplemented his table with items stolen from International Red Cross (IRC) parcels.[1] His passion for playing bridge extended to inviting our Camp Representative up "the Hill" on a number of occasions, which he could not refuse but which caused some adverse comment if only because Gimson would be sure of a decent meal

He was in charge of all prisoner of war (POW) camps in Hong Kong, which meant that because Stanley was not designated as a military internment camp until 1944 we did not come directly under his authority at the outset. This was just as well. Like many Japanese he regarded prisoners, including women and children, as beneath contempt. According to his thinking they deserved no consideration and should be treated as sub-human. One of his earliest interrogations of some Canadians recaptured while escaping involved his adjutant (Lieutenant Tanaka) and interpreter (Lieutenant Niimori) bashing them with baseball bats for an hour in his office. He maintained at his trial in 1946, at which he was condemned to death (later commuted to life imprisonment) for war crimes, that he deserved a medal and that, "Japanese women and children find it better to die than become a POW". From April, 1942, for about five months, Tokunaga had four POW camps under his control and, as prisoners from these camps who were awaiting trial or were under sentence to specific jail terms or execution were always transferred to Stanley jail, they are involved in my story. I will devote a few lines to explaining them.

Immediately following the British surrender all POWs had been segregated by nationality and sent to three separate camps. The British, with some Chinese from the HKVDC, were imprisoned at Shamshuipo on the waterfront on the northern outskirts of Kowloon. The Indians went to Mautauchung, close to Kai Tak airport, while the Canadians and some other units were grouped at North Point, alongside the harbour on the island, in a former illegal immigrants' camp of wooden huts. Shamshuipo housed up to 5000 men and was the largest camp as it had been a British barracks in peacetime. The men of the Royal Scots sent there as prisoners were on familiar ground as they had been based there before the invasion. At Mautauchung the Indians were subjected to unremitting pressure to join the Indian National Army (INA). Some 200 out of over 1500 did so with varying degrees of enthusiasm.

In April, 1942, it was decided to separate the officers from their men, although a small minority were not moved. Accordingly about 500 officers were sent to Argyle Street Camp only 300 metres from Mautauchung, and within sight of Tokunaga in his new house. It had been constructed to detain Nationalist Chinese soldiers who had fled from China and as such was already equipped with searchlights, machine guns, guard towers, plus an electrified fence. The final change came in September when North Point was abandoned and the Canadian soldiers went to Shamshuipo and the officers to Argyle Street. Thus for much of the occupation there were three POW camps, all in Kowloon, and one internment camp for civilians on the island at Stanley.

The final Japanese decision on internment was that all European enemy nationals would be confined at Stanley; that women and children should not be segregated from the men; that the police be regarded as civilians (despite the fact that they had been designated a militia soon after the attack on Hong Kong); but that some key individuals, whose services were still required, should be confined at night to a hotel from whence they would be escorted to and from work each day. Good examples of the latter were Dr Selwyn-Clarke and the chairman of the HKSB, Sir Vandeleur Grayburn.

Although I did not know it then, it was due to the persuasive insistence of Dr Selwyn-Clarke that the Stanley peninsula was the chosen site for our internment. It had been suggested that the Peak was the most suitable place. This was rejected out of hand, not so much because it would have been difficult to secure, but because the internees would be looking down on their masters. The Japanese, ever conscious of their small stature, had a horror of being looked down on both mentally and physically. Time and time again during our captivity I would see evidence of this feeling of inferiority. The Japanese would invariably go to any lengths to contrive to look down on us in the physical sense. They would stand on something, their accommodation was always higher up, or they would make a prisoner sit or lie to receive his beating. In different circumstances it might have been amusing to watch an unusually short soldier trying to slap the face of a tall European – on tiptoe, reaching up, jumping up, and flailing away with his arms while his victim stood tall and bent his head back as far as he could. At times it was pure comic opera.

The Japanese had liked Selwyn-Clarke's suggestion of Stanley, which he had made on the basis of the peninsula being an isolated, healthy spot which could be easily sealed off from the island by a fence across the neck. On two sides the sea acted as a barrier, while to the south was Stanley Fort with its Japanese garrison.

The 3000 or more people who were ferried to the tiny jetty on the western side of the peninsula were dazed and demoralized. They stepped ashore into utter confusion. The area was full of sentries with hundreds of people darting frantically back and forth in the hunt for somewhere to live. All we were told was that certain buildings had been set aside for the Americans and Dutch. For the rest it was a free for all. "First come first served" or "all for me and none for you" seemed the appropriate catch phrases applicable to the British.

We, that is our "mess", dumped our baggage and rushed off to join the scramble. As the police were almost the last to arrive there was not much from which to choose. After a quick look at a few places which were already crammed we opted for a bungalow overlooking Stanley Bay which, although occupied, was so battered and filthy that the majority had passed it by.

Although Selwyn-Clarke had been able to visit Stanley with a small advance party a few days earlier virtually nothing had been done to prepare the area. About the only memorable thing the advance party did that I recall was to find numerous boxes of condoms which had been for the use of the Japanese troops in the area or at the Fort. The finders were later to do a brisk business in selling them to amorous internees. Although we were not at our best physically at Stanley sex did rear its head at times. Both marriages and births occurred, while the Japanese order that "Sexual intercourse is prohibited except between husband and wife or close friend" allowed for a whole range of possibilities. I, like most of us, was too hungry and more interested in finding food to survive.

The attempt to bury bodies that had littered the peninsula since fighting stopped a month previously had been only partially successful. I recorded:

"Along the edge of the lawn [of the bungalow] . . . were several graves; pathetic mounds of earth hastily heaped over bodies, one being a mattress flung over a body with a small pile of earth to keep it down but which could not hide the feet protruding from under it. On some of the graves were crudely fashioned crosses or a steel helmet with a jagged hole. On one cross which caught my eye were pencilled the words, 'To a brave British Tommy'. . . .Everywhere was littered with the debris of war – steel helmets, web equipment, discarded boots and uniforms. A good pair of brown boots attracted my attention and I picked them up to try them for size. I noticed they were of excellent quality, made by Hawkes. Then to my horror I saw the name West marked inside them. They belonged to my friend Captain West of the Middlesex Regiment who I knew had been killed at Stanley. Months later I learned that he had commanded that part of the last defence line at Stanley of which the bungalow was a part. I could not bring myself to wear them."

Needless to say the boots quickly vanished.

Our bungalow, which was called Bungalow "C", was in an awful condition. Aside from the graves the vicinity had live small arms ammunition strewn around like so much confetti; many unexploded grenades (mostly Japanese), mortar bombs and rifle grenades had been left precisely as they had been abandoned. The building itself had a shell hole through the roof, all windows were smashed and the walls scarred by bullets or shrapnel. The water pipes had burst, the drains were blocked and overflowing, blood was spattered everywhere. Grenades had been thrown inside destroying furniture and setting fire to the wooden floor while smoke had impregnated every room with a black, greyish grubbiness. The bathroom was the worst. It contained so much blood, filth and human excreta that a respirator had to be worn when we cleaned it. Little wonder it had been left for latecomers. Even so, forty-seven people were now in a building built for one small family. Its only redeeming feature was the glorious view across the bay to Lamma Island. It was the only thing about the place that war had been unable to touch.

We were a mixed lot. Men and women ranging in age from their early twenties to late fifties. Some had husbands or wives with them; most were single. There were police officers (ourselves), government officials and businessmen. People who would barely have passed the time of day were now lying side by side and sharing the same stinking, overflowing toilet. Some seemed totally apathetic, overwhelmed by the almost instantaneous transition from a life of security and servants to one of squalor and suffering. Others showed signs of willingness to make a go of it. We in the police had advantages. We belonged to a disciplined organization, we knew each other, we had come to Stanley as the largest autonomous group, and the majority of us were fairly fit and youthful. Certainly in our "mess" we did not have that helpless sense of being alone that sapped the will of some single people.

The women slept in the two tiny bedrooms and garage, with the men in the dining/sitting room. One married couple, quick off the mark, occupied the servant's room. I shall never forget the first night. My bed was three planks of wood resting on some bricks, which I had been fortunate to find. It was bitterly cold, with the rooms open to the chill winter wind, for Hong Kong can have frost in the hills during January, so I was thankful for my overcoat and blanket, but sorely missed the luxury of a pillow – too much soft living. I did eventually snatch a few fitful moments of sleep despite the endless night noises all around. People wheezed and snored, coughed and cursed and farted. Some had nightmares and my companions swore and blinded as they stumbled around trying to step over bodies or objects on their way outside to pee. We were not yet accustomed to a diet of rice and water which no sooner had it gone in one end was appearing, not noticeably changed by the journey, at the other.

Nobody saw anything humorous in our predicament. Unlike the cockney soldier who was a prisoner of war in Malaya when, as a punishment, the Japanese had crammed thousands of men into a small camp where they slept shoulder to shoulder in the compound, even on the roofs of buildings. There was no way to get to a toilet. What had to be done had to be done on the spot. One night the cockney was awoken by a trickle of "water" landing on his face. It came from the roof overhead. Sitting up, he shouted, "Be fair, mate. Waggle it around a bit."

Perhaps because the British internees were so numerous (some 2500 out of the 3000) they seemed the most disorganized. The advance party had allocated accommodation on a nationality basis which meant the 390 odd Americans being housed together in a block of modern European prison officers' flats, and the 60 or so Dutch in a single building near what had been the prison canteen. The rest of us had had to contend for everything else. The Americans seemed the best organized entity with a commendable tendency to work together. They buckled down to immediate cleaning up tasks whereas the British community, more divided by class, occupation and prejudice, spent too much effort and energy bickering or complaining. Not untypical of their attitude was the remark of the rotund British matron who, as she watched a group of Americans repairing a store, remarked, "Isn't it fortunate that the Americans have so many members of the working class in their camp?"

Because the major part of my story has, as its setting, the central portion of the Stanley peninsula it is important that the reader understands something of the geography of this rocky, hilly piece of land some 800 metres long by 600 across at its widest point. We will take an imaginary walk around its major features. At the time we were free to roam within the confines of the wire, but walking slowly I found I could get round in ten minutes.

Starting in the north the road from Stanley village bisected the neck of the peninsula at the police station where Police Sergeants Simpson and Whitley had made their stand. It had been taken over by the Gendarmerie detachment responsible for security in the area. At this point it forked. The left (eastern) branch became the approach road to the prison, and for part of its length was in a deep cutting with steeply rising ground on each side, particularly as it neared the main gate of the prison. To the east were fairly high cliffs overlooking Tai Tam Bay, with two pairs of large godowns some 200 metres apart alongside the road. These had been stocked with food by the British in the run up to the invasion. On the west of this road was St Stephen's College, scene of the massacre and "Tooti" Begg's lucky escape described in the Prologue. There were four blocks now packed with upwards of a thousand people, most of the police occupying block 10. Around the college were dotted the former senior staff bungalows, six in all, each with its once lovely garden smashed and torn by battle, each building now bulging with internees. They are lettered A-F on the map.

About 200 metres from the jail there was a short turn off to the left where a single building had been taken over by the Dutch community. Just a few metres further down the main road, also on the left, was the former prison staff club or recreation centre. It would eventually become our canteen. It was generally in this area that I operated when handing over food to be smuggled in to the prisoners in Stanley gaol. Close to this was the ration store which, more than any other, was to be focal point of our lives for almost four years. On the opposite side of the road was "the hill" as we came to know it. Up there were the two houses previously occupied by the Deputy Superintendent of Prisons (the Superintendent of Prisons lived away from the peninsula) and the prison's medical officer. These became the Japanese HQ housing their officers and, later, Formosan guards. We came to dread being sent up "the Hill".

Only a hundred metres from the prison was another left turn that led to the former prison warders' accommodation. On the right of this road, between it and the prison wall, was the main block of flats for European staff. I will refer to it as the Married Quarters in this book. From the top of the bank on which this building was built we were to discover that it was possible to see over the prison wall, and glimpse something of what was happening in parts of the compound inside. At the end of this short road were three additional blocks of flats which were occupied by the Americans (they were numbered A1, A2, and A3). Facing them across a hollow in the ground were the red brick staff quarters of the former Chinese and Indian warders. Blocks 15-18 had been for the former, with 12-14 housing the

Indians. To the south of the Americans was the solitary, two-storey red brick building used as the camp hospital, or Tweed Bay hospital as it was somewhat grandly called.

Unless we went in under sentence or, as happened after a few months, some of us were locked up inside at night, we never entered the prison. Its hugeness dominated the peninsula, with its high white perimeter walls, being well over a kilometre in length. The entrance door was gloomy, black and immense. The only occasion that we could get beyond its northern wall would be under escort down its western side, to swim at the place marked as bathing beach on the map, when we were allowed and felt we had the strength.

If one took the western (right) road at the police station fork it led, ultimately, to Stanley Fort. It hugged the shoreline through the camp and came close to Bungalow "C" before passing the cemetery. This was, and still is, a small military cemetery dating back to the original occupation of Hong Kong. I often came to sit here under the shade of the casuarina trees to gaze over the bay and reflect upon our future, and what was happening thousands of miles away over the horizon. It was a perfect place from which to watch the sun set. Most of the graves held victims of attacks by Chinese pirates or, much more numerous, typhoid fever and "the plague", which nowadays would be translated as malaria. A few metres further on this road passed the Preparatory School, and the jetty at which we arrived, before skirting the open space close to the sea that was to be the scene of the most barbarous, bloody beheading to take place in Hong Kong. After this the road heads for the Fort.

For two months there were no senior Japanese in the camp. Stanley was run, on behalf of the Japanese Foreign Affairs Ministry by a Chinese – Tseng Kok Leung. The only Japanese in camp were a handful of guards who occasionally patrolled the area to boost the usual Sikh police guards, who were now working for their former enemies. Because we were all civilian internees as distinct from prisoners of war Stanley was administered by a Japanese civil ministry rather than the military. This was to change in 1944, but until then our régime was slightly less rigorous than it would have been under Colonel Tokunaga – not that this prevented him visiting, nor the Gendarmerie involving themselves with individuals they considered worthy of interrogation.

The head of the Foreign Affairs department was a Mr Oda, the former Japanese Consul in Hong Kong, assisted by Mr Maejima and Mr Makimura. Oda was at first content to let Tseng run the day-to-day routine in camp through a number of subordinate Chinese supervisors, who had responsibility for various nationalities or groups of internees. For example the man in charge of internees billeted in St Stephen's College was Chang Kai Wai, known to us as "Darkie" Chang, a former employee of the Hong Kong branch of the National City Bank of New York. These Chinese were supposedly Wang Ching Wei men, although some were not. "Darkie" was in fact a Nationalist supporter, and was to become deeply involved with taking messages and money to and from town for our (and his) benefit, and was later lucky to escape with his life to China.

In March Oda decided that having no senior Japanese in Stanley camp was too risky and appointed the former Hong Kong Hotel barber, Yamashita, as camp commandant. His second-in-command was Nagasawa, an ex-shipping clerk. Both took up residence on "the hill", smugly satisfied at their rapid social and physical elevation. It was a strange situation. Behind the perimeter wire we wandered freely about under the control of two Japanese civilian nonentities, a handful of Chinese supervisors, watched somewhat disinterestedly by Indian guards. We soon learned, however, that the Japanese military were never far away. The Fort had an Army garrison, the prison had Japanese officers in charge, the Gendarmerie manned the post in the village, and our rations were issued by the Japanese military under a swine of a sergeant-major called Matsubishi.

Whenever two or three Englishmen are joined together they form a committee – it is called democracy. If ever there was a surfeit of committees it was in Stanley. Not that the Japanese had any dealings with committees, they were purely our way of organizing our lives as internees. The Japanese only recognized one man as having any internal authority and initially this was the American Mr Hunt who, by dint of personality and assisted by another fellow countryman, Neilson, was the de facto leader of the internees. Prior to this the senior British government representative behind the wire was John Fraser, a Colonial Service officer in his middle forties who had been Defence Secretary. In March, 1942, he was superseded by Franklin Gimson when he was himself interned with us. As the Colonial Secretary he had been number two to the Governor and as such the Japanese insisted on channelling all communications to or from the internees through him. He was the only one with direct access to the men on "the hill". After some difficult months he also became the Chairman of the British Community Council (BCC).

This council, like its American and Dutch counterparts, had members elected to it from the British internees. It had an executive committee and a host of so-called working committees which met endlessly to argue and bicker, pontificate and allocate on subjects such as rations, law and order, labour, the canteen, welfare, accommodation, medical matters, water, construction, maintenance, education, power supply, recreation and religion. Virtually every facet of life had its sub-committee. The system was refined as time passed. Typical was the setting up of a Billeting Appeal Tribunal formed by prominent citizens appointed by Gimson, or with his agreement, to deal with accommodation grievances – after food probably the most sensitive subject in Stanley. Gimson, who initially styled himself "Camp Commandant" but was later forced to call himself the "Representative of Internees", remained the only person the Japanese would deal with. They steadfastly refused to recognize the BCC.

Gimson who, it should be recalled, had arrived from Ceylon only the day before the invasion, had great difficulty to start with in being accepted by the majority of the British as having any authority over them. The majority of internees were not government men. They felt government had made grievous errors, been totally unprepared, complacent, shortsighted, and had let them down. Gimson summed up the feelings of many when he wrote, "The shock of defeat and the disgust with the past, together with the foreboding as to the future, reduced morale to the lowest ebb".

It took six months for life to settle into an acceptable routine. Like the rest of us my life was overshadowed by an unremitting struggle to stave off starvation, the craving for a smoke, and petty wrangling with my fellow internees brought about by boredom and the circumstances of our existence. Ninety percent of our waking hours was spent on activities connected with the next meal: queueing for it, black marketeering for it, scrounging for it, working for it, cooking it, or just plain dreaming about it. The more amusing or sensational aspects of this subject are covered in Chapter Six. The other ten percent went on other activities. There were the escape attempts, the operation of clandestine radios, the perverted tortures inflicted on some of us, the imprisonment and executions, the anxiety over the deterioriating health of us all, the air raids, and the occasional humorous highlights that helped to keep us sane. For the remainder of this chapter I will select from my diary the more mundane, if memorable, entries of these first few months, the intention being to give the reader the flavour of everyday existence. Trivial matters, minor personality clashes, slight or imagined grievances all became distorted and magnified in Stanley. I wrote many things in my diary that reflected thoughts and feelings at that moment in time, in those particular circumstances, when I was depressed, angry or frustrated over something. I would not have given most of them a moment's thought in normal life. The more traumatic occurrences will follow.

"25 March, 1942.
The big rumour today is that Russia has entered the war. Hope this is true as it will help us out here a great deal. A great feeling of lassitude has come over me today. In fact I feel quite weak. Other persons have been telling me that they get the same spells. Well, I have just weighed [myself] and find I have lost 10 lbs, being 164 lbs. There are some people here who have lost as much as 60 lbs already.

"The rest of the 'mess' are present, and guess what they are talking about. Not hard to guess, it is food, food, food. Wherever one goes the topic is food. Dog biscuits are voted to be a good meal if we can get them.

"I met old Lammert on my stroll today. He tells me he hopes his son is alive. As far as I know from authentic sources he has been beheaded. Of course I did not tell so, though I believe he has been told. Let's hope his wish is right."

Lammert managed the biggest auctioneering company in Hong Kong, and was a member of one of the oldest European families in the Colony. His son, Ernie, had been in the Volunteers and had in fact been executed near Causeway Bay during, or just after, the fighting, for refusing to salute a Japanese officer. The Japanese set great store by saluting and bowing. If we passed any Japanese, even a private soldier, we had to salute by removing our hats or, if we had no hat, we had to bow. I found this bowing in particular most demeaning, and went out of my way to avoid having to do it. Failure to pay the necessary compliments invariably resulted in a vigorous bout of face slapping which, if we were to avoid anything worse, had to be borne standing stoically. To be fair we were not treated any differently from the Indian guards or Japanese soldiers who were also slapped enthusiastically by their superiors for the slightest irregularity.

In August, 1944, Colonel Tokunaga visited Stanley on his first official inspection of the camp since it was officially included in his command. It was a splendid example of the saluting and bowing game. I wrote:

"The guard [of Formosans] had been drawn up on the main road just outside the canteen. Everybody who passed by had to bow or doff their hats. I saw several people, including women, being called back and made to bow. In order to stop any unpleasantness 'Ginger' Angus had been instructed by one of our people to stand on the road and warn people to bow. Donald Wilson, who is as scared as you can get, stopped dead in his tracks and bowed, nearly hitting his forehead on the ground. The Colonel is a very fat man, the fattest Japanese I have ever seen, and certainly the fattest man I have seen in two and a half years. He looks out of place in this skin and bone yard."

I was amused on one occasion to see that even Japanese soldiers can get fed up with saluting. An important Japanese officer had arrived on the road below our camp to inspect work being done by some prisoners under the supervision of a gendarme. This soldier quickly hid himself behind a bush, obviously wishing to avoid the endless bowing, saluting and standing to attention otherwise required of him. I was surprised to see he got away with it.

On another walk at around the same time I was suddenly confronted by the unbelievable. I stopped to stare for several moments to be certain my eyes were not deceiving me. They were not. There, flapping proudly from the prison flagpole was the Union Jack. I discovered that it had been raised briefly by the Japanese as a part of their film-making of the fall of Hong Kong.

We despised the Sikh police for their behaviour after the surrender so we took any opportunity to annoy them, although these were few as we had to be careful. The younger ones could be vicious. The liberation of India was, to them, just around the corner, and meanwhile we, their oppressors, were in their hands. Former constable Gian Singh, an elderly Sikh with a beard streaked with grey, wearing a dirty khaki turban and a mixture of uniform, was our frequent butt. He was usually on duty, armed with a rifle, at the sentry box on the rocky point near the Tweed Bay hospital. This was on the path which we took for our evening walk around camp. As we passed Gian we invariably subjected him to taunts as to what we would do to him for his treachery (he was not actually a traitor) when the British were back in charge. I am sure at times he did not know whether to present arms or shoot us.

One evening as we neared his sentry box Gian came out holding up his hand to stop us and, putting his rifle between his knees, produced a bottle of Jamaican rum from under his dirty old coat and handed it to us saying, "Sahib, sahib, the Union Jack forever fluttering in my heart."

"30 March, 1942.
I have just heard a most amusing story concerning Shaftain (OC CID) whom I call 'the great I am'. He tries to make out he is such a law-abiding citizen . . . and is at present trying to be the CP's confidant. Well, last night he was wandering home about curfew time (8.00 pm) when he was stopped by a camp guard who pointed a revolver at him and took him into the prison nearby. There he was searched by the commandant and found to possess a jar of marmite. He was asked to account for it and said he had paid $55 for it. He was not believed, and accused of stealing it from the godown. A gun was pointed at his head and threats made. Eventually, after half an hour . . . he was released. Poor old Shaftain, this must have frightened him and shaken his integrity.

"9 May, 1942
The 'History of the Plum Duff' is worth recording. In the days when the flour issue was scarce and erratic it was the custom at the [camp] hospital to save up enough flour and give all the patients a plum duff on Sunday (in those days a great treat). However, the patients got to know that this was a regular custom and therefore refused to be discharged until they had their Sunday meal. Hamilton, the Government Auditor, got stomach trouble and landed up in hospital. He got information while there that plum duff day had been changed to an indefinite day during the week. His informant told him that Friday was the likely day but, on Tuesday, he was discharged from hospital much to his disgust and unwillingness. He did, however, manage by various excuses to continue to feed at the hospital for three more days until the 'great day' arrived. But he got no duff because the doctors

had twigged his plan. He stormed and ranted until a piece was found for him."

A pathetic, but not untypical, example of how otherwise honest people can become totally self-centred and unscrupulous when faced by adverse circumstances. A small peep at the darker side of human nature.

"30 May, 1942.
Last night Langston and Dalziel who were sleeping outside at the back of the bungalow were woken up at about 5.00 am by snarls and growls. Langston, at Dalziel's instigation, got up to have a look. He went to the edge of the garden and looked down the slope to the wire fence. There Dalziel saw him leap in the air and fly back into the boiler room shouting 'There's a tiger down there'. . . . Next morning, on being told the story we were inclined to laugh.

"31 May, 1942.
Slept very badly owing to stomach trouble. During the night we were woken by three rapid shots and much shouting.

"1 June, 1942.
Early this morning there was much activity on the hill behind the camp which was being searched by parties of Chinese and Indian police under Japs. . . . One of the Chinese supervisors told me that an Indian policeman had been mauled by a tiger at about 2.00 am."

Two tiger guards were instituted, one armed with a gong, the other with a gardening fork. The bungalows had no doors or windows so for several nights there was considerable apprehension at night.

"4 June, 1942.
As usual we all slept outside. At about 3 am I heard Colin say, 'Geoffrey! Don't move there's a TIGER eating a bone behind your bed!' Then he said, 'Stephen, nobody move. The tiger is at the foot of Stephen's bed.' My bed was around the corner so I loosened my mosquito net and very gradually slipped out of bed ready to take some action, but what I, or any one else, could do was doubtful. Then Colin said, 'Where is Farrar? My God! He's eating him.' This was too much for Searle who came along to see what was happening. Colin then shouted, 'Don't move, you fool Searle!' Just then Farrar woke up and

it was discovered that what Colin had seen was a black coat lying across Farrar's body with one end lying on his white pillow. The pillow he thought was the bone and the coat the animal."

A tiger was indeed on the loose, probably from a circus that had been located at Causeway Bay. It was subsequently shot and the carcass, which weighed some 240 lbs, was given to an internee called Bradbury to be skinned. He had worked as a butcher at the main dairy farm and was probably the most unpopular man in the camp – a real life Uriah Heap as I will explain later. As the reader is aware this skin is still on display today in the Stanley Tin Hau temple. Bradbury's photograph subsequently appeared with the dead animal in a Japanese newspaper, although I did not see it in the *Hong Kong News*.

This paper was a two or three page sheet produced by the Japanese for propaganda purposes which circulated around Stanley. For some time it was edited in town by a former Royal Navy Commander called C. M. Foure, who many considered a flagrant collaborator. His was a sad story. He had been in command of a gunboat on the river at Canton in the 1930s when Chinese mobs attacked the European settlement, the Shameen. He opened up on the crowds with his machine gun, for which he was dismissed from the service. He came to Hong Kong and "went native" as we used to say, in a low-class Chinese slum. Nevertheless, his editing of the news sheet was not treachery as he was able to put across the rumours, half-truths, and exaggerated Japanese war victories in such a way that it was obvious to an English reader what was fact and what was fiction. Later he was interned with us after completing a term of imprisonment. I met him briefly, and although it soon became clear that he was violently anti-"Establishment" he was not anti-British. He was what we called in those days a "gentleman". Nevertheless, he was something of an outcast from conventional society and had few friends. Most could not forgive him his rabid communism or the militancy with which he had advised the Chinese trade guilds before the war. He was regarded as a traitor to his class if not to his country.

We all lived in fearfully overcrowded conditions, and while some of us allowed these conditions to degenerate into squalor most made some effort to keep their rooms clean, or even attempt to decorate where possible – virtually impossible in the majority of buildings as they were pockmarked and pitted with bullet holes or smeared with filth. Nevertheless, some Americans had managed to decorate one wall and it was admired, with some amusement, by those allowed to see it. The commandant got to hear about it and decided to use this room as a show piece for some visiting Japanese dignitaries, which I believe included a minor member of the Emperor's family. The occasion was the forthcoming American repatriation.

"26 June, 1942.

The Americans have been informed that they will be going aboard the *Asama Maru* on Monday 29th [for repatriation]. This is the third time they have been given a sailing date but I think they will sail this time.

This evening three Japanese officers got out of a car and entered the American quarters. As usual they walked around and looked into various rooms. In one room they saw a map on the wall. This was a home-made map of the world showing the route which the Americans hope to go by to Lourenço Marques, and that which the Japanese will use from America [bringing Japanese internees for exchange]. The Japanese officers were all wreathed in smiles as they examined this map. Then, to their horror, they noticed that Japan was missing! A change came over the scene. They lined up the three men who happened to be in the room and smacked their faces. The Japanese went berserk, ranting and raving.

"29th June, 1942.

So the Americans have gone. Today at about 13.30 hours the *Asama Maru* sailed up the Lamma Channel and anchored about three miles off the Lamma Island Point. Meanwhile in the bay below the barges and launches which were there yesterday were joined by a tug and a Star Ferry. Meanwhile the Police had put a guard around the American quarters to prevent looting of beds, etc. from these quarters by the remaining Britishers and Dutch, as they are going to be occupied later by some of the police and civilians. At 1430 hours the Americans were marched off to the waiting launches.

"30 June, 1942.

At 1800 hours the *Asama Maru* started on her voyage to Lourenco Marques. She is going firstly to Saigon and then to Singapore to pick up more Americans. Before she set sail she gave several toots from her siren, with a final one of nine toots ... [they] certainly did sound mournful and made me think of home. How far away it seems now."

A number of the Americans gave away as much as they could to their friends left in camp. I was fortunate to get a towel, hat, pillow and sheet, all real luxuries. Rosalie Lewis, the madam from the European brothel, was among those who left. She was given a list of addresses by dozens of men who wanted her to write to their mothers. She kept her promise to them all. Her letter telling them the whereabouts and health of their sons was frequently the first news they had had since the fall of Hong Kong. Little did they realize that the letter from the charming old lady which brought them news of their sons came from the madam of a brothel.

"1 July, 1942.
Tomorrow we move to our new billets. . . . We are not, however, going to the American quarters we were promised but are going instead to the Indian quarters [Block 12] which are undoubtedly the most unhealthy quarters in the camp. This sudden change of plans is undoubtedly a double cross on somebody's part, and a nasty one at that. . . . I am certain that wrangling has been going on amongst the Billeting Committee to get their friends into the American quarters which are better quarters – the whole affair is a disgusting episode. The Indian quarters, which we commonly refer to as 'the Peak' and its tenants as the 'Peak coolies' are a series of flats, very small flats.

"2 July, 1942.
To add insult to injury the Billeting Committee asked the police to help them show the people moving into the American quarters to their new rooms. Each new tenant brought a billeting card with them which showed name, age, sex. . . . This way I wasted three and a half hours in the rain. . . . When Barton came along with his Eurasian wife and thirteen children I said, 'Sign this register please'. 'Is it all right if I sign for my children?' he asked. 'Certainly,' I replied, 'but you must put down all their ages and names.' This he proceeded to do, asking each child its name and age. He appeared to be uncertain sometimes of their names, sometimes of their ages. I found it difficult not to laugh. The children's ages were 22, 21 (son of 20 in Shamshuipo) 19, 18, 17, 16, 15, 14, 13, 9, 7 and 3. He seems to have had four years' rest between 13 and 9 years of age. His family took up two rooms."

In the event we made the best of the Indian quarters. The move may have saved our lives as our old bungalow was hit by US bombs in

1945 and a number of occupants killed (see Chapter 11). We occupied two tiny rooms with Geoffrey Wilson, Henry Heath and Lance Searle in one room and Walter Scott (the DCP) and Booker (an ASP) and I in the other. Our "mess" had lost Thompson who had escaped (see Chapter 5) so we were down to five, as Scott and Booker did not belong.

By the end of June we had been internees for six months. I put down some of my thoughts at the time:

"As I write our future is uncertain. Will our food get more? Will it get less (nearly an impossibility)? Will we be repatriated or not? The future holds these answers. Never shall I forget the terrible pangs of hunger.... We have had to make our own food receptacles ... old tins have been used.... The canteen opens every now and again and from this (if one has money), one can get food after waiting in a queue for hours.... A Welfare Society is functioning to supply clothes [I was immensely proud of my shorts that I made from a flour bag with a bunch of grapes and the words 'Best Australian Grape Brand' printed on them across my backside].... Neutrals [in town] are allowed to send us parcels twice a week. Those who have good neutrals as friends are lucky.... But we are better off than six months ago."

CHAPTER FIVE

ESCAPING

"20 March, 1942. A bit of excitement has been caused in the camp tonight by the escape of two, possibly three, different parties. . . . Good luck to them. My heart goes out to them in their effort. . . . As for the Chinese supervisors, they are running around in small circles."

If you tried to escape from Stanley and failed the future was decidedly unattractive. For Kevin Smythe, Brian Fay, Police Sergeant Vincent Morrison and Vic Randall, an Australian engineer from the Hong Kong Light and Power Company, it meant two years' imprisonment, a lingering confinement that brought each of them acute suffering and a long look at death.

During the five weeks immediately following recapture they were held at the Gendarmerie headquarters at the former French Convent School in Happy Valley. Morrison had described his initial reception:

"The cell measured 9 feet long by 8 feet wide and the entrance was through a small door about 3 feet high and 2 feet 6 inches wide. On the day of entry, 10 March, 1942, there were thirteen occupants, all Chinese, both male and female including the corpse of an old Chinese male which remained there for another three days. . . . I was able to squeeze a small space for myself between the corpse and a Chinese female. The floor was of stone, no blankets or bedding were provided with the exception of two or three filthy pieces of sacking. The toilet consisted of two empty kerosine tins which were full to overflowing, and were emptied approximately once a week, with the result that excreta flowed all over the floor. In less than three days I was infested with lice and later contracted ring-worm. Our only food consisted of one ball of cold, wet rice a little larger than a tennis ball, which was thrown into the cell twice a day at 9 am and 6 pm, sometimes accompanied by a little coarse salt and water. These conditions existed for the whole of the five weeks, the population of the cell varying from 11 to 21 persons."[1]

All four were brought before a sham military court on 20 June, 1942, at the Hong Kong Supreme Court charged with "attempting to communicate with the enemy" (maximum penalty seven years); "escaping from a place of internment" (maximum punishment death); "obstructing and impeding the Imperial Japanese Army" (maximum penalty three years). The "trial" consisted of lengthy speeches in Japanese during which the Formosan interpreter remained silent, except for the part where the Japanese prosecutor was apparently demanding the death sentence and, at the end, where the prisoners were asked if they had anything to say. In the same breath the interpreter told them to "Shut up!" Attempts to speak were silenced by angry guards and the court was adjourned for the judge's lunch. At 2.30 pm the verdict of guilty was pronounced but although "our offences were very serious His Imperial Japanese Majesty had been moved to show clemency and we would therefore be sentenced to two years' solitary confinement". All four were sent to Stanley prison.

For much of their time under sentence, until he was transferred to the Gendarmerie as an executioner and torturer, all suffered under a Japanese prison officer called Takiyawa. He was described by Morrison as "an absolute sadist who took delight in beating prisoners for little or no reason". When they complained of the cold and requested additional clothing Takiyawa found an alternative way of generating warmth. Morrison again:

"He made us strip off our clothing and run around the prison drill ground. As we ran he kept beating the laggards with a baton and many collapsed, only to be beaten until they rose again. After thoroughly exhausting us all he asked if we were still cold, and on receiving an affirmative reply he recommenced the running and beating."

Takiyawa had a perverted obsession with keeping everybody cold. During the winter:

"We had only one thin suit of clothing, and were not allowed to cover ourselves with a blanket until 9.30 pm. One night he came to inspect the prisoners shortly after midnight. As I heard him coming I feigned sleep but allowed my blankets to cover me only to my shoulders. I heard all the cells being opened with the exception of Randall's and my own, and then followed the sounds of prisoners being beaten. Next morning I learned that we two were the only ones not to suffer a beating as we had not covered our faces whilst sleeping. All the others had been beaten and some, including Mr [Smythe], had had their clothing and bedding taken from them and had been forced to stand naked until dawn."[2]

"B" Block inside the jail was for remand prisoners awaiting trial and as such was run by the Gendarmerie. To be on remand was worse than being under sentence as it was the time when confessions and evidence had to be extracted for the framing of charges and the forthcoming court appearance. Interrogations often took place in a special room in the ground floor of the prison hospital which was fitted out for torture. It contained devices for the administration of the dreaded water torture which was later used to break the resistance of several internees, and the contraption known as the "Fong Fei-Kei" (flying the aeroplane). This consisted of a bar pivoted like an aeroplane propeller to which the victim was strapped. The propellor was then spun by an electric dynamo with the direction of rotation being reversed at the whim of the torturers. Morrison claims it was found particularly effective on Chinese prisoners.

Another of Takiyawa's tricks was to issue orders that no prisoner was to sleep until 9.30 pm, that is for the four hours from the evening meal at 5.30 pm. Instead, he was forced to sit absolutely motionless facing the cell wall which was only one foot away. It is difficult for a person who has never had to do this for half an hour let alone for four hours daily, week after week, to comprehend how fearful a punishment this was. The slightest move meant a severe beating.

I count myself extremely fortunate that I was not with Morrison and the others. I had so very nearly joined them on their escape bid. For several weeks I had known of their plans and had discussed options and problems with Police Sergeant Kinlock, a courageous and extrovert Scot, who was originally a member of this party.[3] In the event neither Kinlock nor I went. When Kinlock dropped out and was replaced by Smythe only shortly before the attempt was made, I also declined to participate, limiting my contribution to a tin of bully beef. I longed to be free but did have doubts about the plan. When Smythe joined that made my mind up. I thought that he was not fit or tough enough and certainly had no confidence in him. Kinlock and I had undoubtedly made the right decision.

Morrison has written of the mishap that ended their two brief days of liberty:

"On the 8th April, 1942, at 10.20 pm I and Mr [Smythe], Mr Fay, and Mr Randall ... escaped from Stanley Internment Camp and, after spending the following day in hiding, we made our way to Chi Wan village near Lei Mun, arriving at 2.30 am on the morning of the 10th. I left the other three members at the outskirts of the village whilst I tried to procure a boat from someone to enable us to cross to the mainland. I approached a Chinese named Wong who, after I had spoken to him, entered his hut.[4] A short while later a Japanese sergeant came out and covered me with his revolver. I shouted loudly to warn my three friends that the Japanese were present in the village and was immediately seized by more Japanese who came from the hut accompanied by Wong. I was taken into the hut where two Japanese [soldiers] were placed to guard me. The sergeant questioned me as to where I had come from, how many were with me, and what arms and information I carried. Wong acted as interpreter, speaking fluent Japanese. I replied that I was alone, carried no arms or information and that my intention was to get to Free China, but Wong interrupted and informed the sergeant that there were others accompanying me. Shortly afterwards the other three men were brought in. Randall was suffering from a wound received when he was struck by a Chinese who captured him."[5]

There is no doubt that this abortive attempt was encouraged by the success of two separate groups that got away three weeks earlier on 19 March, although the planning process had begun at much the same time.

During those early months we knew nothing of what was happening outside Stanley or, more importantly, of any organized escape routes across the New Territories into China. Later such routes became well established by the British Army Aid Group (BAAG) under Colonel Ride who himself escaped from Shamshuipo in January, 1942. Before that would-be escapers took the plunge into the unknown, with an ultimate destination of the British authorities with Chang Kai-shek at Chungking – a thousand miles away.

Once the decision to escape had been taken, which was not to be done lightly in view of the consequences of being caught, or the likely reprisals on the other internees, the problems to be tackled were daunting – the most obvious being the wide stretch of water between the island and the mainland. Some planning was possible, but good luck was always the overriding factor. An escape from Stanley could be divided into three phases – getting out of the camp; getting off the island and into China; getting across China to Chungking. Certainly at the start, when there was only one perimeter fence which was unlit and erratically patrolled, the first stage was by far the easiest. It was possibly more difficult than the other camps because of the sea barrier.

The first pair to go consisted of W. P. Thompson, who was the senior officer in our "mess", and Mrs Gwen Priestwood who was one of the women living in the Married Quarters. Until they had gone I had no idea what they were planning. Unbeknown to each other both had been giving thought to the idea. One afternoon Gwen and W. P. were walking through the cemetery on the way to watch a softball game when Gwen broached the subject by saying, "I've got a map and a compass and enough money. Will you join up with me? I think we can escape if we plan it carefully." He replied, "Well, I've got a map and a compass too, and a Colt .45. Besides I can speak Cantonese well enough if we ever get to the mainland, but I've only five Hong Kong dollars." To which Gwen responded, "I think we can pool our resources and win through."[6]

The deal was made. Later W. P. would insist he only went with Gwen because she had the money and advised many months later, in a letter smuggled into camp, strongly against escape bids with women.

A crucial part of phase one was planning and preparation. Escapers had secretly to accumulate the equipment needed – map, compass, clothes, food, and cash for payments and bribery en route. Not only was it important to be able to buy food or transport during the journey but Japanese sympathizers could perhaps be persuaded to look the other way with sufficient financial inducement. To depend on charity and goodwill on such a venture was to court disaster. Gwen was a wealthy woman, certainly as far as internees were concerned. She had jewellery and money. With the latter, however, there was a problem. Gwen had two $500 notes, which in the camp, or indeed on an escape bid, were virtually useless. They were impossible to change or get rid of at all. She approached the unofficial leader of the internees – at that time still the American, Bill Hunt – who, she had been told, could get things done. Within days Hunt produced a thousand dollars in small denominations. The team of two now had the kit, the money, knowledge of the language and a weapon. Their disadvantage was Thompson's size. Not only was he European but he was well over six feet tall. Nobody, even at a distance, was going to mistake him for a Chinese no matter how he dressed.

Their preparation was thorough. Food was accumulated, haversacks procured, clothes were acquired, even half a shower curtain for use as a waterproof sheet was eventually extracted from Pennefather-Evans after some haggling over the relative values of a tin of butter and a fountain pen. Water bottles were to be filled with pine needle essence. Camp doctors had declared that a handful of green pine needles, well soaked and mixed with water contained as many vitamins as a couple of oranges. According to Gwen it tasted like barley water. All her jewels were sold or traded for necessary items except for her pearls as the Cantonese are superstitious about pearls, sewing them into burial garments to light the dead into the next world. Stolen pearls were bad luck and would give off no light.

The two of them had spent many hours discussing the venture and studying the routine of the guards at the wire. Their movements had to be known exactly. Where was the wire less taut so they could wriggle under; where was the darkest stretch; when did the guards change or wander off on patrol; how long would they have to get clear? They knew that they must move at night and hide by day, so they needed the maximum number of hours of darkness on the first night, which in turn meant leaving soon after the evening roll call. To increase the length of time before their absence from the bungalow became obvious they pretended to be ill so that the doctors could say they were in hospital. The aim was to get off the island before dawn on day one, say within ten hours of getting out of camp. It was an optimistic ambition.

Gwen Priestwood has described her changing into her "escape outfit":

"Over my lingerie I wore two pairs of woollen pants, three woollen vests, one pink sweater, one green sweater, one yellow sweater – all of wool – and one blue cotton sweater. That's not all. I also had on a navy blue woollen cardigan, a green cardigan and another cardigan and a pair of grey flannel trousers. I put on woollen stockings over woollen socks, hauled on a pair of woollen khaki gloves, and topped myself off with an old officer's cap I'd found. It had no top, and I had patched it up with an old puttee. I was also careful to take my powder compact and lipstick."[7]

Not surprisingly Thompson was appalled by the round woollen woman that confronted him. "Good grief Gwen, you can't go dressed like that! You can barely walk, let alone run. You'll have to take some off." A lengthy, if subdued argument followed. As Gwen adamantly refused to remove anything Thompson was soon forced to concede defeat, although not before thinking that, money or no money, taking a woman on such a venture had perhaps not been a wise decision.

Their first problem was when the haversacks got hooked on the wire as they tried to drag them underneath. There was some frantic tugging, with both expecting a high-pitched yell from a guard at any moment, before they could be freed and the pair rolled into a ditch and thence down into the sandy beach close to Stanley village. The next difficulty was getting through the village. The Gendarmerie had a post in the former police station so the villagers were almost certain to give them away if they were seen and dogs, like dogs the world over, react to the slightest suspicious noise at night with a chain reaction of barking. At one point a torch was flashed in their direction from a doorway. A quick dash between more houses and onto the beach again, followed by an hour of patient crouching in the blackness, convinced them it was safe to move off again.

They skirted the Maryknoll mission building, crawled up the road, dashed across and hurried into the hills beyond. Then they got lost. They had found the water catchment, a concrete-lined trench, which they intended to use to guide them north but after a while it petered out. Gwen wrote:

"We squatted down at the end of the ditch and brought out our military map of the island. We flashed on the light momentarily, while [Walter] twisted the map round and told me to locate the Pole Star.
    'The Pole Star? Where's that?'

'For heaven's sake! Look!' He showed me the Plough and added an explanation of the way in which the pointers are followed to the star.

'If we get separated over in China,' he said, 'you had better remember how to find that star, or you'll just wander about and get nowhere.'

I replied, 'I have my own map, which is in Chinese characters so I can't get lost if I get to China, because I shall ask the way."[8]

After this they headed higher, up the steep ridge looming above them to the north. It was extremely hard going and they had both developed a consuming thirst. "W. P." was in the lead with Gwen struggling gamely along behind, often stumbling, sometimes falling. At one stage "W. P." snapped at her, "For God's sake Gwen I told you to get rid of those clothes. We are just not making progress. If you can't get a move on we'd better slip back into camp before its too late."

"Never! The only way I'm going back to Stanley is as a corpse. I can keep going."

They pushed on. At the first hint of sunrise they started searching for a suitable hide. A concrete pillbox used by the British as an observation or machine-gun post was spotted conveniently nearby. It was deserted, with an iron door hanging crookedly on its hinges. Inside was a pleasant smell of dried grass, a wooden shelf on one wall, and an old clothes line strung across one corner. They gratefully collapsed on the floor.

The arrival of dawn brought intense disappointment. They could still see Stanley. They had covered a mere two miles at most and were still on the upper slopes of Stanley Mound. Through binoculars they could easily pick out bungalow "C". So much for getting off the island on the first night. They were worried that their absence would now have been discovered, with the resultant hue and cry making the odds on success considerably longer. There was little they could do except endure a long thirsty day, praying that no search party would be looking for them that close to camp. "W. P." spent the day repairing the soles of his shoes with some nails he had found in a discarded map board, while Gwen set about concealing the list of names of some 2500 British internees, given her by Gimson, that she was taking out. It was written on thin paper which she cut up into strips, unravelled their solitary toilet roll and wound the strips around the cardboard cone before winding the paper back over them. A long time was spent poring over the map discussing the second night's journey. "W. P." summed up their thoughts when he said, 'If we don't get off this bloody island tonight we never will."

The second night saw more progress, and a desperate search for water, but dusk was to find them still on the island. They moved off Stanley Mound towards the NE, down towards Bridge Hill with the road and reservoir at the bottom. The reservoir contained water although to reach it meant ploughing through mudflats. Thompson suggested they try a deserted bungalow first. With luck, turning on the taps might be all that was required.

"We went gingerly round to a side door, stole inside and in the flash-light beam saw a bed with a mosquito net down. The net down usually means someone is sleeping in the bed. We switched off the light quickly, expecting to hear the grunt of a sleeping servant – we were in the servants quarters.

"Nothing happened. We backed out hurriedly, went round to the front of the house, climbed on the verandah and went into the living room. It was a confused mess. . . . We walked into a looted bedroom and then into the bathroom, [W. P.] tried the taps. Dry again. He swung the flash-light towards the tub. It was completely full of sparkling, clean-looking water. I squeaked with delight."[9]

After striking the Tai Tam Gap road they followed it cautiously northwards, at one stage dropping down behind a bank as a carload of fully armed Japanese rounded a corner. With the approach of dawn they once again realized that another day would have to be spent on the island. By this time they were near the Lei Mun Gap and Chi Wan Hill, overlooking the northern coast of Hong Kong Island. This time they found a derelict bungalow on a barren hill surrounded by barbed wire, the door of which had been sealed with a strip of white paper, with Chinese characters on it, pasted across it. Hopefully it was a warning to keep the inquisitive out. Once inside they took it in turns to sleep. It was to be an exciting day, one in which they came within a whisker of being caught with Japanese soldiers coming within touching distance of them both. Gwen again:

"I was awoken by [W. P.] who was shaking my shoulder. He looked white. He leaned down and whispered, 'There are three Japanese soldiers coming up the path to the house!' My heart thumped. The blood drained from my face. The only place we could possibly hide in the small bungalow was a sort of alcove off the kitchen. It had been used to store coal and was filled with old newspapers, bags and general rubbish."[10]

Within seconds "W. P.", who was well over six feet tall, had curled up in the alcove to be covered over with the newspapers by Gwen who then crawled in beside him. The soldiers shouted out, obviously wanting to find out if anybody was inside. They banged on the door, then walked around the outside peering in the windows and opening shutters. The two fugitives were suffering agonies from cramp and holding their breath to keep back the urge to cough or sneeze from the dust. After some minutes they heard yells from down the hill followed by the sound of the soldiers running off. Then, just as they began to stretch slightly to move their dead limbs,

"A window near us opened, and a Japanese apparently left behind stuck in his head within four feet of us. He started to climb in – and then, in the nick of time, there came another shout from below. He stopped, turned, yelled something, and ran down the path."[11]

For half an hour more they hunched in the alcove. When they dared to crawl out the Japanese were still there at the foot of the hill with an officer, complete with sword, who was seemingly organizing a looting expedition as bundles of goods were being distributed to several Chinese coolies to carry. Through the binoculars the expressions on their faces could be seen clearly.

That night their luck held. They crept down to the little bay near the village of Chi Wan where a junk had been spotted at anchor. After some extremely tense moments when the junk master refused to see them, they persuaded him to take them on board. He had no love for the Japanese, who had used his nephews as coolies for no payment on their looting expeditions, and agreed to get two sampans to paddle them across the harbour to Joss House Bay. There was the Tin Hau temple of the Chinese fishermen at Joss House Bay which was a favourite meeting place for Chinese guerrillas. It was given a substantial sum of money after the war by the Hong Kong government as a reward for the help given to fugitives from the Japanese.

From there they were taken into China and eventually, with the assistance of the communist guerrillas, found their way to Chungking. Strangely, it was usually better to fall into the hands of the communists rather than the Nationalists. The former's hatred of the Japanese was intense, whereas if the Nationalists thought there was more money in it for them they would often hand escapees over. The list of internees wrapped around the toilet roll survived, and it was from this that my mother was first informed that I was alive and in Stanley.

On the same night that "W. P." and Gwen Priestwood got away another party escaped a few hours later. This group consisted of three Americans (F. W. Wright, Viness, and O'Neill) and two British (Martin and Miss Fairfax-Cholmondeley), several of whom had worked for the Chinese Maritime Customs. They fled in the opposite direction. No sooner had they got onto Stanley beach than they made for an upturned boat that they had had their eyes on for weeks. Fortune favours the brave – it was useable. In this they paddled slowly westwards towards Lantau Island where they eventually came ashore near the village of Tong Fuk, a journey of over fifteen miles. At one point they were spotted by a Japanese patrol boat which looked as though it might come over to investigate. Quick thinking saved them. One person put on a conical Chinese fisherman's straw hat pretending to fish while the others lay flat. The Japanese boat ignored them. After some time in hiding on Lantau a junk was organized to take them to Macau. From there the Macau underground took them into China – and freedom.

The mild reaction of the Japanese to these escapes, except to those who were caught, can be attributed to their loss of face, which they had no wish to emphasize. There was nothing that could be termed a mass reprisal, there was nobody singled out for punishment, there was no example made of any individual *pour encourager les autres*, except the sentencing of those recaptured to two years in jail – from the Japanese standpoint a paltry punishment. The only visible sign that security was being tightened was the erection of more, and improved, wire fencing around the perimeter and across the camp, dividing the area into separate compounds. This was inconvenient as it meant much further to walk to get to places such as the ration collection point. My diary of 16 April, 1942:

"The Japanese have decided to limit still more the territory over which we can walk while in camp and today they started to erect a barbed wire fence which will eventually run through our garden, cutting it in half. . . . We asked the Chinese foreman to move the fence so as to skirt the garden as we wanted to tend to the several graves in the garden. . . . He was agreeable to ask the Japanese, but they said NO!

During the erecting of the fence a remark was made by an English-speaking Chinese labourer, which typifies, in my opinion, the whole state of affairs now existing in Hong Kong. As he went past the bungalow carrying an iron stake over his shoulder he said, 'Once upon a time I used to carry a fountain pen, now I carry this bloody iron.' I could not help laughing at such an English remark, and so true."

We did hear rumours that Smythe, Fay, Morrison and Randall had been caught, but it was not until 15 May that this sad news was confirmed by an actual sighting of all four when they were brought into camp by lorry under Gendarmerie guards:

"They were seen by Lance, Henry and Colin, who at forty yards did not recognize them because they had changed so much. However, on looking again they recognized [Smythe]. How can people be so inhuman? They were just a mass of skin and bones with long unkempt hair and beards. They were hardly able to walk. They must have been starved and badly questioned. Lance and Co. came back to the bungalow very much upset . . . an unpleasant sight that of men reduced to animals.
A fine day and very warm."

Unbeknown to me the escape had prompted a visit to Stanley by the greatly feared Colonel Noma, head of the Gendarmerie. He summoned a meeting on "the hill" on 20 March with Yamashita, Nagasawa and the chairman of the three main community leaders (Gimson, Hunt, and a Dutchman). Not surprisingly Noma wanted thorough investigations; indeed he made it plain that he suspected Hunt knew all about the escapers' plans and intentions. He made threats and wanted Hunt to start talking. Unusually, Maejima, the meek civilian from Foreign Affairs, interjected successfully to calm things down, actually getting agreement for the chairman to leave the meeting. Later that night Yamashita explained that some extra disciplinary measures would have to be imposed. There would be two roll calls per day at 8.00 am and 10.00 pm; lights out at 11.00 pm; all internees to be in the vicinity of their buildings at 8.00 pm; chairmen of committees to be held responsible for future escapes; the room from which the Americans had escaped was not to be used again (why this room was singled out I could never fathom); and the camp would be patrolled by Gendarmerie at night. A pretty feeble response; certainly not Noma's idea of a deterrent.

By July, 1942, Colonel Lindsay Ride had established the British Army Aid Group (BAAG) and was in contact with all the POW camps and Stanley. Ride was a former professor of physiology at Hong Kong University and, in endeavouring to find out what was happening in the camp, it was natural for him to make the initial contact with his former boss, the Vice-Chancellor Duncan Sloss, who was an internee. The letter smuggled in read, in part:

"My dear Sloss,
This is an attempt to set up a regular news service between us. . . . The Priestwood – Thompson party brought the British list [of internees] and not the American or Dutch. An up-to-date list . . . is very badly needed and also a report on the treatment, conditions and casualties in the camp. I am trying to arrange the 'escape' or liberation of all children; if this plan ever gets as far as the camp, please do all you can to persuade mothers to let their children go. . . . This communication route is absolutely trustworthy; use it as much as you can. . . . I understand you need money badly. Here is $100 from me as a trial."[12]

Sloss responded positively, although his health was failing. Within a few weeks Ride wrote again, this time with more startling suggestions as to escaping from Stanley:

"Now for your orders. A daring plan of escape for about 50 of you has been worked out, and you are responsible for the inside arrangements. Here is a list of the people to come. . . . The list is to be used as a guide only. The plan involves a swim of about 500 yards and those who cannot swim must be struck off the list. The next to be struck off are those psychologically unfit at present for the task, or for war work when they are out; then rule out the talkers and those not amenable to discipline. . . . The exact number to come out will be communicated to you by my agent. . . . You will have a sea journey, uncomfortable, crowded, but short; you will have an armed escort on board. . . . You will not be able to bring any luggage only what you can swim in.

"You must not warn all these people beforehand . . . [only] those people who would be willing to come out at a moment's notice. There must be no goodbyes. . . . In choosing your men you must not allow a man's value to the Stanley community to sway your choice. It is the Empire that needs men not Stanley – brutal but true – and the Empire needs trained people and lecturers badly. Doctors, engineers, wireless operators, master mariners and young fit fellows for the Army should come out.

And lastly if you can't get anyone to come with you, come yourself. I'll be here to meet you."[13]

This was surely a weird and wonderful plan. It suffered from a total lack of practicability. Just about everything was likely to go wrong. One of the BAAG agents (No.85), a former policeman called Chow Ying Kwan, was supposed to contact his police friends still working at Stanley (Ride seemed to be unaware that the Gendarmerie and Indians formed the bulk of the camp guards), to ensure only they were on duty on the day of the breakout. Their families were to be smuggled out of Hong Kong in advance. On the appropriate day (nominated by agent 85) a junk was to be in position 500 yards off Stanley peninsula to pick up the escapers, and the policemen, who would all be swimming madly out to sea.

Not unnaturally there were problems finding a junk master and crew, as the chances of survival, let alone escape, verged on the non-existent. Not even the smugglers in Macau who had motorized junks could be persuaded to consider the plan. It is possible that this mass escape was to take place under cover of heavy Allied air raids on the Colony, and that it would coincide with similar attempts from one or more of the POW camps. For a host of practical reasons all thoughts of getting hundreds of prisoners out of Hong Kong en masse were eventually shelved. The Stanley scheme died with the others, but it had one consequence on our lives for a period of three weeks in November/December, 1942. Due to some whispering about large-scale escapes linked to air raids at night the Japanese decided that all males between 18 and 35 were to be locked up in the prison every night. It was to be a novel, and at times highly amusing experience.

On 6 November, 1942, Yamashita assembled all internees for a special announcement. Gimson had been told that because of the blackouts and likelihood of air raids men between 18-35 were to spend every night in the prison cells. He read out a long list of the persons affected. Yamashita, feeling in an abnormally friendly mood, then rose to ask in his sing-song barber's English, if there were any questions. There were several. A man called Ingledew started complaining that some people seemed to be missing from the list, and why should they be exempt. Gimson answered to the effect that, "The list has been approved by the Japanese". Then one wag at the back piped up, "Have the cells been fumigated? Are there any possibilities of getting vermin?" Yamashita, smiling broadly replied, "We have new vermin now!" The great roar of laughter that followed left him both perplexed and pleased.

At the appropriate time everybody formed up outside the prison gates carrying their bedding. I was in charge of a group as police officers had been detailed to organize the move, check names and make sure there was the minimum of fuss or delay. There were a number of people who were being "difficult", which was perhaps understandable as none of us knew what to expect inside a jail which had a decidedly unsavoury reputation. In my group one individual was being noticeably obstreperous; it was Ingledew again, who was still loudly protesting the injustice of what was happening and still blaming Gimson. I did my best to shut him up, during which I said something to the effect that he was behaving like a "fifth columnist". This annoyed him intensely.

Once inside we marched through the prison compound along the road lined by the Indian workers, now self-consciously wearing their new Japanese uniform caps instead of their colourful turbans. We were locked into cells in F block which had some 84 cells per floor. We had a cell each which, if nothing else, gave us a little privacy. The cells were clean but small, eight feet by five approximately, with a tiny window high up near the ceiling. From 6.00 pm we were, surprisingly, allowed to exercise for two hours in the vicinity of our block. After lights out at 10.00 pm the mimics went into action and the corridors echoed with hooting owls, screeching tom cats and barking dogs. Anybody entering the jail that first night would have thought they had entered a lunatic asylum. The place was in uproar. If people were not imitating animals they were singing, some were dancing in their cells, while through it all could be heard the raucous

Scottish brogue of Sergeant Kinlock as he tried to coordinate the bedlam of noise.

I am not sure why, but Yamashita and Nagasawa took it in turns to spend the night in the prison with us, although not of course in a cell. The commissioner, Pennefather-Evans, actually invited Nagasawa to come and drink some tea with us. It had been brought in a thermos flask. He accepted, and this was the first time I had had personal contact with him. His English was fair and he spoke a little Cantonese, but the atmosphere was decidedly strained, although he always struck me as being a more reasonable man than Yamashita, who had more of the self-important bullying streak in him. Geoffrey (Wilson), meaning to be funny, asked Nagasawa

"I think it would be a bloody good idea if you were to give us all roller skates. We could run races up and down the corridors. It would be excellent for morale and good exercise!"

Nagasawa smiled stupidly and nodded. The Japanese could never understand our sense of humour, especially how we could laugh as prisoners. They normally treated our merriment with suspicion, always thinking (often correctly) that we were laughing at them. Yamashita visited us as well. We actually shared a precious tin of bully beef, curried rice and a few beans with him. His English, too, was reasonable, but I always had the impression he knew more than he was letting on. No doubt years of listening to gossip in his barber's shop which was full of service officers and passing on the tit-bits to the Japanese authorities had been the reason he secured the plum post of camp commandant. He was actively disliked by most of us, unlike Nagasawa, as he was moody, overfond of the bottle, and totally unpredictable.

At about 6.30 am we were roused and taken back into the camp. Later that morning, 9 November, I received a formal letter from Ingledew. He had taken great exception to my saying he had acted like a "fifth columnist" outside the prison gates the evening before. Part of his letter (which I have to this day) reads:

"I hope you appreciate the seriousness of calling a person a fifth-columnist in our present circumstances, in fact it would be difficult to make a charge which can more vitally affect a person's position in the camp both vis-à-vis the Camp Authorities and his fellow internees."

He finished by demanding a written apology, failing which he intended to "take up the matter vigorously with the Authorities until I obtain full satisfaction". Incredible as it may seem now I took the letter seriously and went to consult a solicitor friend who, for a fee of a packet of cigarettes, drafted a suitable response. In it I wrote:

"I merely stated in the presence of witnesses whom I can, if necessary, produce that 'you are behaving like a fifth-columnist by going over the head of the Colonial Secretary'. No inference was contained in my remark that you were, or are, a fifth columnist, and no such inference can, or should be, construed from this remark."

Ingledew grudgingly consented to let the matter drop. I include it here as a small illustration of how sensitive and petty people became, and how even as prisoners in an internment camp the legal niceties of peacetime civil life, like consulting lawyers, continued.

On the night of 11 November we held a memorial service in the prison for all those killed in the two World Wars. It was conducted by a medical missionary called Dr Laurie: a strange, probably unique, place to hold such a service. We all stood in the long corridor flanked by the cells while the verses of the hymns were first read out by the priest before we sang them. There were three, one of which was "Abide with me". The commissioner read a psalm, we had a two-minute silence and prayers were said. The atmosphere was rather spoilt afterwards when a Chinese electrician who had been mending some lights discovered he had been locked in the block by accident at 8.00 pm. He set up a frightful racket, screaming and banging on the gates trying to attract attention. For about an hour and a half he kept up this performance, yelling for somebody called "Cha" to come and let him out. Needless to say we all stood jeering at him and encouraging him to shout ever louder. He seemed quite unable to see the funny side of it.

Sergeant Kinlock was the real comedian among us. I remember on one evening, when we were forming up to enter the prison, he appeared being wheeled down to the gates seated in a baby's pram, dressed the part in a bonnet. There he inspected a "guard of honour" composed of internees with brooms. Even the Gendarmerie officer who was watching laughed at the crazy English or, in this case, Scottish.

The night of 15 November was one that I have never forgotten as it was the occasion of our band performance. I can do no better than quote what I wrote in my diary:

"The band went into action last night in fine style. We formed up outside the jail at 1830 in three squads, A, B, and C. Every so often somebody peeped through the hatch in the gate as we were waiting outside. Then our motley guard of Chinese arrived under Japanese Kempeitai. The gates opened and we struggled through to form up in three ranks inside, with the band leading. The drum-major, a White Russian policeman, led it with a broom-stick for a mace. Watson had an accordion, Blackburn a mouth organ and the others combs. Kinlock, not to be outdone, had his bedding rolled up and strapped to his chest like a big drum and used two lavatory mops to beat it with great gusto. We set off singing songs like 'Tipperary' along the path that led us round three sides of the prison, about a quarter of a mile in all. We never stopped singing. When the band reached our cell block it stood to play us in, but just at that moment the Japanese executioner arrived [I believe it was a man called Hirano]. Yelling and swearing, his face the colour of bad tomatoes, he made for the accordion player (Watson). Geoffrey saw what was happening and stopped the band, but the executioner had already taken a mighty right swing at Watson who ducked. He missed and a left followed, Watson swaying back so that his face was just brushed.

"After these antics, amid our loud laughter, the Japanese naively started to examine the accordion. Maybe he thought it was some kind of bomb. Everybody dispersed. For some time the Japanese remained outside menacing anybody who came out for exercise. Watson went into hiding."

We planned a repeat performance the next night with bagpipes but Nagasawa told the commissioner in no uncertain terms that it was forbidden. In early December the nightly sojourns in jail were stopped. A pity really as they had been no real hardship, had given us some light relief from the normal monotony, and taken our minds off the darker side of life. Perhaps that was why they were stopped.

On looking back I am staggered we got away with such behaviour. It just confirms how erratic the Japanese were – one minute grinning broadly, the next brandishing a sword and threating to lop off your head.

CHAPTER SIX

ADJUSTING TO HUNGER

"Hunger is like a ghost that can find no peace. . . . It is always there, a perpetual groaning in one's stomach. . . . It pervades every thought; it sets you dreaming of steaks . . . you must fight with all your will power against these dreams . . . or they become your master. It is a hard fight that only those who have been really hungry can understand."

Diary, 3 March, 1944.

Food was foremost in our thoughts throughout our time in Stanley. Lack of food, lack of nutrients, lack of vitamins and minerals in our diet for over three and a half years resulted in malnutrition-related diseases such as beri-beri, suppurating sores, skin infections and dysentery. It was the contributory factor in virtually all deaths in the camp, while at the other extreme it was the reason we seldom had to cut our nails; they just did not grow. For Europeans, accustomed to eating bread, meat and vegetables daily, the sudden switch to rice, rice and more rice, supplemented by a few tiny lumps of stringy buffalo or horse meat with the occasional boiled Chinese cabbage leaf, was devastating. The lack of quantity and quality over such a prolonged period affected not only our bodies but also our minds and personalities. The survival instinct predominated. We lived from one meal to the next, continually planning and scheming how to increase or improve our meagre rations. There was universal scavenging, scrounging and blackmarketeering, with many people resorting to cheating or stealing in order to obtain that little bit extra for themselves.

It would be quite wrong to think everybody was equal with regard to food as internees. Like life outside those with more money (from whatever source) or with generous friends, or those in the right jobs in camp could (and usually did) fare comparatively well. An example of a particular category of people who sought to secure personal benefits, particularly with regard to food, were many of the missionary prisoners. I quote from my diary dated 8 July, 1942.

"... missionaries who, with rare exceptions showed their true character and colours in camp. They were well ahead of all of us in looking after themselves. They knew every angle from years of practice. Where there was a racket you could be sure they were hovering around taking what advantage they could. For example, if there was a committee to hand out clothes they would be on it, and they and their cronies would be well looked after.

They were of course always in the kitchens. ... One woman missionary was caught stealing a partridge from the Indian quarters (they had been sent in as rations because the cold storage depot had been bombed and they were going bad). She was charged and brought before a camp tribunal which found her guilty but the conviction was not registered as it might be to the detriment of her career after the war."

Over two years later the same woman was still at it. Again I wrote of my (our) intense bitterness on the subject:

"19 September, 1944.
Whenever there is extra food going or extra perks to be had you will find missionaries. ... They are in charge, or at least work in most of the diet kitchens; they are to be found in the welfare (committee), and serve in most of the committees dealing with food or clothes. Most of them look well fed by camp standards. ... We have one bright specimen in the diet kitchen down here. She is small, fat, sour faced – a really curdled looking woman – who has been caught several times pinching food, and every time the Church has intervened and pleaded and the case has been dropped. A few days ago she stole a bag of wood belonging to Sergeant Rothwell. ... She is going to be prosecuted. Today she was caught again stealing wood. Both cases are stone cold against her."

There were several sources of food. First, there was the basic ration supplied by the Japanese and meant to be in accordance with a set scale. This could be supplemented by earning tiny extra entitlements by getting on to various working parties such as those employed in the gardens or in the kitchen. In addition individuals could obtain food through the black market, by barter, by buying from the canteen when it opened, by the receipt of parcels from neutral friends in town, by growing vegetables in the garden or, very infrequently, from the distribution of Red Cross parcels. Every source was the centre of some sort of racket, if not outright theft.

I will take the rations first. When we first arrived, and until later in the war when the economic blockade began to bite in earnest, we were issued with some 4 ounces of rice per meal, two or three lumps of gristle or a dessert spoon of fish, with a few boiled cabbage or lettuce leaves. Potatoes were a luxury, as was sugar or milk. To begin with we also got one thin slice of bread per person per day, plus a small allowance of flour. As time went on the official ration scale decreased; bread was stopped, then flour; milk was never seen and, finally, in 1944 the supply of meat ceased although we continued to get some fish. The total absence of meat had some interesting side-effects one of which was the disappearance of cats. On 22 April, 1944, I recorded:

"Another cat has disappeared. Calthrop had the amusing story of an acquaintance of his whose room mates caught it, skinned it and ate it. Tasted like rabbit they say. Two pounds of good flesh! Personally I will stick to rice."

Rations were issued by the Japanese for the two daily meals at noon and 5.00 pm. If one ate only at those times the seventeen-hour wait from the evening meal to the following midday was an agonizing eternity to which our stomachs could never adjust. Our mess pooled all our resources including food which Geoffrey distributed. We all strove to have some sort of breakfast. A typical start to the day in 1942 was described by me as:

"Breakfast struck me as a most solemn affair. At 0700 the rush to the boiler house for hot water (which) is issued daily, and then put on our hot-ring made in camp. Meanwhile the rest of the mess is up and washing, some at the tap at the back or in the bathroom, some in the servant's shower. We have one shower and one bathroom between 19 men. Then the big moment arrives. We solemnly cut our bread into five slices and Geoffrey issues us with a teaspoon of jam for each slice.

The tea is made and poured out (no milk or sugar). Then silence reigns while we eat the only meal of the day in which rice does not take a prominent part.

The bread is made in the bungalow from the flour issue. It is our mess policy to have an extra meal out of the bread issue, also to eat all the bread at once. Others keep it to nibble all day and must wait until 1200 for their first meal."

The ability to bake our own bread was a wonderful luxury that regrettably only lasted for as long as we were given flour. Lance was the expert at this, using a sort of yeast made from rotten potato peel.

The mindless monotony of rice was embodied perfectly by some wit who, on one occasion, had merely written, "Hebrews, Chapter 13 verse 8" on the menu board in the kitchen. Of course the more curious among us looked it up and were rewarded by reading, "Jesus Christ, the same yesterday and today and forever". Equally accurate was the notice about the fish that appeared on 26 February, 1944.

" 'This fish is unfit for human consumption. You eat at your own risk' was the notice hanging outside the kitchen when food was drawn this evening. As far as I know not one person refused it. The fish was fried and seemed to taste all right. . . . The fish is brought in frozen, an improvement on the past when it was merely buried in oil, but in this hot weather it soon goes bad."

Our time in Stanley made us all experts on rice, its cooking, its quality and its consumption. Although ravenously hungry, and always desperate for more of it as a filler, I for one longed for a change, something less bland, something with a different flavour. As I wrote:

"Our meals are mostly composed of rice; rice disguised in various forms but still rice. One can eat a large meal of rice, get up feeling full (if you eat enough) and an hour later you are hungry again. It has neither the nutritious, sustaining or fulfilling power of flour and other staple European foods. It just turns to water."

At one time, when the Japanese were to issue internees with an extra four ounces of rice a storm of controversy swept the camp as to how it should be given out. There were those who insisted, because they felt they might otherwise be cheated, in having it issued in bulk and raw; others, such as our "mess", wanted it as congee (a boiled mush) as it was then swollen with water, thick and warm, thus giving an illusion of quantity; still others preferred it made into rice biscuits. These were about 1½ inches square and 1/5th of an inch thick. They were popular with some people as they were different and dainty, perhaps reminding them of the old days of tea and biscuits in more congenial circumstances. One problem was that they tended to be rock hard, so people with false or weak teeth preferred the soft, sticky congee. Our committee deliberated for two weeks on this difficulty. Dozens of suggestions were received and argued about before the usual British compromise emerged. The extra ration could be drawn as either one small portion of congee plus one biscuit, or two biscuits, or one larger portion of congee, or raw. We eventually chose the last.

Sometimes, for special occasions, an extra effort would be made to bake rice cakes. I described them as "masterpieces, being made from rice ground to a flour, soya beans also ground to a flour, and mixed with margarine and peanut oil. A little real flour was added, plus oatmeal and sugar. All this was then baked and was very filling." I should explain that this lavish variety of ingredients was only available in the early days of 1942 when flour was issued, and we had sufficient pooled financial resources to buy from the canteen or through the black market.

Rice grinding was a tedious and, for the elderly, an exhausting chore. In June, 1944, Professor Burn had the ultimate misfortune of dropping dead from a heart attack while grinding rice to make a cake for his sixtieth birthday. One of fate's unkinder tricks. Each accommodation block had a Chinese rice grinder which was two flat, heavy round stones placed one on top of the other. The rice was ground between the stones by moving the top one with a circular motion. There was a hole in the top stone through which the rice was fed. It was a common sight to see old people crouched over these machines in the entrances to their blocks. An alternative method of cake making was to squeeze the cooked rice in one's hand until it was gelatinous and gooey, add a little flour if possible, and then bake it.

The oven was our prize possession, a marvellous home-made contraption which consisted of a square wooden box lined with tin. In the bottom was a six-inch-diameter hole which was placed over an electric ring, with the article to be baked being put on a metal grill over the ring. One side was baked and then it was turned over. To help keep the heat in, the box was usually covered completely with a sack. Surprisingly good results were obtained. Our "mess" had a special system of sharing out the delicacies it produced. After the food had been prepared, cooked and divided up into five hopefully equal measures, each of us was permitted to choose his portion. The order in which we chose was decided, bingo fashion, with a bag of numbered metal discs. The person with the highest number had first choice, the next highest followed and so on in descending order. It was was quite an exciting game for us. I recall being rather lucky with the discs. The cry of "You bastard, George, you've won again!" was not uncommon. As the junior member of the "mess", my frequent success was the cause of some irritation among my seniors.

There were a number of fiddles, in effect thefts, of rice worked by some unscrupulous internees. One of those caught was a police inspector called Cain. My diary entry for 3 June, 1944, describes what happened, and illustrates our mistrustful nature over all dealings with food.

"As far as I can discern this is what happened. Every person is given an option whether he wants to draw his rice cooked or raw, they cannot draw both. If he draws it raw then it is issued to him in bulk every two days and when he draws his meals he draws everything except rice. In order to ensure that persons collecting meals do not collect more than their proper share there is a checker who marks off their names on a list as they collect their food. The checker has a list of persons who have already drawn their rice in raw form. . . . For some time there has been a constant shortage of potato cakes; this is strange as always more than the correct number were made to ensure against breakages. Therefore it was decided to check up on the leakage. First the servers were watched, but nothing was wrong there. Then it was decided to watch the checkers. It was discovered that Cain was the culprit and a bigger swindle was discovered. Cain, and certain members of his mess, drew their rice raw, but every day, after the serving was finished, he would draw rations for himself and his mess all in cooked rice. This had apparently been going on for about a year. . . . Disciplinary action will be taken against Cain, but it not yet decided if it will be by the Camp Tribunal or by the CP. If he is found guilty the CP should sack him. . . . He has not yielded to sudden temptation in moments of hunger but has carried out a systematic larceny of Camp food."

With another instance involving food vanishing from the kitchen I wrote:

"There is something fishy about the kitchen in these quarters (we had just moved into the old Indian quarters) and it won't be long before we get to the bottom of it. This morning we were given a swill of rice, chives and water. (It was) a disgrace with no meat or potatoes. The cooks will claim they put all the meat and potatoes into the evening meal, but (this) is not true . . . meat is being taken from the kitchen by people for their own use or for sale. The same is happening with the flour issue. . . . The whole affair is an utter disgrace. How people can rob others of the little food they get is beyond me. . . . I have heard of the mysterious 'gumboot steak', so called because it is smuggled out of the kitchen in the thief's gumboots. Those having the money can buy it. Some persons are selling our flour ration at 50 cents per pound. Also some cooks' helpers have specially made waistcoats to slip bits of meat etc. into when cutting it up."

No food was safe. Once, when one of the priests had made some Communion wafers from rice specially donated for the purpose, he made the mistake of leaving them on a window sill for a few moments and forgot to watch them. Within a flash they had gone. It was the basis of his next sermon – wrath and vengeance called down on all. As for all services or other meetings of large numbers permission had to be obtained from the Japanese in advance. I recall that just before Christmas in 1942 when Yamashita was asked for permission for a Communion service he at first looked blank, and then comprehension spread across his face as he replied, "Ah so; it's a church cocktail party".

As mentioned above, efforts were made to curb the dishonesty in the kitchens by appointing people to be supervisors or check on the cooks and their assistants. We also took it in turns to help out in the kitchen so that all had the opportunity of earning a small entitlement to more food. Because a close watch was kept on them, and the work was both hard and thankless, the cooks were allowed a double portion of the meals served up. The situation improved but we never eradicated pilfering entirely. I described the system appertaining in 1944 as follows:

"Sunday is always a fishless day but we always get the best meal of the week. This may seem to be a paradoxical statement ... but in lieu of fish [a teaspoon of] extra vegetables are supplied and from it they make a vegetable cake to go with the rice. ...

"Sergeants Goldie and Goodwin are the chief cooks for our quarters. ... Goldie, who is a far better cook than he is a policeman, is the better of the two. However, Goodwin produces his meals on time. ...

"There are two official cooks who take it in turn day on, day off. Each cook has a rice boiler (a person, not a thing) under him. The cutting up of vegetables, gutting fish, etc. is done by a working squad which is on for two weeks at a time. Every man is eligible for this work, which is hard. The enticement is an extra ration of food so it is a very popular job. The selection is on a rota basis. Henry, who was on for the last two weeks, is now off and Geoffrey is on. Colin goes on tomorrow, and Searle and myself should be on sometime this month. One gets into the kitchen once every three months or so."

Poor old Goldie, having spent years serving up fish for his fellow internees, suffered the terminal tragedy of himself being eaten by a fish. Within two or three days of the Japanese surrender he was attacked by a large fish, probably a barracuda, while swimming at our bathing beach. It took a huge hunk out of his leg and he bled to death. Fate can be cruel.

One could also earn extra rations by doing hard manual work, for example working in the camp gardens, moving bulk rations by hand, acting as a coolie for the Japanese on any work detail, or by doing an unpopular and uncomfortable duty such as night-time kitchen guard. In March, 1944, I described a stint of this:

"This duty is usually given to older men who cannot do hard labour. I find myself amidst empty tubs in a dirty old room called a kitchen, which smells predominantly of fish and has bloated cockroaches overrunning everything, because I offered to substitute for Sparrow who has just come out of hospital. ... Why did I offer? Not because I enjoy sitting up all night in a black room surrounded by draughts, listening to running water, banging doors, creaking windows. ... I am here because the bait is an extra meal. ... The kitchen has no (lockable)

128

1. The author in 1941 soon after being recalled to police duties.

2. The author with Lance Searle (right). "He was one of the bravest men I have known." (p.77)

3. Fu King, the No. 1 boy. (see p.21)

4. 'Tsui Chi-ming was my first teacher.' (p.25)

5. 'Then came the infamous "Rape of Nanking" during which at least 150,000 soldiers and civilians were executed.' (p.33) (*Imperial War Museum*)

6. 'St Stephen's College, a private school for the sons and daughters of the more affluent Chinese.' (p.2)

7. 'The Japanese forced him to heap the corpses into one huge pile for a mass cremation.' (p.9) It was here that the bodies were burnt after the massacre at St Stephen's College.

8. The Luk Hoi Tung Hotel where the author was first imprisoned. (see p.80)

9. 'Henry Heath had been born in the West Indies where his family had lived for generations.' (p.77)

10. 'Colin Luscombe was the rough and rugged type, bursting with energy.' (p.77)

11. 'W.P. Thompson, the senior officer in our "mess".' (p.106)

12. 'Geoffrey Wilson... was clever and a leader, with a touch of the cynic in his makeup.' (p.77)

13. 'We sailed out of the harbour... and headed for the Stanley peninsula.' (p.82) This is the spot where the prisoners landed. The execution ground is to the left.

14. 'Our bungalow, which was called Bungalow "C", was in an awful condition.' (p.87)

15. 'We are going to the Indian quarters which are undoubtedly the most unhealthy in the camp.' (see p. 100) The author lived on the top floor at the far end of the near block.

16. 'Alex Summers... had a working radio receiver hidden in the wall of his room.' (p. 147) The room was in this building.

17. 'There were plenty of people about on the main road.' (p. 148) It was here that the author handed over packages to Wong.

18. 'As the weeks passed Wong and I developed a special code of signals.' (p. 149) A view of Stanley Prison from the vantage point where the author watched for Wong's signals.

19. Where the ration lorry used to come.

20. The kitchen in the Indian quarters.

21. Grinding rice to make flour.

22. One of the quarters in St Stephen's College. Note the bullet holes in the wall.

23. Prisoners cutting grass for fuel.

24. 'Waterton had been able to scratch a last message on the wall of his cell.' (p. 185) (*Imperial War Museum*)

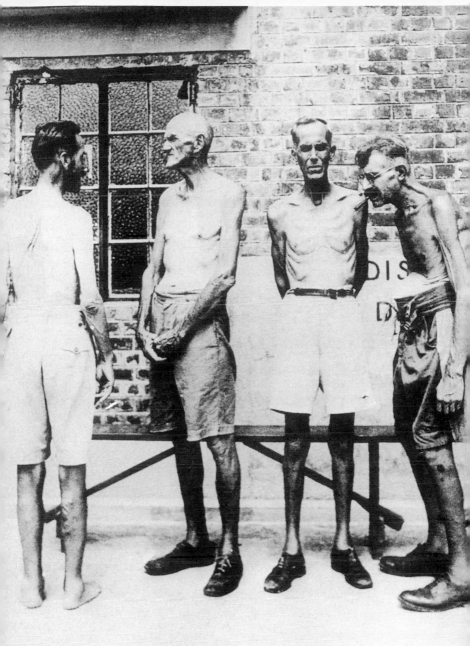

25. 'Lammert [second from left] managed one of the biggest auctioneering companies in Hong Kong.' (p.94) On the right is McKenzie, the Government vet.

26. Mrs Loie, mother of David Loie, wearing his posthumous King's Police Medal for Gallantry. (see p.172)

27. 'By accident a bomb hit Bungalow "C".' (p.240) The graves of those killed in the American air raid on 16 January, 1945.

28. Mr Raven, aged 70, was one of the oldest inhabitants of the camp. On his 'home-made' lathe he made buttons, pipe stems, chessmen and other things unobtainable in the camp. (*Imperial War Museum*)

29. Sub-Lieutenant J. Poole with Japanese war criminals. Left to right: Colonel Tokunaga, Colonel Kanazwa and Sergeant Matsuda. (*Imperial War Museum*)

30. Japanese troops are marched through Hong Kong after the surrender.

31. Japanese war criminals line up for the move to Stanley Prison.
(*Imperial War Museum*)

32. Franklin Gimson, the Colonial Secretary (in trilby), meets Rear-Admiral C.H.J. Harcourt aboard HMS *Swiftsure*. (*Imperial War Museum*)

33. A Japanese envoy and his interpreter come aboard HMS *Swiftsure*. (*Imperial War Museum*)

34. The Author in 1969, then a Deputy Commissioner of the Royal
Hong Kong Police.

doors. . . . Until guards were placed on the kitchen the storeroom used to be broken into and food stolen during the night. . . . Even some of the guards, it appears, are not beyond doing an 'inside' job for two were caught the other day, but owing to the amateurish bungling of the case a charge could not be proved. . . . Until midnight Calthrop and myself kept guard together. He is now lying on a camp bed trying to sleep while I remain awake until 3.30 am. He then takes over until 7 am. It is getting damn cold so I must walk around. Another two and a half hours to go."

I used to volunteer for other working details for the same reason. Often the miserable reward of two tiny biscuits was not worth the energy expended. An example of this was when bulk rations arrived for the canteen, about which more below. These had been purchased for the Welfare Committee out of camp funds and so the Japanese refused to supply a truck to fetch it from the Stanley wharf. I wrote at some length about this experience:

"I certainly backed the wrong horse, today . . . armed with badly made local trolleys and a wheel stretcher our task was to push enormous sacks of bran, beans and peanuts from the wharf to the camp storeroom, a distance of over a third of a mile on a road in bad need of repair and uphill most of the way. There were three to a trolley – two pushing, one pulling. . . . All along the way you would see some of the fellows, at least two of them pulling and pushing while the third was busily making a hole in the sack ready for a portion of [its contents] to be emptied at the next convenient rest into already prepared cloth bags. . . . This is what hunger has reduced people to"

Countless hours of our time were spent in queueing for food either at the kitchen or the canteen. When we lived in Bungalow 'C' mealtimes were signalled by beating a gong made from a shell case, and as there were only 47 of us the queue was not too long. When we moved to the Indian quarters, however, there were 700 people to be served and although the queue was split up the waiting was interminable. If it was cold or wet, or both, it was a miserable experience. Sometimes I sought a diversion by contemplating my companions in the queue:

". . . known for their eccentricity of dress, such as Scott Harsten who spends all day in his pyjamas (lucky to have a pair or pairs). While we waited Searle and I got much amusement watching former taipans and businessmen standing in the queue. There was a perfect tramp with an old mac, filthy trilby and straggly beard. A few persons behind stood an enormous man with cropped hair and smoking a cigarette rolled in newspaper. He reminded me of Boris Karloff as Frankenstein . . . A habit of Dr Ballion, a one-time well known Hong Kong doctor now famous for his meanness, scrounging and scavenging habits, is to walk up and down the queue asking, "Does anybody not want their pak tasoi?" This vegetable, sometimes hardly eatable, is not very popular. He then appears at the server's table with an order for a dozen or so shares. However, as the hunger has got greater even the most fussy eat it so his success has not been great, but this does not stop him trying. . . . Dustbin-picking is not beyond the ken of some people here. . . . Old men are usually the culprits. This life is very hard on old people.

"Several months ago three old men were taken to the hospital after their room mates had made complaints about their filthy condition. At the hospital they were washed by the police orderlies; in one case forcibly. Afterwards their clothes were deloused. They had not changed their clothes for months."

The Geneva Convention, which Japan had not signed, stated that prisoners of war should receive a minimum of 2400 calories per day. In Stanley I am reliably informed the average was 850. At the start of our internment it was probably slightly higher but as the years passed it dropped in quality as well as quantity. When we ceased to get issued with meat or flour the quality of our miserly vegetable ration also fell. At one stage it included lily roots which, I was told, "the Chinese fed to pigs and say eating it causes goitre. Another informant said it was a Chinese delicacy. Some one must be wrong for the Chinese give nothing of value to their animals, especially pigs. Anyhow I noticed nothing peculiar in this morning's meal except (it) . . . was giving out an unpleasant odour." I remember Geoffrey summing up the situation neatly when he said, "If only my dog could see me now!"

Eventually, in 1944, even my youthful consitution began to register painful protests about what my stomach was, or rather was not, receiving. On 1 April I wrote:

"My stomach gave me hell last night; this morning I was doubled up. . . . I did not eat my congee, a bit of extra starving may do it some good. I saw the doctor a few days ago and he gave me all he had – a dose of Epsom Salts. . . . I went along again this afternoon . . . and was offered the diet kitchen (rice cooked in a refined manner) which I refused (as this is the place) where the female cooks guzzle themselves while the patients go short (it is time some one looked into this matter), so I came away after the inevitable dose of salts.

"2nd April.
My stomach is having a field day. . . . My trouble is not nausea against the food but violent pains for an hour or so after eating. By the time the next meal comes round five or six hours later I feel damn hungry so I eat my fill and pay for it like the foolish virgin."

When we had the energy we worked on our small garden to get extra vegetables. There were always endless arguments over the type to grow, with many people opting for Chinese variants of cabbage which, although less appetizing than carrots, tomatoes or sweet potatoes, grew quickly. To wait three months for carrots, for example, seemed an eternity. Our mess patch was close to our quarters so we could keep an eye on it – crucial if we wanted to eat the produce. Some garden thieves had honed their skills to a fine art. Their speed and cunning enabled them to clean out a plot in minutes during darkness, cutting off the leafy tops and planting them back in the ground so that all looked normal – for a while. A glance at Map 3 will show that every possible space was utilized for growing. In early 1944 I was writing on the subject:

"Every Tom, Dick and Harry in the camp has got a garden. All are in various stages of excavation. . . . Sergeants Williamson, Harris and Johnston not only have a good garden but had the foresight to buy a cock and hen when they were averagely cheap and obtainable. Now they have several hens. One day near the beach they spotted a wild beehive. This is now in their garden. . . . Our Russian police have also got a 'poultry farm'" [They were the first to obtain chickens, being wise about such matters, some having been in refugee camps.]

In August, 1944, there was real panic when the Japanese, as part of the military shake-up that had been instituted by Tokunaga, announced they intended to take over all the produce from our gardens. There was the distinct possibility of our being forbidden to touch all these vegetables. It led to a heated debate as to whether to dig everything up at once, even though it was not ready, or leave it and hope for the best. In the end our mess compromised and dug up half of our potatoes.

Vegetables, or rather the paucity of them, was always a bone of contention between us and the Japanese. They always published the precise amount of food, by weight, that each person was supposedly entitled to as rations, but the amount of vegetables was never listed. The reason for this, and the minute portions we actually received, was eventually revealed accidentally by Sergeant-Major Matsubishi in late 1944.

"Bickerton, the interpreter, and Taylor the QM (Quartermaster) went up to HQ to protest about the shortage of vegetables and there met the sergeant-major. Having heard what they had to say he flew into one of his rages and, pointing to a chart on the wall, bellowed, 'That is what you should get!' Bickerton took a closer look and noted the figures (nine ounces per head per day). He pointed out that what we were receiving was not up to the scale laid down. 'Oh well, I'm doing my best, you hairy ape,' retorted the sergeant-major."

It was Matsubishi's normal way of addressing internees, all Europeans were 'hairy apes', which I suppose we were in comparison to the scantiness of facial or body hair on the average Japanese. Considering the temerity of Bickerton, however, Matsubishi's response had been distinctly low key. Another favourite expression of his was to bellow, "I don't need scales. If I say its nine (or whatever number) ounces, it's nine ounces!" Not much different from sergeant-majors the world over really.

To supplement what we were issued with or grew in the gardens we needed cash or generous friends outside. We were allowed to receive parcels containing no more than five articles. 5 June, 1942, was a red-letter day as one of these parcels arrived for Geoffrey, just in time for his birthday. I recorded the event:

"Geoffrey Wilson's birthday, and as he got a large parcel yesterday, sent from Macao by his wife Joy, we decided to have a proper breakfast. . . . We had milk and treacle . . . then bacon and bread. The bacon was the first I have tasted since the war. . . .(it) was superb. . . .

"In the evening we had Geoffrey's official birthday party to which we invited Penny Guerim, Nina Smith and Betty Grant. They supplied some milk and coffee. We had a very pleasant rice concoction with bully beef, bacon, and tomato catsup mixed in the rice. The sweet was made by the girls and composed of flour, pineapple (supplied by the girls) and treacle. Then we had coffee."

Although I did not receive regular parcels, the more senior members of our mess were fortunate in this respect as they had built up a number of friendships in Hong Kong before the war, and of course Geoffrey was married. Even Emile Landau of Parisien Grill fame sent us at least one parcel. Cheating still occurred. The Japanese would publish a list of people who had parcels to collect and one elderly man, a former ship's engineer called Williamson, and founder of the Douglas shipping line, was often on the list. One of our police sergeants with the same name hit on the idea of collecting and eating these parcels, pretending he thought they were for him. There was an almighty rumpus when this trick came to light. Sergeant Williamson (the hen owner) had to pay for everything he had eaten after the war.

The other source of food parcels was supposed to be the International Red Cross (IRC) but they were so infrequent as to be the exception rather than the rule. For example, over a two-year period we received one and a half IRC parcels, whereas I believe prisoners of war in Europe got an average of two a month. After about a year of internment the Japanese permitted the appointment of an IRC representative in Hong Kong. This was a Mr R. Zindell who was a Swiss national, a resident of the Colony. He never impressed us with his efforts on our behalf and was quickly nicknamed "Mr Swindle" which he was sometimes called to his face, although I have no grounds for saying that he knowingly cheated us out of anything. It was more likely that he was terrified of the Japanese and enjoyed the salary and position that went with the post, with the result that he wanted a quiet life. He was never trusted by the internees who were only too ready to believe any derogatory stories about him, such as the one that he had given thousands of sacks of cracked wheat to the Japanese as horse fodder.

Zindell was seldom seen at Stanley and it was not until July, 1944, that he made a proper, public inspection of the camp:

"When Zindial [Zindell] . . . visits the camp he comes by car and drives straight up to the Commandant's House; he is never seen wandering about the camp. It is difficult to get anywhere near him on these visits; you have to make an appointment weeks beforehand, and you can only see him if your application is approved. He is closely guarded by a mass of regulations to which, I suspect, he is agreeable. I would say 70% of the people here have never seen the man. . . . Today must be the first time most of us have ever set eyes on him. . . . This is the first time he has ever been around during the two years he has acted as a J.R.C. [IRC] official. Maybe it is not entirely his own fault. . . . He visited the kitchens, hospital, living quarters. . . . The notes he made in a pocket book I hope were not eyewash for our benefit. . . . Zindial, who was dressed in a well pressed, white summer suit, looked civilized and well fed."

When IRC parcels did arrive it was a day of wild elation, celebration and EATING. One such day was 15 September, 1944.

"Though really tired I did not sleep during the whole of yesterday. The arrival of the parcels made me restless and excited. Geoffrey and Lance could hardly sit still.

"The IRC parcels, having been brought up from the pier during the morning, were issued, two per person early in the afternoon. . . . A committee is fighting amongst itself whether the Klim Full Cream, which came in separate cases, be issued out to the camp per head or in bulk to the hospital. . . .

"These parcels are from the Canadian RC and are a bit different from the last lot, English RC, which we received about two years ago. . . . They are not as well packed as the English ones, and the cheese in most of the parcels is in powder and many of the biscuits are mouldy. Anyhow, neither will be wasted. Some way will be found to make them eatable. The first thing I did, and so did the others, was to eat my chocolate, at least one slab of 5oz. It was delicious and I found it more satisfying than two of our ordinary meals (doubles); it filled me right up. How Geoffrey and Lance managed two slabs I do not know. . . . This morning we had our congee as usual, but also a real cup of tea, milk and sugar and biscuits, butter and marmalade. It left one full and with a real English taste in one's mouth. . . .

"Like last time we found many of the parcels on opening to be empty. Somewhere they had been looted. The boxes on first sight showed no signs of being tampered with."

This time there were no patriotic messages in the parcels as had been the case when the English ones had arrived in November, 1942. Then, one person had found a message scratched on a tin. It read: "There will always be an England. You will not be in Germany long. I am tall, slim with fair hair and violet eyes." Then followed the writer's address. In my parcel there had been the pencilled outline of two tiny pairs of feet, one marked "Sheila", and the other "Pam". I have kept that piece of paper. I would dearly love to know who those girls were.

It was perhaps ironic that it was the Police who initiated the biggest theft of food in Stanley. After only a few weeks of internment the Japanese decided that the huge stocks of food stored in the four godowns alongside the main camp road, overlooking Tai Tam Bay, should be moved. The British had stocked these godowns as part of their policy of accumulating and dispersing wartime reserves of food. In early March, 1942, they were bulging with every conceivable type of tinned food or dry rations. Veritable Aladdin's caves – all inside the perimeter wire of our camp, within reach of hundreds of hungry internees. On reflection the Japanese security measures, considering the value of the goods in store, were lamentably slack. The godowns were merely locked and had a paper seal over each door. Indian guards mounted spasmodic patrols along the road.

We realized what was in these buildings when the Japanese called for volunteers to load the stocks on to trucks. At first there was heated debate as to whether work of this sort might be construed as helping the Japanese war effort, but the argument that the contents of some of the boxes might be "diverted" for internal consumption won the day, so a working party, mainly police, was formed.

At first the thefts were little more than petty pilfering during the loading process while the Japanese or Indian guards were looking the other way. A tin would be tossed into a ditch to be collected later, a crate would be "accidentally" dropped and some of the scattered contents would disappear, guards would be distracted while an item was quickly passed to an onlooker who then slunk away with the prize. "W. P." was particularly enterprising. He wore a pair of breeches tied at the ankles which he gradually filled with sugar poured from torn bags. At a suitable moment he would wander over to some nearby bushes for a call of nature and relieve himself of the sugar into a gunny bag which we had brought for the purpose.

After the first day news of our pickings spread like wildfire. Others wanted to be in on it, and we became emboldened by the ease with which the guards were hoodwinked. It was realized that it was now or never as once the godowns were empty the opportunity of loot would be lost for ever. All subsquently had the same idea in mind, as the godowns were now only about half-full, if larger quantities went missing the chances of them being missed was considerably reduced. A night raid was planned by one party to bring out substantial amounts.

The idea was for Sergeant Karpovich, a White Russian with the necessary skills, carefully to remove the paper seal and pick the door lock on the half empty warehouse. His success, however, unleashed an avalanche of men, mostly police but also some others, all heading for the godown. There was some control on the first night, but when the Japanese failed to notice the seal and lock had been tampered with, and when the more faint-hearted saw the booty to be had, it developed into something of a free for all.

Our "mess" did well, but I remember on one trip noticing "W. P." crouched down in the shadows some little way ahead of me. He was clutching a package of some sort and was obviously checking that the way was clear before escaping back to the bungalow. As I was close I crept up and tapped him on the shoulder. Poor fellow, he nearly had a heart attack. He dropped his loot and fled, darting in and out of the shadows, ducking behind buildings, with me in hot pursuit. Back at the bungalow, when he realized who it was, I was subjected to, and I suppose deserved, the most monumental dressing down. At the time I was quite frightened by the fury of his verbal abuse.

A similar incident occurred when one looter, who knew exactly where a sack of sugar was located by a window in the godown, crept inside to fill up his gunny bag. Unbeknown to him another individual was after the same prize, but, being less audacious, he approached the window from the outside while the first man was carefully and quietly slitting open the sack. The second man stood outside and reached in through the window, but instead of touching the sugar he suddenly found himself grasping a man's hand. Both men froze, grasping the hand but unable to see who they were holding. For a few seconds they remained locked together in mutual terror. Then, as if on a signal, they vanished.

The blackness inside the godown was virtually impenetrable and there was no possibility of flashing a light. A would-be looter had either to locate what he wanted by day during the loading detail, or grope around and grab anything that came to hand, rather like some gigantic game of lucky dip. Neither method would guarantee you came away with what you wanted. One policeman who was partial to custard saw a large stack of tins of it and resolved that this would be his nocturnal target. He spent the night collecting as many tins as he could, only to discover, come daylight, that he was the hungry owner of the largest stock of Colman's mustard in Hong Kong. These raids were not easy. We had to watch for Japanese patrols. If we were discovered there was a very great danger of being shot. We took very great risks but hunger knows no barrier.

This uncontrolled looting was our downfall. Even the dimmest and most short-sighted of Japanese NCOs could not fail to notice that a store that was half-full one day, was only a quarter-full the next morning. Pandemonium. A cordon was thrown round the police block and a search was instituted, although less thorough than we expected. Everyone tried to get rid of the evidence. Food went into mattresses, Japanese graves, and at least one lavatory cistern. In the latter case it was tea that was emptied in so that for days afterwards when it was flushed nothing but cold tea came out. What a waste! Some inspectors and NCOs, who had a grudge against the commissioner, went so far as to dump their stolen goods outside his room, until the senior officers removed them.

About five police were caught, including Sergeant Moss who was grabbed with a sack of rice over his shoulder. They remained under arrest for nearly three weeks, during which time they came in for some rough handling by Indian guards but were never formally punished. I wrote of them on 4 April, 1942:

"Until further notice they have to march up and down the main road in the camp from 12.00 hrs to 17.00 hrs each day, and whenever they see a Japanese they must bow to them. I am sure they do not like having to do that."

The reason behind the lack of enthusiasm with the search, and the reluctance of the camp officials to punish the culprits, was that they had also helped themselves and were deeply involved in black marketeering (see below). A proper investigation meant the dreaded Kempeitai descending on the camp. Neither Yamashita nor Nagasawa relished the idea. They would be satisfied if the food was returned, or at least as much as possible. There was an amnesty announced – items should be left outside the commandant's office and no action would be taken. Some food was returned in that way to keep them happy, but the great bulk of it was absorbed into the system with a high proportion being sold or bartered on the black market for cash or cigarettes. This did not make the police popular. There was an element of envy involved as we had reaped the rewards, whereas the risks we had taken were forgotten.

For the entire time we spent in Stanley the black market thrived. The circumstances of inequality among the internees, the comparative wealth of some and poverty of others, the determination of many to put self-interest first, the overriding need to find the next meal, coupled with the fact that Orientals are natural traders ensured a booming black market. Trading started immediately the camp was occupied. Soon the Chinese supervisors became involved as they were paid a pittance, while internees would pay large sums or hand over valuable items in exchange for food or cigarettes. The Japanese entered into the business with zeal. Several rival syndicates emerged with Yamashita leading one and Sergeant-Major Matsubishi, the Japanese in charge of rations, another.

The objective of the internees was firstly food, secondly tobacco or cigarettes. In order to obtain these it was essential to have either cash to buy or valuables for barter. By and large money was used to buy food from the canteen when it opened, if you were prepared to queue for hours, if the item you wanted was available, and if you could afford the rocketing prices. Valuables such as watches, pens, rings, jewellery, even towards the end gold teeth and fillings, were exchanged "over the wire" via the guards or the Japanese. It is literally true that towards the end of our long sojourn people with gold teeth or fillings could hardly open their mouths without somebody offering to do a deal for their dentures.

I am certain that there was not a single adult internee who was not involved in some form of black market deal at some stage. Our "mess" sold numerous personal items. I remember that Gimson had given us a pair of binoculars to keep for him. During a particularly bad patch we had a long discussion as to whether we could sell them without damaging the war effort (how absurd it seems now). It was quite heated for a while. Hunger pains eventually defeated our collective conscience and Colin was deputed to sell them on behalf of the "mess". Being a bold policeman he let it be known to Yamashita that the binoculars were available. Yamashita turned up at our quarters one night to view the merchandise and agree a price. He and Colin sat on the stairs haggling. They agreed the exchange would be made for several catties (a catty is 1.3lbs) of rice, peanuts and wong tong (palm sugar), although the binoculars were not handed over until Yamashita produced the food – which he did. No doubt he sold them on to some Japanese officer in town at a handsome profit.

On another occasion we worked on Willy Sparrow, a senior officer and the owner of a Rolex watch, to let us do a deal. We assured him we could get an excellent price as we knew the system well. I admit we neglected to tell him that we would be taking our cut. Unfortunately Pennefather-Evans got to hear of our dealings and we were sent for to receive a talking to for behaviour unbecoming police officers. He told us that we had "sold our birthright for a mess of pottage".

The Japanese had instituted a new currency after their occupation called the Military Yen (MY) with an official exchange rate of around MY4 to one Hong Kong dollar. All cash transactions were in the MY of which, in theory, we received a monthly allowance of twenty-five. In the canteen, for example, a tin of bully beef sold at MY2.50 in 1942 and MY8.40 in 1944, and a tin of condensed milk rose from MY4 to MY12.50. I recall that we calculated that a basket of items costing a total of MY42 in the canteen would, only a few years previously in peacetime, have been about MY1.00. I wrote in my diary, "one needs to be a multi-millionaire to buy the above articles". In fact by 1944 money had lost much of its value to us as prices were astronomical and we had so little of it.

"6 April, 1944.

Money is only useful for canteen purchases; elsewhere it is practically useless. Barter is the order of the day. Two months ago it was possible to buy rice at a price, mostly from mothers whose children were drawing the same quantity of rice as a man and were unable to eat it. . . . Recent canteen purchase restrictions, together with the cut in the children's rice, has definitely put a stop to money being used as a tender. . . . (People) will only part with rice for garden produce or cigarettes . . . gardeners will only exchange their produce for other foods or, if smokers, for cigarettes. . . . Rice, of very little food value, but a temporary filler, has been elevated to a god; a god of carbohydrates and water."

By 1944 the black market had burgeoned into big business with the extensive use of IOUs. I can do no better than quote from G. B. Endacott and A. Birch's book, *Hong Kong Eclipse*, on this racket:

"Many internees had no money, and many others found their money and jewellery close to exhaustion in 1944. The simple process of writing a cheque or an IOU produced ready cash and therefore food, if a middleman or agent could be found to accept it. The discount was naturally considerable because of the risk of the IOUs not being honoured. A man's word had to be accepted and the terms varied according to his standing; members of large companies of international repute had 25 yen to the pound sterling, employees of big local firms 20 yen to the pound, professional men 15 yen to the pound, and so on down to doubtful risks who had to be satisfied with as little as 4 yen to the pound. Those still with valuables to sell could have a sterling cheque or the equivalent in food. Prices were outrageously high and £500 would buy about 25/6d worth of food at normal peacetime prices. People were driven by sheer desperation to pledge the future to ward off starvation. The middlemen, Chinese and Europeans, were of course essential to the proceedings which were euphemistically regarded as commercial transactions, and they cashed in handsomely. To regard people goaded by starvation as being free to make commercial bargains was of course plain hypocrisy, and to turn these exceptional circumstances to commercial advantage would seem to deny the morality basic to the decencies of community life. The justification, if there is one, lies in the fact that the IOUs were generally honoured, despite the fact that the Hong Kong government after the war officially released all individuals concerned from the letter of their engagements.

A few held out against the IOU system on principle, and survived on the issued rations. It is estimated that about six million yen passed over the wire between October, 1944, and March, 1945."[1]

As an example, extreme perhaps, of how money was made within this system there is the story of the tin of treacle. A man sold the tin for HK$100. He then took this money and converted it into MY400 at the black market rate of 1:4. Then he found somebody who was in dire need of cash so he handed over the MY400 in exchange for an IOU of £100. So his tin of treacle had been worth £100 – at today's exchange rate several thousand pounds!

Two of the leading figures in all this wheeling and dealing were Gray Dalziel and the man who skinned the tiger, butcher Bradbury. Dalziel was a businessman who did not intend to starve in Stanley. If he liked you it was possible to get a reasonable deal or price through him. He also became something of a fitness freak which, combined with his extra food, which included a fresh egg most days, enabled him to live exceptionally well as an internee. Nevertheless, he died comparatively young. Bradbury had excellent contacts outside camp and a seemingly endless supply of cash from these sources. He became one of Stanley's top usurers. His deliberate exploitation of hunger with his outrageously high interest rates made him perhaps the most despised of the internees. I can recall him now, a man fatter than most with an innocent, boy-like face. All he needed was a blue and white striped apron to look exactly like the cheerful, wholesome butcher one sees in typical meat advertisements. He was eventually, years later, to die a millionaire, but his conscience had been troubling him as he donated large sums to build a church and his will established a trust fund for the benefit of a Hong Kong charity.

I will end this chapter with a quotation from my diary that to me now is a humorous incident, but which at the time we treated seriously and was typical of the state of affairs in Stanley with regard to profiteering. Everybody had a finger in it one way or another.

"1 December, 1944.

Yesterday the guard (Formosan) in charge of the gardeners working in the 'football garden' called them all together and gave them the following lecture: 'I know that the Indians are selling you wine, cigarettes and foodstuffs, and that you place orders with the Indians and collect them at night. Now this trading must stop. You know that this trading is forbidden; you get yoursleves into trouble, and we guards get into trouble. This is a bad thing, and I warn you that you must stop it, Oh, while I remember it, I want to buy some white shirts! Have you gardeners any shirts to sell? If you have bring them along this afternoon.'"

CHAPTER SEVEN

DANGEROUS ACTIVITIES

"Corporal Akamatsu of the Hong Kong Gendarmerie, to give but one example, boasted to me that he and his comrades had butchered thirty British soldiers in the grounds of the Victoria Hospital at Hong Kong, who they had tied up with wire, bayonetted and then burnt with gasoline. 'They cried like a lot of pigs,' said this young monster."

Statement made on 20 March 1946 by Mrs Kane Bush, Japanese wife of Lieutenant Lewis Bush RNVR, serving with 2nd MTB Flotilla operating from Aberdeen.

There is little humour in the next two chapters. They are primarily concerned with the interrogations, torture and executions that took place at Stanley during 1943. The responsibility for the barbarism displayed against helpless captives belonged to members of the Japanese Gendarmerie (uniformed military police) and Kempeitai (the equivalent of the Gestapo, but usually dressed in civilian clothes). Everybody, including the Japanese, lived in fear of them – for good reason, as illustrated by the above remarks of Mrs Bush. They were all-powerful, sadistic and the trained interrogators of the Japanese military machine. They had full powers of arrest over military and civil personnel of any rank or status. Colonel Noma was their commander in Hong Kong for most of the occupation before he was succeeded by Colonel Kanagawa. Both were among the few war criminals from the Colony executed by the Allies. Unfortunately, one of their more brutal underlings apparently escaped retribution. This was the NCO, described as the "Number 1 Gendarme", Yoshimoto. It was he who was present or organized most of the savagery that occurred at Stanley during the course of extracting information or confessions from my fellow internees and their associates. He was nicknamed "Fei Lo" or Fat Boy, which appropriately described his flabby face and figure. For him interrogation was a pleasure. Although not averse to participating personally, he had trained his men to torture without having to give verbal instructions when necessary. A pre-arranged signal such as the tap of a pencil, the shuffle of a foot or a nod was all that was needed to set in train a particular technique. It is alleged his particular hatred was directed at Indians who were accused of opposing the Japanese East Asia Co-Prosperity Sphere. On 25 October, 1945, the *Weekly China Mail* carried the following:

"WHERE IS YOSHIMOTO?

Where is Gendarme interrogator Yoshimoto, lover of wine, women and song and all forms of gambling?. . . (He) was not in the latest drag-net that took 41 Gendarmerie lads into Stanley Prison on Tuesday. . . . He may be in Macao, but that is less likely than Canton."

It is exactly fifty years ago at the time of writing that the main atrocities and beheadings at Stanley took place. I realize now how close I came to being at the receiving end of these horrors as I was, for over a year, deeply implicated in dangerous activities such as smuggling food and messages into and out of Stanley jail. I also had knowledge of one of the clandestine radio sets operating within the camp. Had I been betrayed or suspected I would have been the thirty-fourth person kneeling on the sand near the jetty on 29 October, 1943, awaiting decapitation. That I was not there was due to incredible good luck and, I believe, to the great courage and amazing ability of one man who probably knew of my doings, to withstand prolonged pain, starvation and suffering. He was a small, somewhat mild-looking civil servant of 47 called John Fraser. He went to his death crippled by torture and beatings, his body emaciated and bent, virtually unrecognizable as the man he had once been. His was the triumph of the spirit over physical torment. Despite the protracted attention of the Gendarmerie over many weeks Fraser gave away nothing. His courage was a superlative example of that trite old Army expression, "No names, no pack drill". He was the only civilian among the four men to be awarded the George Cross posthumously for fortitude under the Gendarmerie.

None of us can tell for sure unless we have experienced it how we would react under torture. It is sickening to think that such inhumanity is still being perpetrated every day in countries all over the world. At Stanley a typical cross-section of Hong Kong residents were interrogated and eventually died horrible deaths. Soldiers and civilians, businessmen and bankers, British, American, Indian, Chinese and Portuguese, all were subjected to similar ordeals. Not all could endure without speaking. Names and confessions were extracted leading to further arrests as the secret network of radio and courier links with the outside world and the BAAG were unravelled during 1943. It was a dreadful year.

As will shortly become apparent one of my rugby club friends from pre-war days, who was later beheaded, admitted to his fellow sufferers that he had implicated several individuals under the infamous water torture. As far as I am aware none of them blamed him. Most of us probably have our breaking point; some (a tiny minority) like John Fraser may not; for others a welcomed death intervenes before that moment is reached. Some, like the Police Reserve officer David Loie, perhaps understand their own weakness and have the courage and opportunity to take their own life before their fallibility is put to the test. In this case Loie managed to leap to his death from the verandah of the Supreme Court building on the day of his arrest.

Some desperately but unsuccessfully tried to take their own lives to avoid more torment, like the man who tried putting the lavatory chain round his neck and jumping off the seat, or the White Russian, Mr Khorkel, who Doctor Selwyn-Clarke described as being:

"So severely tortured that he did his best to kill himself by biting and tearing the blood vessels in his left forearm, but he was stopped before he could manage it and mercilessly beaten for his pains ... (he got) near enough to the bars of my cell to beg me to give him some poison or tell him how he could take his life."[1]

Physical torture was officially recognized by the Japanese as a legitimate method of extracting information from prisoners. It was commonplace throughout the Army, and manuals were published on interrogation techniques that carried instructions on the methods to be used, with the proviso that "care must be exercised when making use of the rebukes, invectives or torture as it will result in his telling falsehoods and making a fool of you." Here the manual was alluding to the fact that many people in agony will say anything, true or false, to halt their misery.

The Kempeitai had their own school of interrogation in Japan operated by the War Ministry which included torture methods on the courses. The water treatment, burning, electric shocks, the knee spread, suspension, kneeling on sharp objects and prolonged beatings were all well tried procedures. Perhaps one of the most feared, and most successful in terms of breaking the victim's will, was the water torture. There were several variations. The most sophisticated was to tie the person up in the prone position and place him in a bath with his face under a tap. A piece of cloth, preferably silk, was placed on the person's face and the tap turned on slightly. Drip, drip, drip the water fell on the victim's forehead and the cloth, as it became slowly saturated, gradually sealed his face from the air. As less and less air filtered through breathing became increasingly laboured and painful. At this stage the tap was often turned on a bit more so that the silk became soaked so that breathing became great convulsive gasps for air which sucked water into the lungs. Part of the horror of this torture was the fact that once the person started to suffocate there was no way he could speak even if he wished to do so. He had to rely on the torturer's judgement as to when to stop, which was often not until he was unconscious, sometimes dead.

A rough and ready variation was to play a jet of water over the nose and mouth until the stomach was filled to bursting point. A Gendarme would then jump on the distended stomach forcing the water to cascade out of the victim's mouth and nostrils. One of the HKSB staff, C. F. ("Ginger") Hyde, received this treatment continuously, being revived by injections when he lapsed into unconsciousness.

There were three types of dangerous activity to which this chapter refers: each was taking place independently of the other with the great majority of internees totally ignorant of what was happening. The three were: the operation of radio sets; the passing of messages to and from agents outside Stanley and thence to the BAAG and the smuggling of food or money into camp and the prison. I was involved in the first and the third.

Not long after Smythe and the others had been sentenced to two years' imprisonment I was approached by Alex Summers who I knew had taken over Drage's MI6 post just before the outbreak of war. He admitted to me that he had a working radio receiver hidden in the wall of his room in the Married Quarters. He was operating it with the technical assistance of George Merriman, his tubby (initially), affable number two in the security service. They were listening in on a nightly basis to the overseas news, mostly in morse, and wanted me to pass important items of information to Gimson. They may also have been receiving messages in morse from the BAAG but I was never told this. As far as I was aware at the time their set was built (from parts they had found in camp) and operated by them on their own initiative to keep themselves informed of the war news. At the same time they suggested I might consider passing extra food or letters into the prison, through a contact they had established, for the benefit of Smythe, Fay, Morrison and Randall.

The Japanese superintendent of prisons, 1st Lieutenant Yamaguchi, had apparently asked Yamashita if there was an internee with a knowledge of radios who could repair his broken set. Summers and Merriman volunteered. They put their day in jail to good use. Not only did they contrive to steal two valves for their own set, but struck up a friendly relationship with the Chinese electrician who had been detailed to watch them at work. Valves were the size of an electric light bulb and therefore not easy to smuggle out of the prison. They were both convinced that Wong (I never knew his real name for security reasons) was anti-Japanese, as, to prove his good faith, he had lent them a radio manual and agreed to act as a courier to take food or messages into the prison. Eventually I returned the manual to him.

I was young and anxious to do something useful and exciting so I tentatively agreed with no real thought to the consequences if caught. Nevertheless my policeman's training cried caution. Was this agent Wong a Japanese plant? Summers thought not, as it was he and Merriman who had made the approach, although it was certainly possible he could decide to inform on us at a later stage. After much debate we agreed to take the chance. The next stage was to somehow introduce Wong to myself.

This was fraught with risk. Wong did not know me, did not know I had agreed to become his contact in camp, and he might well refuse to deal with me, fearing a trap to expose him. How was all this to be resolved? Wong had explained that every week he was allowed out of the prison to go into town, and that this meant walking down the main road from the prison through our camp. This was the time a casual contact could be made. Summers, who spoke good Cantonese, resolved that he would use this opportunity for me to be introduced. Not that Wong or I would speak; we would merely see each other and thus be mutually recognizable.

On the day in question Wong ambled slowly down the road, Summers fell in a pace or two behind him whispering what was happening, and telling him to take a good look at me as I came up the road from the opposite direction. Similarly, I had to get a close look at Wong. It was safer if there were plenty of people about on the main road, particularly between the prison gates and Wong as there was always the danger of being observed by Japanese from the prison, or up on "the hill" which overlooked the road. There was also the danger of people becoming inquisitive and gossiping. Our meetings had to be fleeting, just two people passing, no stopping, no obvious conversation.

With the passing months we became skilful operators. If I had something (a letter or small food packet) to pass to him I would drop it into his bag as we momentarily brushed past each other. If he had a message for me he would usually contrive to drop it on the ground while I was watching him approach, so I could quickly retrieve it before anybody else who might be passing. There were often internees searching for cigarette butts for example, which made it easier for me to pick something up without exciting attention. Occasionally, if we needed to speak at more length I would get a message to meet Wong in the transformer shed just opposite the prison gate. This was highly dangerous. I could never be certain if Wong would be there, or if somebody else might arrive if I waited. If this happened how could I explain my presence? This whole operation had its worries. One never knew what was around the corner.

It was up to me to find a regular source of food to smuggle in. No easy matter. I told Pennefather-Evans what I intended to do and asked his help as far as food was concerned. In turn he approached Gimson who agreed I should get extra food, usually in the form of vitaminized chocolate packed in small, specially made, flat tins. I still have one such container. Gimson received this chocolate, along with other items, from sources in town primarily organized by Dr Selwyn-Clarke, but concealed in the daily ration truck which was driven by a Kowloon Bus Company employee whom we all knew as "Jimmy". His real name was Leung Hung who the Japanese were later to describe in their charge sheets as the "head coolie employed in the (Japanese) Governor-General's Department". Poor Jimmy was later to be one of the many Chinese to be arrested, tortured and then beheaded on that awful day in late October, 1943.

Food sent into the jail via Wong had either to be the chocolate or small biscuits as these were easily concealed, and had no wrappings or containers such as tins that the prisoners could not get rid of or, in the case of the latter, open. The maximum I could send in at any one time was two slabs of chocolate or three or four biscuits. With the chocolate I kept the tin and concealed the contents in a newspaper.

As the weeks passed Wong and I developed a special code of signals that he would display to let me know of any change of plan. I would go to the Married Quarters. There from an inconspicuous vantage point I could see over the top of the prison walls into a part of the compound. Wong arranged to hang out a towel at a certain spot if he was coming out on a Tuesday as usual. Two meant there was likely to be a delay, and three that he would be leaving on the next day, Wednesday.

For about eighteen months this system worked well, and I was eventually able to confirm that the items I sent in reached our police comrades and others such as Sir Vandeleur Grayburn, the chief manager of the HKSHB, the circumstances of whose imprisonment I describe below. Then Wong decided he was pulling out to go to Macau. His departure prompted me to make a stupid mistake that could easily have cost us both our lives. I wrote a letter to my mother, and passed it to Wong to give to the British consul in Macau. Although Wong took it without comment and we said our farewells, which ended with his usual "God bless you", I am certain he wisely destroyed it.

My new contact was a man called Lee who had been introduced to me by Wong. Somehow there was never the same feeling of trust between us. My misgivings were confirmed when, after a few weeks, Lee started to put pressure on me. To begin with it took the form of a request for payment for what he was doing, claiming he was taking serious risks for no reward. I did not argue and he reluctantly agreed to accept a modest sum from certain funds. Lee, however, was in the game for gain. Within a short time, like Oliver Twist, he asked for more. Now he felt confident enough to reinforce his demands with the threat of exposure. I went through an anxious few days before deciding to call his bluff. No, it was impossible to pay him more, and if he exposed me he would also expose himself (if he had not been a plant all along). Nothing happened, although it was shortly after this, in the early summer of 1943, that the Japanese began their series of mass arrests both in Stanley and elsewhere that put paid to our activities for good.

I came within a whisker of arrest on 30 June, 1943. Only the quick thinking of Summers and Merriman saved us. I was actually in their room, in which their radio was concealed, when there was a commotion outside caused by the sudden arrival of several Japanese, including Yamashita, Yoshimoto (he was identified to me afterwards) in full uniform complete with sword, three dapper, bandy-legged little men in immaculate white suits and panama hats, unmistakably Kempeitai, plus our Chinese supervisor and an interpreter. Before we had time to think, let alone act, the door was flung open and the whole gaggle burst in, jostling for position in the confined space. I did not wait but left in haste without any attempt by any of them to stop me. I was told later what happened.

Yoshimoto, through the interpreter, opened the proceedings by glaring at Summers and Merriman and shouting:

"You Summers, you Merriman?" It was a question not a statement.

"Yes."

"We know you understand wireless – right?" Another question of sorts. Yamashita had obviously given the names of all internees known to have had wireless knowledge to the Gendarmerie.

"Yes." Having repaired the prison set there could be no other response. Then came the hard one. Yoshimoto, whose tiny eyes had disappeared into the folds of his puffed up face to the extent that Summers recalled wondering how he could see, bellowed his accusation cum question.

"You have a wireless?" Perhaps Summers and Merriman had prepared for this moment in advance because the reply came instantly, given with quiet confidence by Summers.

"Yes, we did have a wireless, but when the Japanese authorities issued the notice forbidding internees to have them we broke it up, and threw the parts into the sea over the wire near the hospital." It was a classic half-truth. A denial would surely have resulted in the inevitable sequence of arrest, beating, torture, imprisonment, more torture, probably a confession followed by death. The unexpectedness of the admission caught the Japanese off balance. It signalled the start of a high-pitched, agitated argument in which Yamashita and the Kempeitai officers joined.

Later a very white and worried Summers and Merriman arrived, both stressing that, if I were picked up, it was imperative I tell the same story. We all spent many anxious hours worrying as to the eventual outcome. Would the explanation be accepted? Would the Japanese search the room? Would my friends be arrested, and would I become implicated? It should be understood that the whole camp was in turmoil at this time with the Gendarmerie having already made six arrests, including Scott the deputy commissioner, two days before – the story of which follows in the next section of this chapter. That evening both my friends were incredulous not to have been arrested. Yoshimoto had seemingly accepted their part confession, at least for the moment, and there had not been a search, which could hardly have failed to find the set. The radio was buried that night and never to my knowledge used again. Both Summers and Merriman escaped arrest and survived internment. Keeping their heads, telling a half-truth, coupled with amazing luck had saved them, and probably myself, from a gruesome fate. On reflection it is also likely that the fact that the Japanese had already found two radios at Stanley, and were in the midst of arresting and interrogating not only Stanley internees but also Europeans still in town, Chinese, and prisoners of war, distracted them. Their success elsewhere made them more likely to accept Summers' and Merriman's explanation. A half-truth had paid dividends. An outright denial could have led to torture.

I believe it would be useful for the reader to have a résumé of the situation with regard to our clandestine activities as at the end of February, 1943, just prior to the mass arrests that began in March and continued over the following weeks until July. It is no exaggeration to say that from July, 1943, until the end of the war our underground system of operating radios, smuggling messages, using outside agents as couriers and planning escapes was, to all intents and purposes, dead in the water. By the end of that year the Japanese had, quite literally, killed off all these enterprises by decapitating the majority of the participants with swipes of their Samurai swords. It is a sad and shocking story.

By early 1943 the forward base of the BAAG at Waichow had been operating successfully for nine months. It was assisting escapers, planning fresh breakouts and gleaning useful and sensitive intelligence from inside Hong Kong from a network of largely Chinese agents, messengers and informers. Outside of the POW camps and Stanley were a number of secret cells coordinated in the main by a New Zealand Chinese called David Loie, or Loie Fook Wing. He was an officer in the Police Reserve with an intense loyalty to the British cause who had built up intelligence and courier activities using a number of his former comrades in the Reserve. Men like Yan Cheuk Ming of the Harbour Department, Chan Ping Fun who worked as an engineer at Kai Tak airport, his wife's brother from the Fire Service, and his common law wife Lau Tak Oi all played key roles in passing on critical information on the Japanese to the BAAG. Loie, who had been forced to continue his civilian occupation as a chemist in the Medical Department, was among the first seized at the end of May, 1943. As previously related, he took his own life rather than possibly betray others under torture. He was later posthumously awarded the King's Colonial Police Medal for gallantry – richly deserved. To this day he remains an outstanding example to the Hong Kong Police Reserve, now known as the Auxiliary Police.

Other Chinese in the town were also heavily involved, many of whom paid the ultimate price for their courage: men such as Yeung Sau Tak who passed on secret documents concerning the Japanese naval dockyard where he worked, or some of the drivers who were still working for the Kowloon Bus Company. I have already mentioned "Jimmy" the truck driver who made countless trips to Stanley bringing in and taking out food, money and messages. There were others, some well known to us, like Lee Lam and his mate Lee Hung Hoi. At the height of its operations the BAAG was controlling, directly or indirectly, a hundred Chinese agents who had held (or still held) posts as diverse as the Governor's chauffeur, a cook at Queen Mary's Hospital and school teachers.

The BAAG had also established communications with a group of senior British bankers who were still at work at the HKSB and elsewhere, but under Japanese control. The chief manager of the HKSB, Sir Vandeleur Grayburn, his sub-accountant E. P. Streatfield, C. F. "Ginger" Hyde and D. C. Edmondston were among prominent banking officials confined in squalid conditions in the Sun Wah Hotel. They were compelled to continue working under threats of severe punishment to themselves and their families if they did not. All made every effort to keep the liquidation of the Colony's finances under their control so as to minimize any long-term adverse effects. Unfortunately the speed of the Japanese victory had prevented the destruction by the banks of some $HK119 millions worth of notes. Such a vast amount takes time to burn. The bank officials were forced to sign these notes and issue them via the Japanese. They were called "duress notes". Important information on the Japanese financial activities was brought out by T. J. J Fenwick and J. A. D. Morrison when they made a successful escape on a Chinese fishing junk via Mirs Bay in October, 1942.

Grayburn did much to alleviate the suffering of internees by sending in more money than he was allowed into the camp. A secret hoard of cash of some two million dollars was accumulated from Chinese sources. Among those responsible for raising these funds was Edmondston. Part of the money was kept in a suitcase under the chief cashier's bed at the Sun Wah, but the bulk was under the false bottom to the bank's wooden trolley-box in which much of the official cash was kept. Mr Perry-Aldworth, the chief cashier, has explained its use:

"These funds were paid over by me from time to time to Dr Selwyn-Clarke, the Director of Medical Services of the Hong Kong government (who was also at large) and who . . . bought bulk supplies of all sorts which included food, drugs, mosquito netting, camp beds and bedding, clothing etc., all of which was sent by various means to the different internment camps and hospitals, both military and civil."[2]

Apart from my involvement with Wong and passing on items of wireless news from Summers' set to the commissioner and sometimes to Gimson, I knew nothing, other than camp rumour, of the existence of the three other radios in Stanley. This was fortunate as they were all discovered. When one of our sergeants, Frank Roberts, was first interned at Stanley he brought with him a wireless receiving set. He reported this to Fraser (former Defence Secretary) who at the time was the senior British government official in the camp. Fraser, after consulting with the internee camp quartermaster William Anderson, decided to give this set to Stan Rees and "Duggie" Waterton. Both these men had the technical knowledge as they had worked for the General Post Office, Rees being on secondment from Cable and Wireless. They agreed to conceal the set in their room, listen in nightly and report important news to Fraser. When Gimson took over in March, 1942, these news items were given to him. It was vital that as few persons as possible knew of the existence of this set (and Summers'). The principle was clear, but the practice far from easy to achieve in a close-knit internment camp where people had little to do except elaborate on, or invent, rumours. Certainly by January, 1943, I feel sure most of us had heard stories of radios operating within Stanley.

William Anderson, who was still working closely with Fraser, became increasingly concerned by these whisperings about a wireless. He and Rees investigated and traced the source back to members of the BCC. Gimson was consulted and he agreed that the news emanating from the Rees/Waterton set, which he was passing to selected members of the BCC, should in future only be given to the former attorney-general. The "need to know" principle was not being tightly enforced. People given accurate news naturally assumed there must be come sort of clandestine source, probably a radio.

This slight tightening of the security screw was insufficient. In the following month, February, William Anderson whose job as quartermaster meant he had a comprehensive knowledge of camp activities, heard that there was a second source of radio news. It was allegedly coming from "F" Bungalow. This was where his namesake, James Anderson, another Post Office official, lived. An anxious Anderson again confronted Rees:

"For God's sake, Stan, is there another wireless in 'F' Bungalow? I'm hearing rumours now that people are getting news from there. This is crazy. We must sort it out or the Japs are sure to get wind of it, then it's curtains for us all."

At first Rees rejected the possibility, but Anderson persisted, stressing that it must be checked out and that he wanted to be able to reassure Fraser and Gimson. Only then did Rees admit to the truth.

"Okay, okay, James does have a small battery set which is a reserve in case the power supply is cut and Duggie (Waterton) and I can't keep our mains set working."

"But he's using the bloody thing."

"Not now. He did listen in for test purposes and I suppose a bit for personal information, but he's stopped."

"Well get the damn thing off him and give it to me and I'll hide it. This whole business is out of control. I'll have to brief Fraser and Gimson."

The set, contained in a small Huntley and Palmers biscuit tin, was duly handed over to William Anderson.

March, 1943, saw the security situation worsen. First "Jimmy" (Leung Hung) the ration truck driver, who was by this time smuggling messages and money on a regular basis, told our quartermaster to expect a highly secret message that he must pass to F. I. Hall, who would know what to do with it. It would arrive inside a cigarette. Anderson duly received the packet containing the message and passed it on. "Jimmy" had appeared nervous and admitted that he, "had the feeling that Chinese spies were watching the ration truck carefully in camp, especially at the canteen (where Hall worked) on its daily delivery." Hall was warned, but at first ignored the advice to keep away from the truck.

The cigarette message was indeed crucial. It contained instructions from the BAAG in Waichow for Stanley to listen in on the 40 metre wave band. Direct radio communications from the BAAG to the camp were to be established using the Rees/Waterton receiver. Rees later told Anderson that he had been given this message, and that Fraser and Gimson knew all about it. As Rees was totally unaware that Anderson had handled the message the fact that he was talking to him about it was extremely disconcerting. Far too many people seemed involved in some way or other, or at least knew the names of persons implicated.

At the time I was blissfully ignorant of what was happening or who was involved outside of my own dealings with Wong, Summers, Merriman and Gimson. Fortunately ours was a small cell, run by quick-witted professional intelligence operatives, and we were blessed with perhaps more than our fair share of luck. Outside our small circle there was a growing group of people involved in some sort of secret enterprise, if only black marketeering or smuggling in items for personal use. At the centre of the illicit radios, and undercover communications with the town and the BAAG, was Gimson. He knew what was happening, he was kept informed and often authorized a specific action, although he never participated personally as far as I am aware with the hands on aspects. A man who knew as much as Gimson was Fraser. Often he acted as a filter for Gimson, with information coming through him before he passed it on. His role was perhaps similar to a chief-of-staff who oversaw the detailed work, coordinated and submitted courses of action. Certainly Fraser knew all the names – probably including mine. Likewise my involvement was known to the commissioner.

William Anderson had been involved from the start; he knew about Rees and Waterton, and about Logan and Addingly who were also wireless technicians sharing both a room and listening duties with them. He knew (as did others) about Jimmy and Hall and the other Anderson, James. Sergeant Roberts was known to have brought in the radio now operated by Rees and the others. He was also, according to his statement made in late 1945, involved in planning an escape with Fraser, Scott and Waterton. Although I find it hard to credit that these two senior government officers would have been involved with a sergeant who would seemingly have little to contribute to the venture, Roberts is emphatic on this. Such close association between the highest and lowest within the police was extraordinary for those days.

There were too many links in the security chain. If one broke the chances were that the whole system could collapse with fatal results. This is precisely what happened.

During March two events occurred that, in retrospect, were of considerable significance. The first was the "official" visit to Stanley of a Chinese called Tse Chi, alias Howard Tau. He was well known in pre-war Hong Kong as a dance-hall manager with the irritating habit of starting every conversation with the words, "Call me Howard". It had stuck as his nickname. He was a known collaborator whom the Japanese had sent into the camp to sniff for information. He went around visiting people (including our "mess" – we scrounged a bottle of alcohol off him), asking questions, listening to gossip, all the time trying to cover his real intentions by assuring everbody that if they had complaints he would personally take them up with his friend Mr Oda in the Foreign Affairs Ministry; a thoroughly unpleasant, oily individual whose ingratiating manner and Japanese connections made him instantly suspect. I was amazed to see that he spent a long time with Scott.[3]

The second occurrence, about which I heard much later, was the arrest of a Dr Harry Talbot. It was the first arrest of anybody attempting to smuggle things, in this case money, into Stanley. Talbot was an internee who had been receiving medical treatment in town and who had been persuaded to bring in the extra cash for Grayburn. At the gate he was searched, the money found and he was arrested. Talbot was questioned in the Stanley Gendarmerie post.

"You take money into camp against Imperial Japanese regulations". Before he could reply the next question was screamed at him.

"We know you bad doctor. You operate on Madame Chang Kai-shek. You say bad things about Japanese. We insist on good manners. You must always obey Japanese regulations or we will put you in jail".

There was a pause for this to sink in. Talbot seemed uncertain whether a reply was called for and was about to speak up in his defence when the Chinese/Japanese interpreter, who had lived for ten years in London and spoke with a broad Cockney accent, whispered, "I'd fuck off if I were you while the going's good!"

Talbot was released back into camp but was later re-arrested and received three months' imprisonment.

When Grayburn heard of this incident he, accompanied by his assistant Streatfield, immediately went to the Japanese authorities to take the blame, saying they had given Talbot the money for the camp hospital. For two weeks nothing happened. Then Grayburn and Streatfield were seized, badly beaten up in the hope of their revealing the bank's connection with the BAAG, and eventually sent to Stanley jail to serve a 90-day sentence. I recorded Grayburn's arrival:

"Diary 13 April, 1943.
Grayburn brought to Stanley chained to Streatfield . . ."

And the next day:

"Some of our quarters being on higher ground than the prison it is possible to see into it. Recently twice a day a number of prisoners have been exercised outside one of the four blocks. The usual procedure of walking round in a circle with hands behind the back. Today amongst those unfortunates a tall European dressed in a lounge suit was seen.... Walking up and down on the grass verge was another European dressed in jacket and shorts. The one in the suit was Streatfield but owing to the distance it was impossible to be certain if the other was Grayburn."

I was, in the next few weeks, able to smuggle in letters and a little food for Grayburn from his wife who was now an internee. Lady Grayburn generously gave me a pair of her husband's gold cuff links which I am ashamed to say I was later forced to sell on the black market to stave off starvation. I have always deeply regretted doing this.

Following "call me Howard's" visit, William Anderson overheard mention of a Gendarme raid while working at the Japanese HQ and immediately alerted Gimson and Rees, strongly advising that radio reception should cease and the set be buried. This action was taken. Several weeks of radio silence ensued in camp. No raid took place so by the end of May Gimson was suggesting to Rees that his set reopen. As we now know if things seemed quiet in Stanley the months of April and May had seen some ominous events outside.

It was the period in which the bankers Grayburn, Streatfield, Hyde and Edmondston were arrested, and also the linchpin of the underground organization in town, David Loie. Early in May Dr Selwyn-Clarke was seized and charged with no less than forty offences. He was initially incarcerated in a cell under the Supreme Court.

"Everything was taken from me except my shirt and trousers and I lay on the concrete floor, crawled over at night by cockroaches from a nearby latrine.... The investigation cubicles were near enough to bring at intervals the heart-rending sounds of pain.... As for my own share, I lost count in the end of the Kempeitai's repeated efforts to make me incriminate myself and others.... (When eventually sentenced to death the courageous doctor replied), 'The sooner the better. I am extremely tired of your methods of investigation.'"[4]

Selwyn-Clarke was not executed. He was imprisoned at Stanley and later in Kowloon. After the war he was deservedly decorated and later became the governor of the Seychelles.

Suspected BAAG agents in town were being picked up. We did not know the details but my diary for 13 April records ominously the execution of several Chinese near the Stanley preparatory school: "Some (were) in such a poor state of health that they had to be moved by wheelbarrow for execution."

It was considered too risky for Rees to reopen his set in his flat. He and Waterton had quarrelled seriously and were no longer sharing accommodation, so Gimson persuaded William Anderson to take it on. He was most reluctant.

"In view of my other activities I was not keen to add a new commitment.... (I) finally agreed to operate the set for a time from my office cum living quarters conditionally that no persons other than the Colonial Secretary (and) Rees were informed.... I was given this assurance, also a promise from Rees that should he be questioned ... my name would not be disclosed. I likewise gave a (similar) undertaking."[5]

The next event of significance was the arrest, release and disappearance of "Darkie" Chan, the Chinese camp supervisor responsible for the St Stephen's College blocks. For months he had been working with an American called Chester-Bennett in town taking messages and money in and out of camp for our canteen. "Darkie" was dragged off to the Gendarmarie HQ well aware of what was coming. Nobody was more surprised than himself when Nagasawa appeared to speak up on his behalf, saying that nothing could be proved against him and that he should return to Stanley. He was released. Wisely he fled at once to Free China. Nagasawa must have had a lot of explaining to do. It was not long after this that he was replaced by Mr Maejima from Foreign Affairs and posted back to Japan for military service. The Japanese were now poised to strike.

At about noon on the 28 June, 1943, I was present when our Chinese supervisor, Yip, arrived at our room and announced to Scott that he was wanted "up the hill". Slowly, without any outward sign of the turmoil of doubt and fear that must have seethed within him, he calmly finished his meal of bully beef. Waiting outside was Yoshimoto. Anderson happened to be at the Japanese HQ when Scott arrived. He later wrote:

"I saw W. R. Scott (Deputy Commissioner of Police) being escorted by Gendarmes (Yoshimoto with two other Japanese and one Chinese interpreter) to House No. 2 (then occupied by Chinese Camp Supervisors). Later I heard screams coming from the house and had no doubt that Scott was being tortured . . . I received confirmation later."[6]

Now there was real fear. Scott was a key figure. He knew most of what was going on and certainly that Rees, Waterton and others had been operating a radio, although he did not know of Anderson's recent take over of this duty. If Scott cracked. . . . Anderson informed Gimson of Scott's arrest followed by a hasty discussion with Rees as to what to do. There was little to be done except pray. At 3.00 pm Scott was still receiving the undivided attentions of the Gendarmes.

My diary for that dreadful afternoon merely states:
"About 2.30 p.m (Inspector) Whant was collected by Yip. Later about 6.00 p.m several Japanese in plain clothes appeared and went up to Rees' room. A guard was put on the door and later Rees was removed. About this same time Hall and Bradley were taken away."

As part of the round-up Yoshimoto, with Yamashita and several other Japanese, burst in on Anderson's room at about 6.00 pm. Anderson later described what happened:

"I was asked by the interpreter to hand over the wireless transmitter I had. I replied that I had no transmitter. There was then a conversation between Yoshimoto and Yamashita while two Gendarmes made a perfunctory search of the room (during which one) half pulled out the drawer which accommodated the wireless receiver . . . but fortunately he only saw the books I used to conceal the set."[7]

A discussion followed, with Yoshimoto and Yamashita peering at the camp nominal roll checking on the name "Anderson". Yamashita was heard to say, "There's another Anderson J. L. He's a wireless engineer." They clearly believed they had got the wrong man as the whole party dashed out heading for James Anderson in "F" Bungalow. William Anderson again:

"I had been granted a lucky break, but had no doubt I would receive another visit. Within a few minutes . . . I transferred the radio set to a gunny bag which I deposited in a small storeroom at the other end of the building (known as American Block No. 1)".[8]

The lucky break lasted barely thirty minutes. When the Gendarmes returned to Anderson's room they drew their revolvers and locked the door. Without a word Yoshimoto lashed out with all the force his fat frame could muster, striking Anderson on the face and sending him staggering back. Another Gendarme booted him in the leg before hurling him to the floor with a jujitsu throw. This was the signal for everyone to pile in. Anderson felt the blows raining down from all directions as he curled up in the foetal position in a futile effort to shield himself. Then, while a Gendarme sat on his chest, Yoshimoto began screaming and swearing, demanding the radio he said was in the room. His denial provoked a renewed assault, this time with a bamboo stick. Anderson's groans were now being drowned out by the chorus of yelling and shrieking from the Japanese who all joined in demanding the disclosure of the radio. The unfortunate quartermaster later said, "I well remember seeing the face of Yamashita and I felt sure he was genuinely sorry for me".

Anderson hung on, the thought of his promise to Rees strengthening his resolve. Next his legs and hands were bound and he lay bleeding and helpless on the floor. The finale is best described by himself:

"One Gendarme left the room and returned with a fire bucket full of water. I remember the thought passing through my mind, 'I was being prepared for a bath but which kind I knew not'. I did not guess I would have to swallow this water. A towel was picked up and fastened round my head and I saw no more. The bawling by all continued and water was forced through my mouth and nostrils in large doses. This was a painful torture but I was so waterlogged that had I wanted to talk I was physically incapable of doing so. The water torture ceased and the towel was removed from my head. I was forcefully turned over on my side facing the door which was opened and outside stood Rees. The door was closed and I was asked where was the wireless set. I quickly decided it was useless to continue my denial and I said I had a set. Yoshimoto booted me on the body and yelled why did I not say so before. I replied that I was asked if I had a wireless in my room and

I replied I had no set in my room but there was one in a store room. I was freed from my bonds and told to take Yoshimoto to the store. This I did and handed over the radio set. We all returned to my room where the set was uncovered, checked up with notes Yoshimoto had taken from his bag; in fact he spent some time checking his notes and examining the set. It was clear he had a full description of the set. (Rees told me in prison that he was forced to describe the set in detail when arrested in camp.) The Gendarmes appeared to me to be satisifed that they had got what they wanted because there was much laughing and light talk between them, possibly feeling they had done a good job.[9]

"They also unearthed the J. L. Anderson 'biscuit tin' battery set but appeared to take no interest in this set."

28 June had been a long day. At the end of it Scott, Rees, Whant, Bradley, Hall and William Anderson were in custody at the Gendarme post in Stanley village. All had suffered cruelly at the hands of Yoshimoto and his thugs. Regrettably the Japanese were far from finished. During the week that followed the inhuman interrogations continued, justifying a second bout of arrests on 7 July. These included Fraser, Waterton, Roberts and J. L. Anderson. It was also during that week that the arrests of the military personnel that will feature in the next chapter took place.

The only person we know for certain who broke under extreme torture was Rees as he himself later admitted. Quite rightly in my view, he was never blamed for it, not even by the people whose names he revealed. Nobody can resist for ever, and Rees was among those singled out for repeated and prolonged "interrogation". It was while in the cells of Stanley prison that Anderson learned of Rees' confession:

"Fraser asked what I (William Anderson) had been arrested for and I replied, 'in possession of the Rees wireless set'. This news surprised him. He then asked if I knew how I was given away and I replied, 'Stan (Rees) talked through water torture'. I asked him how he came to be arrested and he said 'through Stan'. I knew that Rees had been taken from his cell by the Gendarme for questioning on the third and fourth days after our arrival in 'G' Hall."[10]

The arrest of the second group of internees on 7 July culminated in a pathetic scene which I witnessed being enacted near the Indian

Quarters – the unearthing (literally) of a fourth radio which, as far as I am aware, had never actually been used. There was a touch of humour on this occasion, introduced by "New Moon" Moss, the former Director of Marine. He had acquired his nickname because of his continued insistence, to anybody who would listen, that the British would recapture Hong Kong when the Chinese had had a chance to reap the harvest, and there was a new moon for the attack. I wrote:

> "The Gendarmerie were back on the rampage in camp today. All in plain clothes. Waterton of the Wireless Department and also (J. L) Anderson of the same Dept. were arrested; so was John Fraser. . . . The fourth was Sgt Roberts. . . . At about 1.30 pm (we) heard loud shouts in Japanese coming from the commandant's house followed by screams. Later on Waterton came down with three Japanese and one Chinese. They were armed with spades. Waterton was made to dig a hole at the end of No. 18 Block in the Indian Quarters. He was kept at it for about 2-3 hours and in the end a grey box was unearthed."

At this stage one of the guards went into the Block and reappeared with "New Moon" Moss who was brought to the hole and confronted with the radio in the box. I watched anxiously as a protracted argument ensued. After a while Moss walked away, and the guards hustled the wretched Waterton into a car and drove him off. Moss had obviously been accused of being associated with the radio; but how had he got off as he shared a room with Waterton? I later heard at first hand what had transpired. According to "New Moon" when he saw Waterton he realized straight away that he had been tortured and named him as the person who had helped bury the set. Moss was certainly not as daft as he sometimes seemed as his response had been that, yes he did help but had never looked in the box. He had been asked one night to assist with the burial but had been told it was Waterton's family silver. As there was so much stealing in camp he needed to hide it. The Gendarmes had swallowed this unlikely story – another half truth. Moss lived to tell the tale, Waterton did not.

On about 17 July the Japanese celebrated their success with a party in the prison. My diary reads:

> "From all accounts it was some party. One individual got very drunk and they locked him up in a side room. Then he started to break up

the furniture so he was let loose into the yard. From the yard he started to fire his revolver and everybody dived for cover. Then one of the Japanese officers came out and shot him in the shoulder and he was carted off. This was all seen by the people living in the rooms overlooking the prison."

CHAPTER EIGHT

EXECUTIONS

"Hundreds of innocent Chinese were executed by these fiends without trial, and it was the usual thing for them to say, 'It is time we executed some more, my sword arm will get out of practice.' This is no exaggeration whatever. . . .

"Every day and night I was forced to witness the torture of Chinese who were subjected to brutal beatings, water poured down their noses, their finger nails set on fire, made to walk on burning charcoal etc. . . . The conduct of the Kempeitai was unspeakable and it was impossible to believe that they were products of the land which gave me birth."

Statement by Mrs Kane Bush, nee Kane Tsujimura, the Japanese wife of Lieutenant Lewis Bush RNVR, 20 March, 1946.

Everybody in the jail knew Hirano. Although I am uncertain of his rank I believe him to have been a senior NCO. He was slightly taller than the average Japanese but with a square frame made more so with the flabbiness of overindulgence and lack of exercise. His head was close-shaven, while the skin of his face was coarse and pitted like the skin of an orange – a typical turniphead. When he grinned, which was usually when witnessing or inflicting some suffering, there was a distracting gleam of gold from among the brownish yellow stumps in his mouth. He was a man in his thirties who spoke little, but to whom fellow Japanese and guards were deferential, respectful, never failing to bow or salute when he appeared. Above all he was a man who understood fear, a man who dealt in death. He was the executioner.

Hirano was pleased with his job, proud of his prowess with the sword which he carried at all times. In October, 1943, he was specially happy at the prospect of overtaking the Supreme Court executioner, Takiyawa, in the unofficial competition between the two as to who could decapitate the most people. He knew there were over thirty due to come under his sword, which would boost his score to record levels. He relished the prospect, and spent much of Thursday, 28 October in the prison workshop supervising the sharpening of his Samurai sword for the work ahead. His one regret was that the weapon that was to shed so much blood was merely an ordinary Army issue Japanese NCO's sword. (I still have an exactly similar one in my possession.) It was not of the finer quality of an officer's sword, it had no history, it had not been handed down from generation to generation and bore no master swordsmith's mark on the blade. Nevertheless it was a well made, heavy-duty instrument eminently suitable for the job in hand. Hirano spent a long time that day listening to the screech of the grindstone, watching the sparks fly, every now and then testing the blade with the ball of his thumb.

The cutting edge had to have the keenness of a cut-throat razor, the entire blade must be polished to perfection. He did not want any botched job. One blow one head was the rule; anything less would degrade the dignity of the occasion and ruin his reputation. Still, to maintain this standard for thirty or more consecutive strokes was asking a lot. There was no knowing whether some idiot would faint, or refuse to kneel or move at the crucial moment and spoil the purity of the experience. Even Hirano had never been required to do this many before. Indeed the authorites had insisted that several stand-by executioners be available, induced with the princely fee of MY5 per head (literally). Among them would undoubtedly be Takiyawa. Hirano made a mental note to try to ensure that those victims who showed signs of collapsing be given to his assistants.

I do not know what happened to Hirano after the war, but if his sword had been preserved and could be identified today it would be worth a small fortune. The Japanese sword forms an integral part of the nation's history, and is still generally considered one of the finest cutting weapons ever devised. Mysticism surrounds the lengthy process, involving fire and water, of tempering the slightly curved steel. Some blades date back to medieval times when the sword was the chief weapon of the Samurai warrior. It is a single-edged weapon, remarkable for its three exactly similar curves – edge, face line and back, its cunning distribution of weight giving maximum efficiency of stroke. Connoisseurs examining a blade lay it along the length of their arm to look for the wavy milky line that shows up as the metal catches the light.

The 10th century saw the cult of the sword at its peak. Men devoted their whole lives to acquiring the skills of swordsmanship. The distinction of wearing it, the rights it conferred, the deeds wrought with it, the honours bestowed on an expert swordsmith – all these things conspired to give the weapon an importance beyond the comprehension of modern society.

A Samurai carried at least two swords, a long and a short. Their scabbards of lacquered wood were thrust into the girdle, not slung from it, being fastened in their place by cords of plaited silk. The short sword was not normally employed in actual combat. Its use was to cut off an enemy's head after overthrowing him, and it also served a defeated soldier in his last resort – suicide. The Samurai adopted in "hara-kiri" (disembowelment) a mode of suicide so painful and so shocking that to school the mind to perform it without flinching was a feat not everyone could aspire to. Assistance was often rendered by a comrade who stood ready to behead the victim immediately the stomach had been gashed. I would stress that decapitation was considered an honourable way to die. Hirano and his fellow Japanese believed the condemned were being granted a privilege in being killed in this manner.

After the war thousands of these symbols of rank and status were surrendered to the Allies. A lot were destroyed, but many also found their way to the West as souvenirs of returning servicemen. Today the international market for Japanese swords, a specialized and expensive area of antiques, feeds partly on the availability in the West of these weapons shipped home fifty years ago. Events have turned full circle, with the Japanese now the keenest buyers, anxious to recapture their history. At enormous cost these swords are returning to Japan.

Interestingly, one of the greatest collectors was the late Field-Marshal Sir Francis Festing who had amassed over 400 by the time he died in 1976. Sothebys sold the last 40 weapons from his hoard in 1993, with Japanese dealers being the dominant bidders, for the staggering sum of £754,000. A katana (an especially long sword) made by the master swordsmith Yamaura Masayuki in 1839 fetched £265,500, while a 17th century blade surrendered by the Japanese commander in Sumatra to his opposite number went for a mere £78,500. In 1945, during a meeting at which I was present at the Gendarmarie HQ, my friend Geoffrey took the sword of Colonel Kanagawa, who had by then succeeded Noma as head of the Gendarmerie, who parted with it grudgingly and with the words, "You look like a gentleman, please look after sword. I sure you return it later." It was after the Japanese surrender but before the arrival of the Allied fleet. Kanagawa, who a few days previously could have had us executed on the spot, was politeness itself, insisting we sat down and giving us cigarettes. He was hanged (a disgraceful way for a Japanese officer to die) for war crimes and Geoffrey kept his sword.

Stanley prison was run by 1st Lieutenant Yamaguchi. He was directly responsible to a Major Kogi who held the posts of Commissioner of Prisons, Public Prosecutor, and head of the Army Legal Section in Hong Kong. Yamaguchi's second-in-command was a Sergeant-Major Imiaye. Under him were a number of Japanese NCOs, men such as the sadist Takiyawa who had been on the prison staff until early in 1943 when he got the job of Supreme Court torturer and executioner. The Gendarmerie were not officially prison staff although they had the run of the place, and absolute control of remand prisoners under interrogation and awaiting trial. They ran "B" Block for this purpose. It was from here that terrified men and women were dragged to the "Grill Room" on the ground floor under the prison hospital, to face Yoshimoto and his merry men.

The bulk of the warders, prison officers as we now call them, were the original Chinese or Indian staff who had merely exchanged their British masters for Japanese. These men were under a thoroughly unpleasant Indian head warder, Rehimat Khan, commonly known as Redbeard. It had been his job before the war and he took immense pleasure in humiliating and beating his European prisoners. The other Indian warders fell into two groups – those that followed Redbeard's lead and revelled in the power they now had, or those who retained some loyalty to the British. A number of these went out of their way to show small kindnesses at considerable risk to themselves. The most prominent of these was Redbeard's number two, Sirdar Ali.

In 1945, while Rehimat Khan languished in a cell awaiting trial for his misdeeds only a few metres away, Sirdar Ali was presented with a sword at a special ceremony in the prison compound. It was a token of tribute for his conduct during the Japanese occupation. On 25 October, 1945, no less than 170 Chinese and Indian warders attended this parade at which the acting, later commissioner of prisons, Mr C.J. Norman, made a speech of thanks and handed over the sword, after a minute's silence to remember those who had suffered and died.

Among the most loathed of the Chinese warders was Sar Yuen Chui, a notorious Japanese toady who William Anderson was to describe as "a perfect brute ... a beastly individual, hated by his own nationals." Like Redbeard he too became an inmate of the jail in 1945.

Immediately inside the gates were the administrative offices and quarters of the prison staff, their dining hall and kitchen. Separated from this area by another wall and gate was the prisoners' compound with its cell blocks, seven down the eastern side. These blocks were lettered, with the important ones in this story being "B", "C", "D", and "G". "B" Block was where prisoners on remand were held. As mentioned above it was run by the Gendarmes and as such was a place of particular horror as inmates were subjected to varying degrees of brutality and torture here to obtain confessions, or "evidence", to secure a conviction at their trial. After conviction (nobody that I am aware of who actually got to trial was ever acquitted) those sentenced to imprisonment went to "D" Block – "the cooler" – while those sentenced to death awaited execution in "C" Block. "G" Block was normally used to hold persons temporarily, immediately after arrest, and was staffed by mainly Chinese warders. From there progress was usually to "B", then either "C" or "D".

From the end of June, 1943, until almost the end of December the grim process of interrogation, torture, trial and sentencing of those arrested earlier in the year took place. For the scores of men and some women of all nationalities those months were a succession of unspeakable horrors. Some survived and eventually recovered, some survived but were physically crippled, others died horrible deaths. All who lived bore the scars on their bodies and minds for the rest of their lives; none could forget, only a few could forgive. I will use the experiences of William Anderson, our camp quartermaster, to illustrate what went on in Stanley prison during that period. Fortunately I did not have first-hand exposure to the treatment meted out to him. Anderson lived to tell the tale, so I have used quotations from his detailed post-war sworn statement, much of which has never to my knowledge been made public before.

On 29 June the Stanley internees (W.J. Anderson, Rees, Scott, Whant, Bradley and Hall) were deposited in "G" Block, in cells on the top floor. The Chinese warders were comparatively lax and Anderson, whose cell was opposite the stairs, was able to keep an eye on the comings and goings. He was also able to communicate by sign language and tapping with Selwyn-Clarke and A.C. Sinton, who were in cells close to his. Two days after their arrest he saw the arrival of what I will call the "military party" consisting of servicemen rounded up from the Kowloon PoW camps. Those lodged in "G" Block that Anderson recognized were Colonel L.A. Newnham (formerly Middlesex Regiment), Captain D. Ford (Royal Scots), Flight-Lieutenant H.B. Gray (RAF), Sub-Lieutenant J.R. Haddock (HKRNVR), Sergeant R.J. Hardy (RAF) and Sergeant R. Ruttledge (Royal Canadian Corps of Signals).[1] Later, while on remand, Gray was able to teach Anderson the morse code through the wall of their adjoining cells. About a week later J.A. Fraser, D.W. Waterton, J.L. Anderson and Sergeant F. Roberts (HK Police) appeared. The key participants in the tragedy were now assembled.

The only person not mentioned by Anderson at this stage was Captain A.M. Ansari of the Rajputs, who, although a serving officer, had already been incarcerated with the civilian group along with several other Indians. He had been the senior officer at Matauchung camp, and as such deeply involved with escape bids and in encouraging his men to remain loyal to Britain. It was Ansari's second session in Stanley jail.

As early as April, 1942, he had been singled out for special treatment for his staunch support of the Allied cause. Repeated beatings had no effect so he was sent to Stanley, where torture and starvation brought him to the point of death before he was returned to Matauchung for hospitalization. The British C-in-C India, General Sir Claude Auchinleck, heard of his ordeal and had the following message sent to Ansari by BAAG agents:

"I have just heard of your brave refusal to do anything in the way of cooperating with the Japanese. By your behaviour you have been an example to all of the highest standards of devotion to duty which we have learnt to expect of officers of the Indian Army. [Ansari was proud of the fact that he held the King's commission after training at Sandhurst, rather than the more usual Viceroy's commission]. I hope you haven't suffered too severely in body – your spirit is certainly unimpaired. We look forward to your safe return to India."[2]

Tragically this was not to happen.

Anderson was able to "talk" by midair finger-writing to Fraser. It was then that he learned that Rees had revealed names under torture, including those of Waterton, J.L. Anderson and Roberts. The two of them agreed not to involve each other, with Fraser stressing that "the Colonial Secretary [Gimson] must be kept out of this at all costs". After this brief conversation Fraser was unable to speak with Anderson again until 19 August, after his two week interrogation by the Gendarmerie. Shortly after this Anderson stated:

"I saw J.[Jimmy] Leung (ration truck) being brought into 'G' Block by the Gendarmes. He occupied a cell nearly opposite me. He looked surprised when he saw me looking out of my cell door opening. . . . He specially asked me if 'Darkie' Chan had been arrested and when I replied 'no' he seemed relieved. He also said voluntarily that he would not 'talk' and I replied that was the spirit of all our friends."[3]

When all the prisoners were later moved to different cells on the ground floor Anderson was deprived of his ability to see out. It was a major setback, but not for long. In the door was the usual spyhole, a small glass window about 2 inches in diameter, which was covered over by a moveable brass cap on the outside. A close inspection of the door revealed a crack in the woodwork below the spyhole, and of the cell a tiny piece of glass plus an old chopstick. Using the glass Anderson whittled down the chopstick until it was thin enough to pass through the crack. With "a slight upward movement and a little pressure I was able to move the spyhole cap to the right or left." It was through this hole that he saw Pennefather-Evans, Commissioner of Police, being brought in. It was to prove a most rewarding observation post.

On one Sunday afternoon in early August Anderson heard a commotion in the corridor. He sprang up and gently pushed aside the cover. He saw a European man being thrust into cell No. 10, a

Chinese man into No. 4, and a Chinese woman into No. 35 next to him.

"I was able to have a good look at the European, who concerned me most, but hard as I tried I could not recognize him. I spent days worrying who he might be. I can never forget him as I gazed on him that Sunday. He was of small stature, wore a blueish badly torn shirt, and a pair of shorts also torn. He had long hair, a grey beard, eyes were sunk in his head, cheeks hollow and an emaciated body. 'Poor devil,' I thought, 'I don't know where you have come from but you sure have had a hell of a time.'

"In my cell were iron rods which passed through to the adjoining cells. Formerly the rods had hooks to support hammocks. The hooks had been sawn off by the Japanese in case, I gather, the hooks might be used for suicides.

"Before the Chinese woman arrived in cell No. 35 I had spent hours with a piece of wire picking the cement holding the iron rod which passed through to this cell. I hoped to be able to remove the iron rod. I continued with this operation after the Chinese woman's arrival and I was agreeably surprised to hear her picking from her end. I had a new thrill and a determination to release the rod quickly.

"The second day after her arrival I was at the spyhole when I heard her cell door open. She passed by on the way to the wash house carrying clothes. On the way back she dropped a basin of water at my cell door. She asked, and was allowed to mop up the water. I was at the spyhole when she stopped and said, 'Please try to get the rod out. If I cannot speak to some one I will go mad. I have a strong piece of wire and when I pass your cell again I will drop it and kick it under your door.' Well, I was on my hands and knees three times when the woman passed before I collected the wire.

"In another two days the rod was sufficiently loose to talk easily through the space between rod and wall. I remember the thrill when I could see the light in cell No. 35 and when I asked if my new friend could see me. Her reply was, 'Yes, I see your eye.' The rod was soon completely movable.

"Names were exchanged, the lady was Gladys Loie, 'wife' of David Loie, Assistant Chemist at the Hong Kong government laboratory, an officer in the Police Reserve and our No. 1 man in BAAG Waichow communications. She was a former nurse in the Medical Department . . .

"Mrs Loie (as she was known) was most anxious for news of her husband who she was told had been arrested in his office by the

Gendarmes. From that moment she had neither seen nor heard of him but was afraid he had been killed by the Gendarmes. I could not give her any news and tried to assure her that as he had not been seen he might have escaped. She described her arrest and torture by the Gendarmes."[4]

Gladys Loie could not at first remember the name of the European who Anderson had glimpsed in such an appalling condition. The Chinese man had been her brother Lau Tak Kwong. She told Anderson that the European had been in a filthy makeshift cell next to hers in a garage attached to the Stanley Gendarme post. She was full of praise for the way he had borne his pain and degradation. At times he was interrogated in his cell with his moans and cries terrifyingly audible through the wooden boards separating them. The man never talked. Sometimes he was taken away during the night, always returning semi-conscious and covered with blood. For much of the time he was deprived of all food. When a meal was produced it was a small ball of rice twice a day.

Mrs Loie said she spoke a lot to this gallant man, mostly about their families or about Hong Kong people they both knew. All she could remember as to his identity was that he had a house in Taipo. That was enough for Anderson. "I then knew who the European was and said his name is 'Fraser'." To the very end this courageous man, who had won the Military Cross in World War 1 and was to be awarded the George Cross after his death, never revealed a single name to the Japanese – and he knew them all, almost certainly including mine.

On four occasions during this period before their "trial" Anderson was taken to the "grill room" to confront Yoshimoto. Each time he mentally tried to prepare himself for a repeat of the awful ordeal by drowning, far from certain he could hold out indefinitely. He could admit to knowing those already implicated, but he knew of others, who, as far as he was aware, had not been arrested – principally Gimson. For some unknown reason Anderson's resolve was not tested again by the water torture. He was beaten, booted and slapped, but nothing worse. A typical Yoshimoto questioning session went something like this:

"Where you get radio sets?"

"From Rees."

"You sure, only from Rees?"

"Yes."

"We know Anderson [J.L.] give you a set."

"No." Slap, slap, slap.

"Anderson give you set. We know."

"No."

"Why you take sets?"

"For storage."

"Why you not hand to camp superintendent?"

"I didn't know I had to."

"Did you listen to broadcasts?"

"Yes, to London, San Francisco, Manila, Japan."

"Why you listen?"

"For private information, to compare with the news I heard or read in the papers."

"To who you tell news?"

"No one."

"Did you tell Gimson?" There was prolonged questioning about Gimson's activities, punctuated by vicious kicks and blows when Anderson denied knowledge of his affairs.

"How often you listen in?"

"Three or four times a week."

"Who was with you?"

"No one." More blows to the chest and shoulders, this time with a heavy ebony ruler.

"Did you listen on 40 metre band?"

"No, never."

During one session Yoshimoto lost his cool, leaping from his chair in a fury yelling, "Do you think England will win war? Never! Never!" He brought his sword (in its scabbard) down on the table with a mighty crash and paced back and forth across the room, screaming, "Japan's 100 million people will fight for a hundred years! We will never surrender! We will never be defeated!" Then, quite suddenly, as if he was emotionally drained, he threw himself back in the chair and with trembling hands fumbled to light a cigarette. With his piggy eyes fixed on Anderson's face he leaned across to offer him one from the packet. Anderson took it, and immediately Yoshimoto left the room.

Eventually, Anderson had to put a thumbprint on his innocuous

174

replies and Yoshimoto returned to make a short speech stating what good work Anderson had done in the camp as quartermaster, how he was sorry he had beaten him and that he hoped it would be forgotten. A truly incredible performance for Yoshimoto – inexplicable, but on reflection not unusual as spoilt child behaviour is a universal Japanese character trait.

It was on 7 August, 1943, at the height of these interrogations, that Sir Vandeleur Grayburn died, only a week or so before his sentence was due to finish. He was 62, and the weeks of prison starvation and neglect had quickly undermined his health. His constant high fever and the mass of boils that broke out all over his right leg received no treatment despite several admissions to the so called hospital. I would stress here that one of the Indian orderlies, Gholum Mohammed, did his best to comfort him, but, without medicines, and with his every action watched with suspicion by the other warders, there was little he could do.

Police Sergeant Morrison witnessed the end:

"On Friday [6 August] morning he [Grayburn] felt much better. . . . He had a better appetite. . . . After the evening meal he told me of his travels in Norway and of his brother who had been a tea plantation manager in India. As he spoke he seemed to age very suddenly and interrupted the conversation in order to urinate. After making an unsuccessful attempt to urinate he sat down and continued the conversation for a short while, at the end of which he again tried unsuccessfully to urinate. The tin dropped from his fingers and his legs failed him. . . . I assisted him to bed as best I could, being very weak myself and he remarked, 'That was very remiss of me,' after which he went into a coma."[5]

Various orderlies and warders were called during the night and next day, including Redbeard who muttered, "Very sorry", and disappeared. Even Dr Talbot, who was also under sentence, was allowed to examine him briefly. He pronounced jaundice and septicaemia, but without drugs nothing could be done. At 7.30 pm on the Saturday he died. When we heard the news in camp I wrote in my diary:

"The body was to be released at 3 pm. A party of police were detailed to receive it. They brought the dead box [coffin] along and waited some while outside the prison gates. The gates were opened and the box taken inside. . . . Chinese convicts brought the naked body in a blanket and placed it face down in the box – all very grim and sad. Our men then placed a sheet over the body and took it to the mortuary, an improvised construction made by us in the camp. The body was in a decomposed state and emaciated; death had obviously occurred about two days ago."

A week before his death I received from my agent (Wong) a letter from Grayburn to his wife. It was the last letter he wrote. I was able to tell Gimson before the Japanese did so that Grayburn had died.

Throughout these weeks Anderson continued to use his spyhole to great effect, recording the comings and goings. He witnessed Sinton being slapped by the Chinese guard Sar Yuen Chiu when he complained of being ill; he saw Scott being similarly treated when he cried out for treatment for his diarrhoea; and he himself received the same medicine when Sar Yuen Chui heard the click of the spyhole cover fall back into place when he released it in a hurry. Fortunately the Chinese had no idea what caused the noise.

During this period Anderson and others became highly suspicious of a fellow prisoner, an Indian called Bushir Ahmed, the son of a Hong Kong government school teacher who was known to have broadcast Japanese propaganda. This man was observed to have considerable freedom, receive special food from the warders and to be able to talk freely to fellow prisoners on exercise. If he was not a deliberate Japanese plant, Ahmed was certainly out to save his skin by ingratiating himself with his captors and passing on information. He was a man to avoid.

An example of his treacherous behaviour is given by Major C.R. Boxer (the officer I had seen meet the Japanese peace mission on 14 December, 1942). Boxer had the opportunity of talking to Colonel Newnham during this period of interrogations and confirmed how Ahmed had betrayed him. Newnham and Ford lay in adjoining cells and Newnham was anxious to communicate with Ford so that they would both tell the same story to Yoshimoto. After trying in vain to tap out a message on the wall he decided to trust Ahmed who was visible in the cell opposite. Ahmed appeared to be friendly and willing to help, signalling that he could get messages to Ford.

Newnham took the gamble and signalled a number of messages, one of which contained the phrase "Keep Boldero out of it" (refering to Lieutenant-Commander Boldero, RNR, who was another officer involved in escape plans and smuggling messages between POW camps). Later all these messages were produced, written in English, at Newnham's interrogation. Ahmed had been promised his life to betray the others.

At Newnham's first session with the Gendarmerie on 10 July he went out of his way to absolve General Maltby from knowledge of all clandestine camp activities. Like Ford and Gray he took full responsibility on himself. On a subsequent occasion of 19 August in front of Major Kogi when Newnham asked to alter his statement Kogi flew into a rage and savagely slashed him about the face with a bamboo cane, cutting one eye and bellowing, "I'll get you the death sentence for this".

19 August marked the point at which the Gendarmerie, and the public prosecutor (Kogi), were satisfied they had extracted sufficient evidence in the form of statements and confessions to secure an automatic conviction at the trial. It was also the day that Pennefather-Evans and Whant were released. Nobody had been forced to implicate them, which was a relief for me as the commissioner was well aware what I had been up to. This was the date that the accused were formally handed over from Yoshimoto to Kogi, from the Gendarmerie to the Prisons Department. This procedure involved each prisoner being marched in front of Kogi in what was called the "Adjudication Hall" inside the prison. One by one each man was called forward. Anderson again:

> "I was marched in in military style by a Gendarme. When halted and turned left I was a pace behind chalked feet marks [on the floor]. I was forcefully pushed forward and my feet struck by Gendarme Katanawa's [sic, this was Takiyawa, now the Supreme Court torturer and executioner working under Kogi].
>
> "Kogi sat behind a table – book in front of him and on his right sat a Japanese interpreter."[6]

Referring to the book, Kogi reeled off a string of questions in rapid succession, anxious to press on, but still trying at this late stage to implicate Gimson. After checking personal particulars came:

"You listened to enemy radio news. Who ordered you to listen to enemy countries?"

"Nobody."

"Did you know Gimson?"

"Yes."

"Did you listen to enemy news on Gimson's orders?"

"No."

"Did you communicate enemy radio news to Gimson?"

"No."

Kogi raised his voice to repeat the question, to which Anderson again replied "No."

"You are handed over to prison custody to wait trial by court martial."[7]

For the next two months all prisoners were housed in "B" Block on remand, awaiting trial. On arrival they were stripped naked while all possessions except for shirts, shorts, towel and toothbrush were taken away. Regulations for remand prisoners specified they sit in the squatting position facing the wall while in their cells. This was at first a painful as well as tedious exercise for Europeans, and was enforced to ensure silent contemplation of their "crimes". Meals were a few miserable leaves of water-spinach with a lump of rice. These were handed out while the prisoner stood rigidly at attention, not daring to touch the food until all had received their ration and the order to eat given. Exercise, which consisted of walking in a circle between "B" and "C" Blocks, each person three paces apart, was allowed for half an hour twice a day. It was the time for whispered conversations under the noses of the guards. To be caught resulted in being dragged aside for a beating, which happened virtually every time.

The only other relief from squatting staring at the wall was to get on the daily cleaning details. Two parties of about six men were tasked with washing floors and ward cleaning for an hour in the morning and afternoon. It got the prisoners out of their cells, gave them further opportunities to talk, and was thus a sought-after perk. The problem lay in getting selected or, having been chosen, keeping one's place. The Japanese had deliberately put Ahmed in charge of choosing who should be on these work parties. He selected those who could do him a favour, or who he thought might let slip some useful titbit of gossip which he could pass to the authorities. Ahmed was the recipient of favours from other warders as well as the Japanese. Redbeard was a close friend of his father and another warder was his uncle, so he felt increasingly confident that he would avoid the fate that so obviously awaited convicted prisoners.

The first cleaning party was composed of Chinese, the second of Europeans and Indians. In the latter case there were three semi-permanent members – Ahmed, Ansari and Hyde, with the other three selected from Fraser, Scott, Chester-Bennett, William Anderson, Waterton, Newnham, Ford, Hardy, Ruttledge, Edmondston, Wong Shui Poon and N.S. Grewal. As the weeks passed Ahmed dropped Hyde because he ceased to give him anything from his food parcel; then Fraser, Scott and Anderson who it seemed were not prepared to promise Ahmed favours after the war, particularly with regard to his father who was still doing pro-Japanese broadcasts. Ahmed's determination to keep his head tended to conflict with his resolve that, should the allies win the war, he avoid retribution as a collaborator. It proved an impossible task. He was eventually half-carried, pleading and sobbing, to the execution ground alongside many of those he had tried to betray.

As far as I am aware Ahmed's behaviour was exceptional among the prisoners, most of whom went to great lengths to help each other. Food parcels were an example. These were permitted under Japanese regulations for remand prisoners, with the exception of the military party. Friends outside could send them in, often on a daily basis, although sometimes (in Fraser's and Scott's cases always) they were devoured by the Japanese at camp headquarters. Those Europeans who received extra food in this way shared it with those not so fortunate. Each of the Stanley internees undertook to "take care" of one of the military party. When Fraser got his first parcel he gave half to Newnham and several others such as Souza, Wai Po Chuen and Wong Shui Poon divided theirs among needy prisoners.

About two weeks before the trial, set for 19 October, an event took place which was seemingly of no consequence at the time, but afterwards was strangely significant. On that day both the Andersons, Roberts, Souza, and two Chinese were called to the entrance of the ward to have their thumbprints taken. Several Japanese officials arrived and the group was told they would be going for trial. After half an hour these six were returned to their cells.

*

19 October started badly for Fraser who was, rightly I suppose, regarded as the man mainly responsible for organizing the subversive activities in Stanley. He was sick that morning with dysentery, and while still in the cell block had removed his underpants to sponge himself clean when he was spotted by an Indian guard called Mohammed Khan. Khan beat him unmercifully with a heavy truncheon, possibly doing serious injury to the base of his spine. At around 9.00 am all the accused were divided into three groups to appear before the court. The first had 27 prisoners – Fraser, Scott, both Andersons, Rees, Roberts, Waterton, Hall, Bradley, Sinton, White, Souza, Yeung Sau Tak, his wife, Mrs Loie and twelve other Chinese. In the second party of 15 were Edmondston, Hyde, Monaghan, Chester-Bennett, Ansari, Ahmed (still seemingly confident he would be acquitted), Majid Feroz, Raghbir Singh, Lall Singh, N.S. Grewal, G. Kotwall and four Chinese. The third group comprised the military prisoners – Newnham, Ford, Gray, Haddock, Hardy and Ruttledge.

All three parties were marched to a waiting room adjoining the Adjudication Hall to await the start of the trial. Then, with no explanation, the six military personnel were taken back to their cells. They were not to be tried that day. The first group of 27 were ushered into the courtroom at around 9.30 am to be lined up in fours, facing a long table with five empty chairs behind it. Waiting for them was Takiyawa, who was what I would call the chief court orderly. Everybody had to stand precisely on the footprints chalked on the floor. Takiyawa made a great show of pushing people into line, using his sword scabbard to hit the feet of anyone whose toes were not exactly aligned. "Everyone stand to attention. No movement allowed," he screamed. Throughout the long hours of the proceedings Takiyawa took great delight in cudgelling anyone whose arm moved, or even whose face twitched. He was in his element.

When Takiyawa was satisfied, the members of the court filed into the room and took their seats. On the right sat a smug-looking Major Kogi, well pleased to see so many victims arraigned on capital charges. Next to him was Army 1st Lieutenant Timuro, then in the centre, the president, a tired, wizened old man in the uniform of a lieutenant-colonel called Fujimoto. On his left another officer whose name I do not know and finally, in the left-hand chair, legal 1st Lieutenant Yamaguchi. Completing the court were two Japanese writers and a Chinese interpreter. Each member at the table had a case book in front of him.

Yamaguchi opened the proceedings by calling the roll. Next, each individual had to come forward in turn to hear the statements he had signed read out to the court. Yamaguchi read them, frequently adding a few questions of his own such as, "Did you do so and so?" or, "Why did you do so and so?". The accused was expected to respond quickly. If he tried a long explanation he was usually told to "shut up", which gave Takiyawa the opportunity to thump him. Roberts kept quiet until the end when he responded (typical Roberts), "I have no guilty knowledge," to which Yamaguchi sneeringly answered with his stock phrase, "We know the Gendarmes know better." Sinton was asked by Kogi:

"Why did you send a chit into Stanley camp for Bradley with the coolie on the ration lorry?"

"Because if I sent it through the Japanese official channels it would take six weeks to get there and a further six weeks to get a reply. Since these chits dealt with essential drugs, etc, for camp use speed was necessary. I had a reply within 24 hours through the ration lorry coolies."[8]

To which Kogi yelled, "Nevertheless you fooled the Gendarmes. You are guilty. Next one."

Fraser came in for a long bout of questioning, still framed to implicate Gimson, about the wireless sets or messages to Waichow (BAAG). I quote from Anderson's statement:

"Fraser replied boldly and clearly, his voice ringing resonantly through the courtroom, that he alone was responsible, that he acted solely on his own judgement."[9]

Scott was only queried on the so called "Waichow letter" which he was accused of receiving. He denied it, heatedly protesting his innocence which provoked a bout of sword beating from Takiyawa and, "we know, the Gendarmes know better," from Yamaguchi.

This rigmarole was endless. When Yamaguchi finally finished, Kogi rose to address the court. For the remainder of the morning he droned on and on in Japanese. The interpreter was given no opportunity, nor did he make any attempt, to translate. By this time the president had slumped forward with his head resting on his arms, fast asleep. Nobody had the courage, or felt it necessary, to wake him. After some time he raised his head, yawned, stretched his arms and spoke briefly to Yamaguchi. Yamaguchi rose, took Fujimoto's arm and the pair of them tottered off to the toilet where the president had a quiet smoke before returning.

Meanwhile Kogi continued, his voice rising to a shriek when he emphasized some crucial point. At this stage the interpreter did make a few feeble attempts to put across the gist of the prosecutor's oration. Anderson's understanding was that it was primarily to do with the prisoners hindering the Japanese in bringing about a new order in Asia. At about 1.00 pm Kogi stopped, wiped his sweaty brow, bowed to the court and sat down, to the enthusiastic applause of the other members. The interpreter turned to ask a question, and there was a minute or two of gabbling in Japanese, after which he turned to the accused to announce, "In the eyes of the law you are all guilty of high treason and the prosecution demands the death penalty."

The farcical trial was drawing to a conclusion. No defendant was represented, no defendant was allowed to speak in his own defence and nobody was permitted to query their statement. Anderson has described what followed:

"The president then spoke to the members on his right and left. Each shook his head as if indicating they did not wish to speak. The president then fumbled with the pages in his book . . . on the table in front of him. . . . Yamaguchi came to his rescue. He opened the book and indicated certain places with his finger. The president then called all the names of the prisoners, repeated by the interpreter, and each accused acknowledged. Again the president lost his place, and once more he was assisted in finding what he wanted. Then he said, looking at the book, and repeated haltingly by the interpreter in English, 'The judgement of the court is that all are sentenced to death.' Again there was a nodding of heads by all members of the court. Next the president announced, 'The court is adjourned'."[10]

It was the signal for the unfortunate Roberts to collapse in a heap, fainting from the shock of the sentence and the strain of standing still for so long.

Back in "B" Block a meal of rice was served, their first food since

4.30 pm the previous day. Anderson comments that during the meal Fraser chatted away, seemingly quite unperturbed by the terrible turn of events. Rees came over to apologize to Anderson for getting him into such a dreadful mess. Anderson was the only one of the opinion that the proceedings were not yet over. There was still hope he believed in the president's final words "The court is adjourned", arguing that it implied the court had to reassemble. On reflection Fraser supported this view so the group cheered up a little, nobody daring to mention that of course the court had to reconvene to try the second group of fifteen prisoners.

By 1.45 pm they were back in the court waiting room together with the second party. While awaiting the court they were subjected to another demonstration of sadism by Takiyawa. First Waterton was savagely assaulted for some fancied offence during the morning hearing, then Takiyawa turned on the married couple, Yeung Sau Tak and his distraught and sobbing wife. He subjected them first to a torrent of verbal abuse and ridicule before dragging them out in front of the others. "Now I show you how I do head chopping. All watch closely." Grinning broadly he drew his sword and forced the wretched Mrs Yeung to kneel on the floor. She was close to collapse, while poor Yeung must surely have felt he was about to watch his wife be decapitated. Takiyawa, however, merely swung his sword down stopping just short of the neck. "There – you see, very simple, very easy!"

All afternoon the second group went through the same courtroom procedures. By 5.00 pm they were back in the waiting room, all except four having been sentenced to death. The court were eating cakes and fruit. Then Takiyawa reappeared and proceeded to thrash Hyde and Monaghan with his sword scabbard, intermingling the blows with heavy kicks. They had been whispering in court.

At around 6.00 pm Anderson's group filed back into court. Another roll call. A short consultation between the president and the member on his left before he rose to speak. He mumbled, hesitated and lost his place in the book again. Nothing was translated, but when he started to read out the numbers of each prisoner all knew something of critical importance was happening – but what? There was absolute silence as Fujimoto slowly read out a list of numbers. It was a long list. the interpreter then pronounced:

"The court confirms the sentence of death on those whose numbers have been called." The remaining numbers were then read out, which included those of William Anderson, James Anderson, Souza, Roberts and Mrs Yeung. Their sentence was 15 years imprisonment each.[11]

It was then that the significance of the taking of thumbprints two weeks earlier became apparent – none of those people had been sentenced to death – the Japanese had decided everybody's fate long before the trial.

Of the two groups tried that day 33 were to be executed. Takiyawa showed his delight at the sentences by giving Waterton a pitiless thrashing with his sword scabbard before turning once more on Mrs Yeung. The hapless woman was hysterical with grief, and clinging desperately to her husband who had been sentenced to die. Takiyawa pounded her with his sword, boots and fists, at the same time shouting and swearing at the top of his voice. While this appalling scene was being enacted the prison interpreter was trying to match up those on his list for execution with the actual people. Laughingly he pointed at each prisoner in turn saying, "You?" and made a sign by drawing his thumb across his throat. Those not sentenced to death had to shake their heads and say, "Fifteen years".

The condemned were left behind while the others were marched back to their cells half-carrying, half-dragging the screaming and struggling Mrs Yeung. It had been a monstrous day.

Hirano was up early on 29 October. He had slept well and, as he buckled on his sword belt over his freshly laundered uniform, he was delighted that his day had come. He was in charge of the actual beheadings, he would strike the first blows, and only when he considered his sword was losing its keenness or his arms their strength would he delegate his duty to others. He had briefed and practised his assistants the day before and inspected their swords. They were Itano, Kawada, Nishida and Sahara from his staff, plus his rival Takiyawa from the Supreme Court who was certain to be there, itching to exercise his sword arm. Thirty-two men and one woman – it was a lot. From his previous experience he knew things could go badly wrong. It could be a messy business with blood everywhere, prisoners fainting, or not being killed cleanly. If revolvers had to be resorted to to finish off victims it would be a sign of failure. Hirano hoped that he would be able to send these miserable

Chinese and Europeans to a speedy, and what he believed to be, an honourable death.

From the verbal evidence of actual witnesses, mostly Indian warders, it is possible to reconstruct the events of that grim Friday of fifty years ago.

Duggie Waterton had been able to keep a tiny Bible with him in his cell. Shortly before the end he had carefully written a farewell message to his wife and children inside the Bible telling them to be brave, and that he loved them deeply. It is, I believe, virtually impossible to imagine, far less convey, the emotion, the sadness and perhaps the bitterness that goes through a man's mind when he writes to his loved ones in those circumstances. Waterton passed his Bible to a sympathetic Indian guard asking him to get it to his family somehow. The warder, weeks later, thrust the Bible into the cell of Lieutenant H.C. Dixon, RNZNVR, an officer serving a sentence in Stanley. Incredibly, Dixon was able to keep it and ensure that Mrs Waterton received it after the war.

Like numerous other prisoners Waterton had also been able to scratch a last message on the wall of his cell. It read:

"D. W. Waterton. Arrested Stanley camp July 17th 1943. Court martialled October 19th 1943 and condemned to death. NO DEFENCE. Executed date calendar stops."

Underneath was a column of squares representing October, 1943. Each square up to the 29th had been crossed through. Another condemned man, White, had scratched a full list of the 21 Europeans executed, also with a calendar. Many of these messages, which were noted by Anderson, were later removed on the orders of Redbeard, but at least one survived. It is both a will and a final touching message of love from James Kim to his family.

On the previous day a working party of prisoners from "D" Block had spent an exhausting afternoon digging two long, deep trenches in the open ground west of the prison walls, within a short distance of the jetty and preparatory school. All knew their purpose.

The condemned prisoners had all been kept in solitary confinement since sentencing and, despite repeated requests for visits by a priest, none was permitted. The only concession was that as they were assembled that final afternoon inside the cell block they had five

185

minutes together in which to talk and compose themselves. Mrs Loie was sobbing. At this moment it was the Indian, the Sandhurst-trained Captain Ansari, who spoke to them, giving an impromptu pep talk. Clearly and calmly he asked them to die bravely. This officer, who had a pre-war reputation within his regiment for being "difficult", now again expressed the sentiments of total loyalty to the Allied cause. Anderson was told that the essence of what he said was as follows:

"Everybody has to die sometime. Many die daily from disease, some suffer painful, lingering deaths. We will die strong and healthy for an ideal; not as traitors, but nobly in our country's cause. We cannot now escape the enemy's sword, but no one should give in to tears or regrets, but instead face the enemy with a smile and die bravely."[12]

After these words of encouragement Wong Shui Poon, who had worked at St Paul's College, said prayers. They were then roped together in groups of three with hands tied behind their backs and, escorted by Japanese and Indian guards, were led to the prison's administrative compound where they were put into the "death bus" for the short drive to the place of execution. The blinds were pulled down before it drove out of the gates ahead of two Japanese staff cars. At the time, being aware of the sentences, I recorded:

"29 October, 1943.
    In view of recent rumours about supposed sentences imposed on the European prisoners in gaol an incident which happened this afternoon has upset everybody. . . . At about 2.00 pm a big, light brown car flying a military flag went into the gaol. It contained three Japanese civilians . . . behind came another car. . . . A few minutes later the big prison van left the prison with three Indian guards standing on the step at the rear . . . it was followed by the two cars. . . . As it made its way slowly along the road to get round the prison corner it passed a few internees who heard a European voice from the van call, 'Good-bye'. I believe it may have been Fraser or Scott. . . . When the van arrived at the wharf other people saw about thirty prisoners, and what they swear to be three Europeans amongst them, being marched by guards along the short distance to the execution ground."

There they were lined up in single file and told to sit down while guards blindfolded them. Among the Japanese officials watching were Kogi, Yamaguchi, his second-in-command Imiaye, and a doctor. Hirano was standing with drawn sword by the graves waiting for the first trio to be led forward the last few paces. It was Ansari, Scott and Fraser. Ansari knelt, hands still bound behind his back, eyes bandaged. Without prompting he leant forward to expose his neck, his face a mere inch or so from the sand. Hirano raised his arms, the sword slanted back above his head, glinting brightly in the sunlight. He glanced towards Kogi, who nodded. A momentary pause as he sighted on Ansari's neck, then down swept the blade in a silent, silver blurr. It was an expert's stroke, removing the head with a dull thud. Blood from severed arteries spurted up over Hirano's polished field boots and soaked the bottom of his trousers. His sword had lost its shine. He stood motionless while the body and head, which had not fallen into the pit, were pushed in. Now it was Scott's turn, then Fraser, then . . .

Hirano began to tire and lose concentration quite quickly, so others took their turn, including Sahara and Takiyawa. The butchery became even more cruel and bloody as some victims moved, or inexpert swordsmen only partially severed a head. Some waiting prisoners who had broken down had to be dragged forward squirming and squealing and forced to kneel. Wong Shui Poon was struck by Sahara, whose blow only wounded him so that he lay shrieking in agony with his life blood pouring from his open neck. Still alive he was booted into the grave where he lay crying piteously until Sahara leaned over to thrust the point of his sword into his stomach.

Takiyawa made a similar mess with Kotewall. He also was thrown in while still obviously not dead. This time Takiyawa apparently finished him off with revolver shots. It is of interest to record at this point that Takiyawa's eventual fate was perhaps appropriate. After the Japanese surrender he was seized, half-drowned, then lynched by a Chinese mob before being hanged, still alive, from the Star Ferry terminal and left to rot.

According to Anderson's account the nightmare continued for over an hour. God alone knows the mental torment and terror those near the end of the line had to endure before their turn finally came.

At last the graves were filled in by the Indian guards. Then the Japanese, who had been laughing and joking throughout, suddenly became serious. Water was sprinkled on the soil, while all the Japanese bowed deeply before departing. Despite it being such a botched job it called for a rowdy celebration that night. Anderson again:

> "No Japanese officer appeared that evening to supervise ... the roll-call and search of prisoners ... but that night, emanating from the Japanese officers' gaol quarters, there were the sounds of loud voices, laughter and gramophone or radio music, and the rabble as from a drunken party."[13]

The next day –

> "in the prison workshop revolvers were cleaned and bent swords were straightened and sharpened."[14]

CHAPTER NINE

LIFE GOES ON – JUST

"One of those depressing days when 'barbed wireitis' descends on one like an impenetrable cloud. Over two years is a damn long time to be in a place like this. And how much longer is difficult to guess."

14 February, 1944

The only advantages of Stanley as an internment camp were its relative spaciousness in terms of the overall area and the view. Its disadvantage from the point of view of escaping was the sea. I used to spend my time, when I had the opportunity, sitting under the casuarina trees in the old cemetery looking out to sea to Waglan Island and admiring the beauty of the bay, or gazing east across Tai Tam Bay, my thoughts thousands of miles away with my family and friends. Sometimes my mind wandered to Simpsons in the Strand – those delicious sides of roast beef – and other grand eating places. But it was a dangerous habit; it only made one more hungry. Talking about food other than that in the camp was sensibly banned in the mess. How we all dreamed of freedom.

At the time of that entry in my diary I had been twenty-five months in captivity and I could not know there were another eighteen to follow. Ignorance is indeed bliss. Life was a constant battle against physical lethargy and mental decline, both brought on by inadequate food.

Most of us, myself included, could find ourselves driven to distraction by the minor faults and foibles of our fellow internees. In Bungalow "C" there had been no privacy whatsoever. For 24 hours every day, month after month, our every movement was subject to public scrutiny and comment. We shared everything from spoons to toilets, we watched each other perform our most private ablutions, we heard every quarrel, the endless moaning and bickering.

189

At night we could never escape the snores, coughs, groans and farting. It was only marginally better when we moved to the former Indian Quarters in July, 1942. There we had seven of us in two tiny rooms with a squat-type Asian lavatory. Geoffrey, Henry, Lance and Colin had one room while I (as the junior) shared the adjoining one with Booker and Scott, neither of whom were in our "mess". I slept on a dilapidated camp bed which I had managed to acquire, Booker on a rubber mattress, with Scott on a sagging sofa which took up much of the room. As the months grew into years I found myself developing an irrational and quite unreasonable revulsion for Booker, who was a middle-aged superintendent. I recorded my frustration with, and mockery for, the man on several occasions:

"17 March, 1944.
Booker appears to have lost all sense of balance – mental as well I suspect. He walks with the jerky action of a marionette, laborious and unsteady. The first few steps he takes are pitiful. . . . His trouble, he tells me, is at his knee joints. At night when he gets up he staggers like a drunkard all round the room. When he comes back [from the toilet] he laboriously pulls himself into bed, accompanied by grunts and puffing and what now, after months of living with him, appears to be the inevitable belching . . . when he eats his jaw creaks as if it needs oiling.

"31 March, 1944.
I have just had five minutes of listening to Booker sucking his false teeth as he shoots them in and out of his mouth, punctuated by belching. It aggravates me to the extreme. I want to yell at him, but what good will it do? So I suffer in silence rather than have to put up with a long bout of tantrums from this miserable old ignoramus.

"5 April, 1944.
Booker is crouched over his table eating lettuce. He reminds one of a rabid wolf eating rabbit's food. Oh, for some oil to lubricate his jaws!"

Moods were not confined to individuals. The whole camp would go through periods of comparative high spirits, when the war news was encouraging for example, then be plunged into a trough within 24 hours when the cigarette ration was stopped. This craving for a smoke affected virtually everyone. In those days and circumstances the non-smoker was a rare bird. To be deprived of tobacco was almost as bad as being without food. Smoking took the edge off the hunger pangs. Cigarettes were also an alternative currency. Many took to smoking dried pine needles, used tea leaves, eucalyptus or sweet potato leaves. Everybody experimented. If it was not too obnoxious, you would be offered it with the usual remark of, "Try it old boy, it's not too bad." Doctor McLeod once suggested I try a new brand – used hops which, mixed with a pinch or two of real tobacco, produced an acceptable puff. The trouble was finding some hops. It was a common sight to see old men shuffling along the main road through the camp, heads bowed, shoulders hunched and backs bent with their eyes darting from side to side. They were cigarette butt hunting. The butt ends from a packet of ten cigarettes made one extra cigarette – there were no filters. By the time there was a final butt end it was more ash than tobacco. This was smoked by sticking a pin into it and then held by the pin.

There was also in the back of the minds of most of us what would happen in the event of a land attack on the Colony. We were sure that the Japanese would without hesitation, qualms or remorse try to exterminate all of us in the various camps. We in the mess did look around for possible places to hide. The choice was not great.

"19 October, 1944.
The Formosan guard . . . offered cigarettes for sale at MY30 a packet . . . there were some raving idiots who bought them but, foolish as this is, it is better than the bare-faced degrading begging – it makes me sick to see it – of cigarettes from the guards. It is always the same people who do it; they are like a lot of Chinese beggars with outstretched, clutching hands. The guards, rightly so, treat them with contempt and when they have grovelled enough they may get a cigarette among four or five."

It was a great personal tragedy when I lost my favourite smelly old pipe. Re-reading my diary I see I gave my pipe a personality, writing about it as if it was a real person:

"17 May, 1944.
I lost a good friend this morning, I fear for ever. Brown, a 'Dunhill' and an aristocrat, was never meant to live the vigorous life I led him, yet he stood it well, but not without the outward signs of a refined person who has had to rough it. The last time I saw him, the time I put him in my pocket without the care due to one who has been so

faithful, he was badly chewed at the mouthpiece and his stem was bound up like a gout-ridden old colonel. Made to be smoked with the best tobacco he had to put up with fag ends, not even the best quality fag ends, but those of cheap Chinese cigarettes or that foul smelling Suk Yin [low-grade powdered tobacco]. . . . I discovered my loss when I came back from the garden and looked for it everywhere. . . . Desperate, my Cantonese rose to new heights as I explained my predicament to the Formosan guard. He let me go and look for it, but it was not to be found. I was a very miserable fellow until D. Wilson, for whom I had done a favour, hearing of my plight suddenly produced a pipe, which he gave me."

There were ways to alleviate some of the tedium. For the first two years we had regular camp concerts and plays but eventually the Japanese got wise to the fact that the majority were making fun of them so they were stopped. The Japanese can always see the funny side of others' misfortunes but hate to be laughed at.

Strolling round camp was a universal habit. We all wanted to see what was going on, to gossip, pick up the latest rumour or just sit and contemplate the view, dreaming of better times. Sometimes these walks proved rewarding or entertaining. I remember watching the arrival of two new sentry boxes which were being brought up from the village on an engineless lorry pushed by sweating Indian guards with a Japanese NCO, complete with sword, sitting at the steering wheel.

A familiar figure, often to be seen wandering slowly along his beat was the so-called "Blind Knight of Stanley", Sir Grenville Alabaster, the Attorney General. He acquired this nickname because of his partiality for wearing dark glasses, even on the dullest of days. He was the subject of much ridicule, being regarded as the archetypal, semi-senile senior civil servant. I expressed the popular view of him when I recorded,

"[He] is a quaint little figure of a man who would look more at home on his strolls if he was guided by a dog. When he speaks to you he peers at you over the top of his glasses. Partly because of the ridiculous figure he cuts, and more so because of his firm conservatism, rigid orthodoxy and his fantastic adherence to red tape, he is regarded by many as a foolish old man."

I must add that when I did stop for a chat I found his conversation quite stimulating, particularly so when he spoke of the Hong Kong of his youth. Outward appearance can be deceptive.

Often it would be Japanese or other guards, who all had nicknames such as "the Christian", "the Schoolmaster", "Dopey" or "Gold Teeth", that provided some comic relief or out-of-character behaviour. One such occasion occurred on 30 April, 1944.

"1 May, 1944.
Last night, just before lights out, there was quite a disturbance in front of the block behind ours ... a babble of voices in the dark, English, Chinese, Hindustani, and broken English raised in furious argument and presided over by what appeared to be the voice of a drunken Indian. Such phrases as 'I am an honest man', 'I no fright', 'I do my duty' could be heard coming in excited broken English from the Indian guard who eventually marched the arguers off to headquarters proclaiming to all in a plaintive, self-righteous voice, 'I no fight anymore'.

"It appears that the Formosan guard ('Dopey'), accompanied by the Chinese supervisor and European block head [Newman] were on their usual rounds from room to room calling the roll when the Indian guard on duty near the block, for some unknown reason, took exception to this and tried to stop them. The Formosan and Chinese rightly protested, but the Indian was in no mood for argument. He pulled back the bolt on his rifle, loaded it and pointed it at them, threatening to shoot them. Then started the expected oriental argument into which Newman was swept. The Indian stood his unsteady ground and all were marched off under arrest."

An event that will surely be recalled by every former internee at Stanley was the monthly Japanese ceremony of the Imperial Rescript (edict).

"10 September, 1944.
An interesting ceremony is held outside the commandant's house on the 8th of every month when the Japanese Imperial Rescript, issued by the emperor on the outbreak of the Pacific War, is read to all the Japanese military and Formosan guards in camp. On the lawn is a table, and beside it a chair on which rests a portrait of the emperor. Formed up a respectful distance in front of the portrait are the Japanese and Formosans in uniform, who bow to the portrait. Lieutenant Hara

then appears carrying the Rescript wrapped in red silk. He approaches the chair from the side, bows and asks whether the emperor will grant his permission to stand in front of him and read out the Rescript. Permission is granted."

In the early months a fair amount of softball was played and we were, at times, allowed to go swimming under guard at the small bay SE of the prison known as the Governor's beach. By the second year in camp the softball had stopped and the bathing was infrequent as the inadequate diet did not make up for the energy expended. We had to conserve our meagre physical strength for more essential activities. Although it was pleasant to swim, or dive off the rocks searching for sea urchins to eat, I found the effort to struggle back up the long, steep steps too exhausting. Each block took it in turn to go swimming and during one session Geoffrey and Colin found a discarded wooden bench abandoned on the beach. Somehow they managed to climb back up the steps half-dragging, half-carrying this bench that they felt would be a useful addition to their room. As they were being counted through the gate by the Chinese supervisor he saw what they were up to and tried to stop them. Geoffrey and Colin ignored the shrill Cantonese and frantic gesticulations and pushed through the gate. The Chinese found it impossible to stop them while continuing to count the other internees at the same time. He dare not stop counting in case he got it wrong which would have meant an entire camp roll call. He gave up and let them through.

I have already mentioned that bridge was a favourite pastime of Colonel Tokunaga, and that Gimson was obliged to accept invitations to join the Japanese up "the hill" on some of Tokunaga's visits. Tokunaga did not speak English, although he made his bids in English during a game, and was normally partnered by a Japanese interpreter called Niimori who had lived in the US and spoke with a heavily accented American drawl. One evening when Gimson was trying to explain some native customs in Ceylon Niimori asked him suddenly,

"Do you know anything about fucking?"

"Yes, a bit," replied Gimson hesitantly.

"Well I used to own one," said Niimori proudly.

"Is that so?" Gimson was intrigued, and wondered what was coming next.

"Well, it's like this. I used to run a rodeo in the States and we had a fakir who, when he wasn't drunk, used to walk on hot coals and sleep on a bed of nails."

"Ah, I see," said Gimson, now realizing what he meant.

The constant fight to keep one's health was a losing one. Few people, if any, were able to keep sickness at bay. The dreadful diet was the cause of our many and varied illnesses, and the primary reason so many of the elderly died of diseases that, had they had normal nourishment, would not have proved fatal. We were fortunate, however, in the siting of Stanley camp which did much to prevent epidemics breaking out, and in the large number of doctors and nurses who were interned. There were some forty doctors, two dentists, six pharmacists and nearly a hundred trained nurses, sufficient for three health clinics to be set up. We all owe so much to these staff. I particularly recall the sisters and nurses from Queen Alexandra's Royal Army Nursing Corps, together with those of the Colonial Service equivalent, the Queen Elizabeth's Nursing Service.

Some drugs were sent in, sometimes smuggled, by Dr Selwyn-Clarke while he was still free, some came from the Red Cross and a few, intermittently, by the Japanese who had no wish to see typhoid or cholera, for example, sweep through the camp. The old leprosarium was taken over as the camp hospital. Tuberculosis was serious, dysentery affected most during the first year as peoples' stomachs struggled to get used to the watery rice rations, and malaria was always present. The effect of the poor food and consequent lack of essential minerals and vitamins has been well described:

"The result of the bad feeding was malnutrition and its associated diseases. Beriberi and pellagra were kept down mainly because of medicines sent in by Dr Selwyn-Clarke; home-made yeast was produced in an old ambulance van used as a laboratory and bran was purchased from the town. Cuts and scratches would not heal and remained septic; dried bones were used for calcium to treat rotting teeth, and the cutting of finger-nails and toe-nails was unnecessary as they hardly grew. Vegetables were later boiled in seawater to overcome the shortage of salt. More frequently malnutrition resulted in inertia, giddiness, inability to concentrate, irritability, and obvious loss of weight, though this was perhaps not entirely disadvantageous in some cases."

I had one session in the hospital in early 1945 when an operation on an anal fissure caused by roughage could no longer be postponed. My brief diary account does less than justice to the pain, which was excruciating as I could not be properly anaesthetised due to acute shortages of drugs. I wrote:

"I walked along to the operating theatre, got onto the table, and there I was trussed up like a chicken – knees bent back to my chest, or nearly there, – and strapped down. The local anaesthetic only half worked; it was not pleasant when the cutting started, but it could have been much worse. I was brought back on a stretcher and spent an uncomfortable hour or so while the searing pain wore off."

I will always remember the difficulties we all experienced with washing, shaving and cleaning our teeth, difficulties that were almost insurmountable when water shortages became acute in 1944.

"9 April, 1944.
One is now reduced to cleaning one's teeth with ashes. Better than nothing but not as good as toothpaste, and one missed the fresh antiseptic feeling in one's mouth after a good brush. Four razor blades have now lasted me for four months and will have to go on lasting for many more. Razor blades are a fantastic price, and it is either blades or food. At one time when it was impossible to buy blades, even at a price, I made one last six months. . . . I have to chisel bits off to make them fit my razor.

"10 June, 1944.
In desperation I have found a substitute for soap, which I have now used for over a month. It is wood ash, and today I scrubbed my whole body with it. I found it quite effective. Little did I think when I left England that one day I would be reduced to eating two bowls of rice a day, cleaning my teeth with lye and rubbing my body with wood ash. It is really very funny."

One of the mental patients developed a mania for washing, having about a dozen baths a day. This was a former seaman called Broome, who, when he was not washing, was always throwing water about his room yelling, "God damn those deck passengers, they're always a bloody nuisance!" What happened when he ran out of water I never found out.

With regard to the two dentists mentioned above only one was properly qualified. The other, Sammy Shields, was a dental mechanic (technician, as they are now called). He was as popular as dentists can ever be as he seemed prepared to take on even the most neglected mouth with the most crude, makeshift equipment. Pennefather-Evans survived having eleven teeth out at one session, but the record belonged to Brian Fay who had 25 extracted. He persuaded Sammy to keep them all as some sort of special exhibit. This mammoth extraction put Fay into hospital with a badly swollen face. When Sammy showed them to me on one of my visits I failed to see anything about them to make them worth preserving. The "real" dentist was a government man who appeared a somewhat disinterested practitioner, so his clients were few compared with the enthusiastic Sammy. His assistant was a Sergeant Pile.

I went to Sammy once. It was a painful experience as he used an old foot-driven drill which seemed to be linked in some mysterious way with a dilapidated Singer sewing machine, the handle of which was turned vigorously by Sergeant Pile. By 1945 when the Japanese surrendered Shields had dealt with thousands of teeth and by way of recognition of his skills he was awarded an honorary degree in dentistry and allowed to practise as a fully qualified dentist in Hong Kong. He became a wealthy man – and I feel deserved it.

One of the ways that we attempted to maintain a degree of normality in Stanley, where we had a complete cross-section of Hong Kong's society and the professions, was with the maintenance of discipline and law and order, linked to a system of courts (or tribunals as we called them) and punishments. The police functioned under their officers in an official capacity, wrong-doers being put in front of courts with lawyers, (usually paid in cigarettes or food) prosecuting and defending and judges pronouncing verdicts and sentences. We were at pains to persuade the Japanese that this was a system to be recommended as everybody greatly preferred it to the prospect of minor infringements being dealt with by the Gendarmerie. By and large it worked well.

Sir Atholl (better known as Sir "Alcohol") MacGregor, the Chief Justice of Hong Kong, was normally the chairman of the Tribunal which had the authority to punish people according to a special scale which included corporal punishment, not exceeding six strokes of the cane, for juveniles under sixteen in the presence of parents or guardians. Adults could be fined, and if a policeman was found guilty of an offence the likelihood was that the commissioner would dismiss him from the Force. An example:

"18 August, 1944.
The camp Tribunal have found Sub-Inspector Cain [not his real name] guilty of stealing rice [a heinous offence in our circumstances]. He has been fined a maximum of MY25 and has had several privileges stopped. What step will the CP take now? He must be firm [i.e. dismiss him], but will he? This case has lasted for at least two months – a case that should have ended in two days. At times I thought the Tribunal was trying to shirk the issue. Jack Armstrong . . . defended Cain. All the bad boys in camp go to him, so much so that he has got the reputation of a crook lawyer (somewhat unjust). He knows all the tricks of the trade and tries to lead the Tribunal, mostly non-lawyers, down obscure alleys by arguing on technicalities. . . . Brooks [solicitor] prosecuted. He is a bit slow and nearly lost the case."

To my knowledge Cain was not dismissed as his real name appears on a post-war list of officers who were imprisoned in Stanley. Pennefather-Evans had been lenient. He was a very religious man with Christian ideals of forgiveness. He was a member of the Oxford Group movement and never ceased trying to inculcate principles of Christian fellowship into a largely sceptical force. I hasten to add that I found him a very fair and decent man. One particular attempt backfired and had its amusing side:

"25 November, 1944.
The CP has been around bothering the 'mess' about the Oxford Group Movement. He has been visiting them in their rooms, and then tells them all about it. He explained to them how they would be welcomed at Group meetings, and at these meetings he was no longer the CP but a 'brother' – so there was nothing to fear. Well, the other day he got a little more than he bargained for when five of the men took him at his word and attended a meeting. There one of them got so emotional that he started to confess with vivid descriptive detail all about his horrible past. The CP listened until he could stand it no longer and jumping up said, 'As commissioner of police I order you to stop. Sit down!' I

wonder if it was a legpull on the part of these five men? The men are extremely suspicious of his newfangled religious ideas. They distrust anything unusual like this, and object to him coming into the privacy of their rooms to discuss such matters. They could understand it from a clergyman but not from a C of P."

The category of internees least affected by life behind the wire were the children. True they went hungry but they seemed to get used to it and had a fairly carefree life with their friends, usually playing wargames around camp, digging in the sandy soil and wearing the minimum of clothes. Many remembered no other life, had never seen a river or a cow and felt that the whole world was Stanley. Barbara Redwood wrote of one small girl who said, "When I grow up I'm going to have four children – one to grind the rice, one to do the washing, one to go to the canteen and one to collect the water!"

Another small boy asked, "Will John get an extra ration for cutting wood when he grows up?" Birthday parties were celebrated with tastefully worded invitations with an extra effort made to bake a cake, but some children had a hazy notion of what Christmas was about. A little girl, when asked who she hoped would come at Christmas, instead of saying Father Christmas piped up, "Uncle Nimitz" (the American admiral commanding in the Pacific).

Nevertheless schools were soon organized with the help of the fifty or so teacher internees. Some fifty senior children had classes in St Stephen's College with over a hundred juniors in the Prison Officers' Club hall. The main problem was the acute shortage of writing materials and paper. Studies were taken seriously with regular school reports issued and examinations taken up to, and including, matriculation standard (university entry qualifications).

A few children were orphaned while at Stanley which was particularly tragic. One example that I well remember was the seven-year-old son of "Ginger" Hyde who had been among those executed. His wife, who had taken the news of her husband's awful death so bravely, succumbed a year later to cancer of the bowel. Regrettably, even this was not the end of tragedy for this unfortunate family. The boy, who was adopted by Lady Grayburn, was accidentally killed years later by a ricochetting bullet while acting as a target marker in the butts when doing his national service in the Army. At the time I wrote:

There were many burials at Stanley, but only one coffin. Because of the impossibility of producing innumerable coffins the camp made do with one with a sliding bottom. This was used again and again, the only exception to my knowledge being one Sergeant Flaherty who was privileged to have a box all to himself due to the ingenuity of his wife – a story I shall tell in the next chapter. This solitary coffin was kept in the makeshift mortuary, a shed at the corner of the prison wall. It was to there that we banished poor Sergeant "Timber" Wood to practise his clarinet. He was in fact a good musician, having served in a Guards band, but his endless playing tended to get on people's nerves so he was compelled to sit inside the mortuary. He appeared not to mind.

As police officers, we were expected to attend funerals of policemen or their families. The following two passages from my diary illustrate the procedure, atmosphere and ones feelings (sometimes rather unsympathetic and frivolous) on these occasions.

"4 February, 1944.
The wife of Sergeant Graves died yesterday with the baby she was giving birth to. After a previous baby, also in this camp, which died at birth and for which a caesarean operation was necessary she had been warned not to have another.
"Neither my brother officers nor myself knew Mrs Graves but felt it our duty to attend the funeral. Our duty was very trying as we watched the rain driving before the wind. A few did not appear but Geoffrey, Henry, Lance and myself, already soaked through, entered the cemetery . . . we saw the CP standing apart up the pathway. Wreath held in his right arm, hat clasped to his heart and rain streaming over his brows, he struck the attitude of the noble martyr. Quite unnecessary. I felt he welcomed the opportunity the occasion gave him.
"We took ineffectual shelter under a withered pine tree to see the procession come into sight and slowly pass the convicts parading prior to going back into the gaol. The Rev Martin, shoes and rolled down socks showing under his oilskin, over his head a Chinese [waxed]

paper umbrella, conducted the service. . . . The service over he hurried home. Only the police pall-bearers remained to remove the coffin which is used for every funeral.

"13 October, 1944.
Monty Johnson DSM, a superintendent in the Police Reserve, died from TB yesterday . . . , Monty was one of my room mates at C Bungalow. There he used to spend most of the day playing picquet with Oscar Eager while Belle, his wife, was the terror of the ladies' room. . . . Oscar asked our 'mess' to be pall-bearers. We fetched the coffin from the mortuary . . . and placed it on the wheeled stretcher which acts as a hearse. Above the coffin was placed a white sheet . . . and on top of the coffin and sheet were placed Monty's medals, cap and cane. The service was conducted by the Rev Upsell, Chaplain of the Forces. There was a good attendance. . . . After the service, when everybody had left, we helped to remove the coffin which was going to be used again this evening. It was all very depressing."

On 19 January, 1944, we got wind of a major change in the status of Stanley internment camp. From that date its name changed to 'Military Internment Camp, Stanley'. Instead of the civilian Foreign Affairs Bureau being responsible for our administration, from then on the Army would take over. As the military were to be in overall control we thought it strange to be told that our new commandant, Mr Hattori, and his deputy, Mr Maejima, were both senior officials in the Foreign Affairs Bureau. We had expected military men. On 27 January we were informed that a formal handing over of responsibility parade would take place on the 31st.

This news generated considerable speculation and argument as to how it was to be conducted. The Japanese instructed that all internees were to parade in groups, for example women and children, or single men, each under the command of a senior person. It would be his, or her, responsibility to call the group to attention, salute and report to Hattori, who would put in his first appearance on the day. We seemed to take all this very seriously as my diary records considerable turmoil over how the various categories of internees would salute. It all seems so petty and futile now.

"27 January, 1944.
The big parade is off until Monday. . . . How to salute is the big

question. In most cases the person i/c [in command] is a civilian and in the female categories it will naturally be a woman. The only people who can salute as we know it are the police. Our 'old man' is i/c of the category I am in, the single and unattached men, which is more than half the camp. I suppose the Japanese mean bow. All sorts of interesting suggestions have been put forward. The answer, I suppose, will be for the civilians to wear a hat and then take it off. This is one of the main snags of being a military camp when all but the police are civilians."

When the great day arrived it was a complete and utter shambles. We spent some two and a half hours sprawled around in the hot sun while the Japanese and our supervisors tried to sort out the counting. There appeared to be five more of my group on parade than on the ration states. It took for ever to reconcile this error. There was no attempt to call names, names did not seem to matter, only numbers counted. We claimed to have 857 single men on parade, which the Japanese had to check and recheck as the ration records showed 852. What a farce! My diary records:

"Never have I seen such a rabble known as a parade! Never have I seen such a time to count a known number of persons. . . .

"Activity started at 1.35 pm when I fell-in outside my block. The right markers had already fallen-in on the green in front of the block. Calthrop, our section marker, was in position sitting on a stool, muffled up despite the blazing sun and reading a book. . . . There was not a Japanese to be seen. Kwan, a nasty little Chinese representative, was lounging around peering through his thick-rimmed spectacles. Fall in! Everybody sauntered across to their positions. We all sat down, some on stools, Lance on a chair; books were produced. . . . After about half an hour's wait four Japanese in uniform, with swords clanking, arrived with Gimson and Bickerton, the interpreter. Hattori, the biggest Japanese I have seen, led the way. He was wearing a civil uniform, black field boots, breeches and buttoned-up tunic of greenish serge, cloth peaked cap and curved sabre at his side. This uniform, except for badges of rank, is very similar to their Army uniform. Behind came Maejima, thinner and smaller, wearing the same uniform and glasses. Walking with him was his assistant who has replaced Nagasawa, a youngster, who can hardly be over twenty, wearing a military uniform with the badges of a full lieutenant on his collar, and of course the inevitable sword. Somebody behind me said, 'Here comes Mickey Rooney in uniform'. Then came a Gendarmerie NCO wearing a sword. After him came Nagasawa, overdressed and looking out of place in mufti. Finally Yamashita wearing European style breeches, but no sword. All were dwarfed by Hattori."

Now the fun started.

"The CP in charge of the whole parade called us to attention, bowed to Hattori, who saluted and shook hands. Hattori asked, 'How many?' and the commisioner replied, '857'. It seemed ludicrous to call this a parade. Some at ease, some at attention, some with arms folded at the front and voices talking all around. Hattori did not appear to mind.

"Numbers were then checked. Something was wrong. Roll states were produced and more re-checking. After half an hour we were told to sit down. Books were produced and the local newspaper. . . . The figures were still wrong. Everybody was jabbering away in increasingly agitated voices except Hattori. He produced a cigarette and, as if on a signal, clouds of smoke came up from our ranks. . . . We stood up again. Still five up on the ration figures. . . . 4.30 pm came. . . . We all felt tired waiting in the sun for three hours on empty stomachs. . . . A little while later after a final count the CP bowed to Hattori, who saluted. The parade dispersed."

The assumption of control by the military meant that they were now responsible for supplying our rations. It also meant that the Indian guards were augmented by Formosans, who were billeted up on "the hill" in the large house opposite to the commandant's. They first put in an appearance on 2 February, 1944, when a party of ten were marched around the camp on a familiarization tour by Yamashita. Their specific duty was to police the interior of the camp, replacing the Chinese supervisors, while the Gendarmerie and Indians controlled the "wire". They wore cheap Army-style uniforms with a red star on the left sleeve. We were not expected to salute them, although we had to acknowledge their presence in some other unspecified manner.

The next event of note instituted by the new régime was the compulsory signing of a "no escape affidavit" by all internees. Our seniors had agreed we should comply and I must admit that, although it was done reluctantly, few, if any, internees had shown much interest in escaping after the dreadful purges and executions of the previous October.

"24 February, 1944.
Outside the headquarters were Gimson, Bickerton and Bickford. You were handed a form by one of the latter two. It was headed 'Affidavit' spelt with one 'f'. The contents of the form written in Chinese and English were 'I. . . . (name already typed in) hereby swear that I shall make no attempt to escape while interned by the Japanese Military'. . . . You then entered the building. . . . We were given a pen. . . . You scratched away and the deed was done. . . . You were glad to get it over. . . . The whole proceedings took but a few minutes. It was the first efficient thing I have seen here."

20 June, 1944, was surely a day that four men would remember for the rest of their lives. It was the date that Fay, Smythe, Randall and Morrison were released from prison on completion of their sentence. They were taken immediately to the camp hospital where Dr Utley examined them, and Sammy Shields probed and peered at what was left of their teeth. I can do no better than repeat what I said about them in my diary at the time.

"Brian [Fay] was showering when I arrived [at the hospital]. He was shaving with the same meticulous care as of old when he used to spend hours in the bathroom titivating himself. . . . This shave and the care he took over it can be forgiven for it must have been sheer joy to be clean again. As he shaved off his beard his gaunt features became apparent. Sagging cheeks, a tight strained look around his eyes and hollows under his jaw bone, left one in no doubt as to what he had been through. He was still as upright as ever but his once powerfully built frame was emaciated and his limbs like sticks. His close-cropped hair and the missing two front teeth of his upper jaw did not convey the impression of a good looking man that Brian is. The remainder of his teeth are rotten and will have to be pulled out. . . . Despite [all] this [his] medical examination proved him to be the fittest of the four.

"Morrison is undoubtedly the unfittest; he is one sick man. One can see an example of him in any of those numerous photographs taken of malnutrition cases, either for war propaganda purposes, or to open one's purse to give to societies that look after these unfortunate persons. He is covered in a deathly, unhealthy pallor, his arms and legs are like spindles, his stomach protruding unnaturally and his chest is sunken . . . half his sentence was spent in hospital – the prison hospital! He said, 'I am a religious man now. All my prayers came true.'

"Kevin Smythe looks like a Jewish rabbi with his white, thin face and beaked nose, framed in a stringy, black beard. He sits in bed enjoying the fuss made over him. . . . He is as run down and emaciated as the others. Smythe has always been a very selfish man, inordinately proud of his possessions, a man who thinks of nothing but himself and so impossible to fit into a communal life such as ours. . . . Frankly I do not wish him to stay with us [join our mess] because I feel he cannot alter, but if he has to stop with us then I say give him a chance, he has been through enough. . . . The others [in our mess], however, are quite strong about it; anyhow they know him better than me and do not want him at any cost to come and live with us; it is hard but hard times make hard minds.

"I have a great admiration for Vic Randall, that tough, rough-edged old fellow from 'down under'. Over 50 years of age this 'old card' has come through it all with his spirits as fine as ever. As he lay in bed he looked like a toothless old Santa Claus who knew what starvation was, but refused to let it get the better of him. . . . He has aged, and shows the signs of the hard life he has had to lead but his humour and guts overrule it all. . . . Vic pointed to his stomach, 'That's where I want it,' and pointing to his toothless mouth he said, 'How the hell am I going to get through those tins without a pair of crunchers? Give me a pair of crunchers and bugger the rest of them. Sammy said he may be able to fix me up with a pair from odds and ends [discarded teeth extracted from other people]. Damn that I said, iron ones will do.'"

I will elaborate on our efforts to keep Smythe out of our "mess" and on how we saw his character at the time, not because I hold anything against him after all these years but rather to illustrate how minor character defects can become exaggerated and distorted, so that they become a fixation. Dire circumstances bring out the good and the bad in people. My diary records how I felt and reacted at the time to what we perceived as an utterly self-centered man.

"22 June, 1944.
All the talk in the 'mess' tonight is about S coming to live with Booker and myself; this is tantamount to staying with all of us. . . . S's reputation still clings to him. . . . His one object, he frankly admits, is to get food at any cost no matter how and where, and that food will be for himself. . . . Geoffrey and Henry have already emptied a trunk

and filled it with what little [reserve] food we have. . . . The trunk has a lock and . . . they seem to visualize the arrival of a kleptomaniac. S has refused an offer to live with the CP. He has been pushed on us and now there are all sorts of schemes afoot to divert this unwelcome tenant.

"26 June, 1944.
The campaign against S coming to live with us has begun. . . . I visited him [in hospital] and made out that the Indian Quarters were a terrible place, but S denied this. . . . 'My dear George I am interested in one thing and that is food, and I can assure you that I have looked into this matter very carefully. Your food is the best [incorrect]. . . . I believe you people live well and I should like to get in on that'. [Smythe moved into the Indian quarters on 7 July].

"10 July, 1944.
S may be interesting as a psychological study. . . . If ever a man is completely ruled by his own greed it is S. He is a slave to his utter selfishness and obeys the slightest whim of his stomach. . . . Anything that has contained food he licks clean with his tongue. . . . It is known that he has eaten pickings out of a dustbin. . . . When he came into internment he brought, of all things, four bottles, large pint bottles, of eau de cologne. . . . Now he is complaining that his former mess mates have used three and a half of these bottles while he was in prison. . . . What a creature! But we can't be too hard because hunger is a terrible thing.

"16 July, 1944.
Vic and Co. call Smythe the 'Camel' due to the peculiar way he walks. . . . Personally I think a better name is the 'My Man'. Everything is 'my' this and 'my' that.

"17 July, 1944.
Last night I was woken by the sound of S being sick in a basin about two feet from my head. He had bouts of vomiting and diarrhoea throughout the night, and this morning the lavatory was in a filthy state from vomit and shit; he should know by now how to use an Asiatic [squat] toilet and be accurate! . . . We warned him time and again to go easy on his stomach, accustomed to two years' gaol food. . . . He ignored our advice and ate everything from raw curry to

sour bran, so lack of sympathy this morning was not to be wondered at.

"6 August, 1944.
'My soup', as Smythe calls his horrible mixture of hot tea, peanut oil, raw curry, Wong Tong, garlic, salt and pepper mixed together and drunk without any attempt at cooking it, is a good example of his uncontrollable gluttony."

For six months Japanese civilians sat on "the hill", despite Stanley being a military responsibility. Then, on 1 August, the Army finally took over direct day-to-day control. For the first time an Army officer, 1st Lieutenant Hara, took up residence, with a new Japanese/American interpreter called Niimori (a man whose evil reputation had preceded his arrival, and about whom I shall elaborate in the next chapter). Maejima departed, and we were left in some suspense as we speculated on whether the change boded good or ill. The first announcement was not encouraging. All privileges such as bathing, concerts, lectures and newspapers, were cancelled for five days while Hara and his henchmen took stock.

Then came the order that all rice weighing would no longer take account of the weight of the sacks. The immediate effect was a cut of some 5 percent from our daily 12 (sometimes less) ounces. Not life-threatening, but still a bad omen. Rumour had it that the Japanese were less than happy with our welcome to them, that we looked sullen and hostile during roll-call, not like the more friendly faces they knew at Shamshuipo camp. They showed their irritation by smashing twenty panes of glass in a door in our block that had V for Victory signs stuck to them. Two days later, however, our spirits rose, and I recorded:

"3 August, 1944.
Good rations have come in. The ration people say that the quantity is the best we have had to date. There are 500 catties [a catty equalled about 20 ounces] of sweet potatoes, 400 catties of yams and roughly 200 pumpkins to last the Indian Quarters for three days."

This amounted to two ounces of raw rice per head per meal or, when cooked, a small mugful. On the same day came the news that all our gardens would be worked on a communal basis, and produce from them would go to the camp kitchens rather than to our private hoards. This caused consternation, but Gimson was able to get Japanese agreement that the existing crops could be harvested before the final handover. Another idea of Hara's was to enlarge the recently started poultry farm. Half the eggs would go to the hospital and the rest sold in the canteen with the proceeds being spent on chicken food. This was definitely a good idea. We tentatively welcomed it, reserving judgement until we saw (or rather ate) the results.

Working parties became an important regular feature of our lives. Large numbers of the Police volunteered for gardening for example, for which we had to pass a medical, and thus qualified for the double ration to which labourers were entitled. On 1 September I wrote:

"There are 150 of us employed on the gardens. As I am on a full day tour of duty I receive a 'double ration' at each meal. This means that for a month at least I shall be eating twice as much food as normal . . . [but] hoeing under a blazing sun and over rock-like ground can leave one like a damp rag."

Towards the end of 1944 we faced what could have been perhaps the most critical crisis of our internment – the water supply from the mainland was cut off and rationing instituted. From 11 November all water from external sources ceased, and Hara gave orders that wells were to be dug. We had news of this impending calamity a few days beforehand.

"7 November, 1944.
There is no water in camp except for one small well, and how can this supply the needs of over 2,000 people? . . . Hara realizes the seriousness of the situation and has been in constant conference with Gimson. . . . Gimson has suggested [a move to] Shamshuipo POW camp but the Japanese will not consider it. . . . Digging has started. There are dry latrines to be dug and pits outside all the kitchens to contain cooking water. . . . The water diviners were out this morning – there were plenty of aspirants – and certain places marked out as possibilities. . . . Seven gardeners, including myself, were sent to the Prep School to block up a stream nearby, and dig a pit to contain the water. . . . Gimson and several Japanese officers were present to see us dig. . . . Hara wants the job finished by the 10th. . . . This is too much

as there are 80 tons of earth to be removed from a pit six feet deep. . . .
Why this water shortage? . . . The trouble appears to be lack of coal
for pumping water from the large reservoir at Tai Tam Tuk.

"24 November, 1944.
This pit, which is meant to be a well, is 14 sq. ft. – bigger than the
room I share – and is already 8 ft. deep without showing the slightest
sign of water.

"27 November, 1944.
This afternoon we struck water at 16 feet. I must say we did not expect
it. . . . It is not too safe at the depth we are now; there is always the
fear of collapse as the soil is sandy. . . . Hara and the sergeant-major
were down watching us work. . . . Hara was smoking a cigar, he turned
to Lance and gave him three-quarters of it saying, 'You smoke?' The
cigar was passed round the squad. . . . Hara was also shown how to
water divine – it worked, much to his delight. The sergeant-major also
had a go, and it worked for him as well."

The Japanese were highly sceptical about water divining. I remember
that when we were ordered to start digging for a well Wynn-Jones, a
senior government official, told Hara that he could locate a suitable
site by water divining. He was given the go ahead. Wynn-Jones
wandered up and down with his little stick, watched with scornful
amusement by a Formosan guard. When the stick twitched, which it
did occasionally, the guard was still unconvinced and thought he was
being made a fool of. In order to test the veracity of the system the
guard resorted to spitting on the ground and getting Wynn-Jones to
walk over it while he stared at the stick. Needless to say Wynn-Jones
had the wit to give it a slight jerk at the right moment.

Although not strictly in chronological order I will end this chapter
by quoting some of my thoughts on my twenty-seventh birthday as
they reflect my mood at the time, and illustrate I still had faith that
we would win the war and that freedom would eventually come.

"17 April, 1944.
Twenty-seven today; the third birthday in this camp. . . . One sits and
watches the hours and days parade slowly past while great events are
taking place. . . . You feel frustrated . . . yet you know it is no good;
you must stretch your patience knowing that release will come. . . .

"Looking back over three birthdays here I naturally think what have I gained, what have I lost? On the debit side three of the best years of my life ... and my 4th Cantonese exam still to be passed. ... I can still pass examinations, still be confirmed [in my rank]. On the credit side I am a great deal wiser about human nature, its strengths and its weaknesses, its endurance and its limitations, its cheerfulness and its resourcefulness. When I leave here I shall leave with a truer perspective of life. ... We will leave realizing that the simple things, those we took for granted, are the ones really worth having. ... Meanwhile a little part of England flourishes here, not free but certainly with English ideals and habits."

CHAPTER TEN

SOME CAMP CHARACTERS

"There was one individual who was not so timid as us. This was Sergeant Hutchinson who, arriving on the scene and finding he was too late, without a moment's hesitation entered the cesspool and swam around in the liquid excreta pulling off solid lumps from the sides."

Diary, 15 June, 1944.

People and their personalities have always fascinated me, an interest no doubt heightened by my profession. The story of life at Stanley is the story of people under pressure, of people pushed to the edge of despair and of others who wielded total power over life and death. The circumstances of our existence as internees brought the instinct of self-preservation to the fore in most of us. In some, character defects were magnified and distorted, while in others the most dreadful adversity, acute suffering, or imminent death revealed a sublime courage (I am thinking of men like Fraser and Captain Ansari now) that even they probably never realized they possessed. I will devote the next few pages to a handful of camp characters, some of whom have already been mentioned, who for a variety of reasons I remember well. Two were well known before internment, others achieved their notoriety as internees, none of them were particular friends of mine, while three were Japanese, about whom I learnt more after the war.

A few individuals lost their sanity in Stanley. Some were obviously mad and treated as such, while others wandered about doing irrational acts which attracted momentary prominence but whose mental state never warranted medical treatment or hospitalization. One such was Sergeant Hutchinson.

Hutchinson was, I believe, a pathetic example of a love affair gone wrong. I recall him before the war as an extremely smart, handsome man with an excellent career in the Police ahead of him. Shortly before the Japanese invasion his girl friend rejected him and he went to pieces. He never recovered from this blow, and incarceration in Stanley further unhinged his mind.

By mid-June, 1944, poor Hutchinson was a shadow of his former self, barely recognizable as the keen, efficient police officer of a few years before. His physical deterioration was obvious to all. His skinny body was always filthy, his broken nose, straggly beard and uncombed hair gave him the appearance of some half-starved ape. The wild look in his eyes left one in little doubt as to his mental state. His career in the Police seemed finished. He had always been hard working and ambitious. In camp this urge to work had not deserted him. I wrote:

> "Nobody but a madman could work as hard as he does in the conditions here. All day long and into the night he works. I really believe that one day he will be found dead by the garbage in his garden, for when he is not acting as dustman – a job he does most efficiently – he is doing some other strenuous labour."

The incident involving Hutchinson that I shall never forget occurred at the large camp sewage tank. Since internment we all had our turn at menial tasks; some I volunteered for, others I did because they had to be done. On 15 June, 1944, I found myself in a queue at the sewage tank waiting my turn to assist with its cleaning. This revolting job was in fact quite popular with the gardeners as the muck was used as manure. That morning the tank was besieged by enthusiastic gardeners dressed in their oldest clothes and armed with hoes and buckets, all clamouring for their turn to scoop out the human excreta.

I remember waiting for over an hour in the driving rain, chilled to the marrow and engulfed by the nauseating stench, while those ahead of us attacked the first tank. It was a slow job as everybody wanted the best, the most solid muck, none of the liquid stuff! The object was to ladle the lumps out with the hoe and drop them down into a bucket. On that occasion one man, a born scavenger, had had his turn and filled his buckets but had brought along his son with a second one. He was hanging round encouraging his son to pick up the muck that missed the buckets with his bare hands. The young lad complied without a murmur.

When our turn (Geoffrey and Henry were with me) came it was impossible to hook out any solid matter because it was out of reach of our hoe and we were damned if we were going to get into the tank. We contented ourselves with several buckets of liquid and were about to call it a day when Hutchinson pushed his way to the front of the queue. My diary described what happened next:

> "Hutchinson who, arriving on the scene and finding he was too late, without a moment's hesitation entered the cesspool and swam around in the liquid excreta pulling off solid lumps from the sides that were out of reach. . . . [There were] hoots of laughter and shouts of exaltation to 'Good old Hutch'. . . . Up the iron rungs and out of the manhole appeared this cesspool Father Neptune, a disgusting and indescribable sight. He was covered from head to foot in this stinking faecal matter and, as Geoffrey aptly described it, 'Shit was protruding from his ears and sticking in his beard and hair.' Deluded fool! Others benefited from his efforts."

Our hospital held several characters who were certifiably mad and were looked after by attendants, usually police, who thereby earned two biscuits a day as compensation for the mental strain. One of these patients was a man called Frain who had once been a seaman. He would sometimes appear in the canteen dressed in a jacket with sergeant's stripes sewn on both sleeves and across the front. Covering his chest were rows of home-made tin medals.

One night Frain was seen smoking long after lights out by a Formosan guard and told in no uncertain terms to put it out. Frain complied, but repeated the offence in the early hours of the following morning. Unfortunately for him he was spotted again by the same guard who screamed, "Come here. Bow!" Frain bowed and was immediately struck on the head. He turned to one of the attendants nearby who could speak some Cantonese and said, "Tell him I'm sorry." "Come here," yelled the guard. "Bow Again." Frain reluctantly did so and was hit again. Then with a note of desperation in his voice Frain pleaded. "Tell the guard I'm mad." To which the guard responded, "I know you're mad. If you were not mad I would have shot you." Once more Frain had to bow, once more he was whacked on the head.

Frain may have been insane but sometimes I wondered if it was not all part of an act to ensure a more comfortable existence. I would dearly like to have known, but never will as the poor old fellow died before our release.

For a long time he sold hospital property through the window of his room at night to guards who crept up to receive it. But perhaps his greatest triumph, and one about which he was forever boasting, was his coffee trick. After receiving two IRC parcels, both of which contained coffee but no tea, he exchanged his coffee for tea and chocolate. No sooner had he done this than the Reverend Short, who was involved in hospital welfare, arrived on the scene. "Have you any coffee, Frain?" "No," replied the old devil truthfully. "Well here is some for you," says the well-meaning priest as he puts some into Frain's outstretched hands.

One of the camp's most prominent but unloved characters who was anything but mad was a Malayan Chinese woman known to all as "Ma" Flaherty or, when she was out of earshot, "The Bitch". She had been a bar girl (although her appearance could hardly be described as girlish) in Wanchai where she had managed to sink her hooks into Police Sergeant Flaherty. What he saw in her physically I will never know as she was short, vulgar and round, her puffed up cheeks reducing her eyes to the merest slits – from which I would have thought vision was well nigh impossible. Flaherty had kept her for many years prior to the war and was one of those six policemen who, out of a misguided sense of loyalty, had married their mistresses in a moment of hysteria within hours of the British surrender.

'Ma' Flaherty was one of the few Chinese wives who accompanied their husbands into captivity. She was a domineering, loud-mouthed woman whose passion was making money. At this she was extremely clever, if completely unscrupulous. Within weeks she had wormed her way into the black market, quickly becoming, in partnership with Gray Dalziel, the queen of the system. At one stage she had a working alliance with the Japanese sergeant-major, getting foodstuffs through the wire which she traded at enormous profit with the internees.

Flaherty himself was totally tyrannized by her, and earned the camp nickname of "Fohki", meaning servant or helper. The poor man developed Hodgkin's disease in Stanley, the early symptoms of which are loss of weight, tiredness and general ill-health. As virtually all internees had these symptoms Flaherty's sickness was not diagnosed for what it was until the cancerous condition had spread to all his lymph glands. Today, if treated early with drugs and radiotherapy he would have had a chance; fifty years ago in Stanley he was doomed to a dreadful death.

Sometime before he died Flaherty had pleaded with "Ma" not to have him buried without a coffin. The idea of his being buried in the camp coffin with the sliding bottom, and left to rot wrapped in a sack appalled him. "Ma" Flaherty promised to do her best. When Flaherty died on 23 June, 1944, she kept her word. With her money Larry Neilson went around camp buying up doors with which to make a special coffin. Considerably more doors than necessary were acquired, the surplus finding their way into Neilson's catty (stove) as firewood. This caused outrage and some weeks after the funeral Neilson was arraigned before the Camp Tribunal on charges of stealing and destroying camp property, it being deemed that doors were permanent fixtures and belonged to the whole camp.

Flaherty's funeral was a freakish event at which Geoffrey and Colin represented the gazetted officers. The previous night "Ma" Flaherty, with several helpers, had struggled with her husband's stiffening body to get it into his best suit. Flaherty was then put on show in his purpose-built coffin for several hours for friends to "pay their last respects". Many came out of curiosity, not so much to see the wretched deceased but rather to witness "Ma" Flaherty in action.

For the burial the top of the coffin was decorated with Flaherty's hat, pipe, pillow, walking stick and a packet of cigarettes. All these items were to be buried with him at his request. When the mourners (in the minority), and the inquisitive (in the majority), had assembled round the grave with the coffin beside it, with all the personal items balanced precariously on top, Father Myers stepped forward.

With a name like Flaherty the deceased could only be a Roman Catholic, so Father Myers had been prevailed upon to "do the honours". At the time I perceived Father Myers as a brash American who was always to be heard haranguing anyone prepared to listen on the latest Allied war move. He had firm views on all things political or military, but his spiritual council was normally much less forthright. On this occasion, however, Myers launched upon a veritable eulogy. There were moments when Flaherty, if he was listening inside his wooden box, might not have recognized the man being lauded as himself.

The really bizarre bit came towards the end. Myers announced in a particularly pious manner that Flaherty had told him shortly before he died that, "When I go to heaven I will talk with God about the conditions in this camp, and see what He can do about them." I suppose Myers meant well but it seemed something of a breach of faith to reveal what was said between a dying man and his priest. His actions did little but expose poor Flaherty to further ridicule.

Her bereavement did nothing to soften "Ma" Flaherty's hard-headed business acumen. She was quickly back at work and to such effect that within two weeks her room was raided by the Gendarmes. They found a rich haul of rings, brooches, gold articles, money and a mass of I.O.U.s. All these were confiscated and "Ma" Flaherty arrested.

She had run foul of Yamashita, who was himself up to his ears in black market deals and had finally resolved to remove her from the scene, thus effectively curtailing the activities of his seargeant-major who was running the rival syndicate. Precisely what triggered this sudden swoop after all these years I do not know, but perhaps Yamashita had got wind of the fact that his days as commandant were numbered (he was replaced by the military a few days later), and felt that now was the time to act with the likelihood of Kempeitai investigations implicating himself before his departure minimal. "Ma" Flaherty got three months in jail.

Before going into the prison she made hasty arrangements with some of her cronies to look after her affairs during her enforced absence. Of great concern was what to do with her hen. Eventually she persuaded Dr Harry Talbot to look after it.

After her release the first thing she did was to seek out Talbot to demand her hen back. He refused, saying that as he had been feeding it out of his meagre rations he regarded the bird as his. He neglected to say that the hen had faithfully laid an egg a day for most of the time he had been responsible for her upkeep. "Ma" Flaherty was enraged. She took the matter to the Camp Tribunal – she demanded justice.

The Chief Justice and several senior judges sat on the Tribunal. A thoroughly undignified bunch they looked, wearing filthy, torn shirts and shorts made from flour sacks. "Ma" engaged a lawyer for an undisclosed fee of cigarettes. Talbot did likewise. What a farce. The top legal minds of the Colony's judiciary assembled solemnly to deliberate on the ownership of a chicken. The irony of it was that all participants pontificated on the legal niceties of the case with the utmost seriousness.

The proceedings lasted several days, with the final judgement being that Talbot should return the hen, whereupon Talbot's lawyer stood to announce, "My Lord, I regret to inform you that my client ate the chicken last night". The camp was greatly amused for several days. "Ma" Flaherty had been outmanoeuvred for once. Undaunted, she was soon back into the black market rackets. This was greatly facilitated when she enticed one of the Formosan guards to sleep with her. This arrangement worked well until early June, 1944, when the commandant was temporarily out of camp, and the boyfriend's brother, a corporal, decided to raid her room to see what he could find for himself, and to get his own back on her for getting his brother in her clutches.

Some 80 lbs of egg yoke were seized and "Ma" Flaherty was hauled up the hill by a gleeful guard. With her went a Greek Jew by the name of Druculis who was known to be implicated in "Ma" Flaherty's trading. At the guardroom things got rapidly out of control as the sergeant-major arrived with other guards. The sergeant-major had both "Ma" Flaherty and Druculis badly beaten with bamboo poles. "Ma" Flaherty had her hands tied and was suspended by a rope from the ceiling. This severe treatment extracted further names, and resulted in her hospitalization with three broken ribs and not a square inch of her body free from bruising. Druculis was assaulted by three guards with poles and, after being severely bashed around, lashed out in a fury, knocking out one of his attackers. His head was then laid open by a vicious blow. Incredibily he was later released. That he escaped without imprisonment or execution for striking a guard was further proof that the Japanese were up to their eyes in the black market and did not want any whisper of it to reach higher authority – the Gendarmarie.

There were two old China hands in Stanley who are worth mentioning; both had acquired the rank of general in the Chinese Army before the war. One was "One-arm" Sutton, the other "Two-gun"

Cohen. Both had lived fascinating lives of adventure before the fall of Hong Kong. Sutton was to die an internee, but Cohen was still seen around the Colony for many years after the war. Frank Sutton was born in 1884 and so was in his early sixties as an internee. He came from a family that boasted Lord Chancellors, ambassadors, secretaries of state and distinguished soldiers among its antecedents. His grandfather had been a parson who owned 10,000 acres of the English countryside. Sutton was educated at Eton and afterwards qualified as an engineer.

Prior to World War I he had worked in South America, where he had married. At the outbreak of the war he hurried home to enlist. During the Gallipoli campaign he lost an argument with a Turkish grenade when he tried to toss one thrown at him back whence it had come. He was not quick enough so it exploded in his hand. It cost him an arm but gained him an MC – a story he never tired of telling. As a result of his wounds he was transferred to the War Office where he claimed to have played the leading part in developing the Stokes mortar, which was a light weapon throwing a 10lb bomb up to 1000 metres. It proved ideal in the trenches of Flanders, and was the precursor of the modern infantry mortar. According to Sutton he was able to sell the design to the American government for a considerable sum.

In the 1920s he moved to Siberia to dig for gold, at which he was reasonably successful, until the Bolsheviks took an interest in his activities forcing a rapid move east into Manchuria. There he became a soldier of fortune, selling his services to a number of minor warlords, all of whom valued his engineering skills and expertise with weapons. He ended up serving the famous Manchurian war-lord Marshal Tsun Tso Lin (known as the "old" marshal) who controlled an army 300,000 strong. At this time China split into three sprawling states, mutually hostile to each other, under powerful war-lords. It was the heyday of a number of European adventurers such as Sutton and "Two-gun" Cohen. At Chungking Sutton achieved great fame and approbation by successfully defending the Mint against odds of ten to one, and killed the attacking general, Ma Jui in single combat. For this he was rewarded with the responsibility for organizing the Marshal's main ordnance depot and armaments factory at Mukden, becoming, in effect the Manchurian equivalent of the British Master-General of Ordnance. As such he received the rank of general, made a fortune and became a millionaire – a rarity in those times and today's equivalent of a billionaire. With the arrival of the Japanese, however, things took a turn for the worse militarily so Sutton decamped with his wealth to Canada.

There he bought real estate, including an island where he set up his own race track and tamed horses, but the slump, and the fact that in his own words he was, "Taken for a ride by some Jewish gentleman," left him impoverished. He hurried back to China. The East was where he made money, and the West where he spent (or lost) it. So it was back to work with the war-lords, this time in Yangtse valley where he was gainfully employed making machine guns. Unfortuately his master lost a battle and Suttton was captured. According to him (but I have my doubts on this) he escaped by killing the general who had captured him.

After an unsuccessful attempt to seek employment with Chiang Kai-shek he came to Hong Kong to start a factory making machine tools. Just as business was picking up the Japanese arrived.

Sutton was a big man, over six feet tall, who brought his golf clubs to Stanley. Despite his loss of an arm he could play golf and tennis, holding the balls with his stump. He was a great talker. He enjoyed nothing better than to ramble on for hours, stammering slightly and often repeating himself, about his Chinese adventures. If one had the time and patience it could make for an interesting afternoon.

He was always dreaming up new ways to make money. Perhaps the most outlandish was his idea to become, as he put it to me, "The Shit King of China". The proposal was that, as night soil was a valued fertilizer in the countryside, he would build a network of single-track railway lines in rural areas, and at intervals construct latrines. The villagers would be supplied with special wheel-barrows, the wheels of which fitted the track. As they wheeled their produce to market they would stop to do their business in the strategically placed toilets. Sutton would sell the contents and make millions. He claimed to have interested T.V. Soong formerly Chiang Kai-shek's minister of finance, in this original scheme. Other plans included running a fish market, building a two-square-mile miniature China (in Hong Kong) and motorizing the fishing junks. The last proposal has long since been done. Sutton died in camp on 22 October, 1944, as my diary records:

"F. Sutton, known as 'One-Arm' or 'General' Sutton died at 10.10 this morning. He went into hospital suffering from beriberi, a lacerated stomach and general malnutrition, and seemed to give up all desire to live — a strange thing in a man who has led so successful and adventurous a life. A large man, these [camp] rations were entirely inadequate for him, and he went in for making grass stews . . . the grass played hell with his stomach. During the last two days he was paralysed from the waist down . . . [and] was worried that he was being swindled in a deal he had made for some rice! China has lost a well known personality."

"Two-gun" Cohen, a legendary figure who had been Dr Sun Yat-Sen's bodyguard, had risen to a position of prominence in China that many would have thought impossible for a European. He was an amusing and wise old bird.

In Stanley I would have thought his nickname could equally have been "Two-pipe" Cohen. When seen approaching with his empty pipe in his mouth you knew for certain how the conversation would begin.

"Morning Wright-Nooth, nice day. You wouldn't have a small fill of tobacco would you?"

If you made the mistake of producing some he would pocket the pipe in his mouth and fish out one twice the size which he stuffed to capacity with your precious tobacco. Of course one soon learned the trick. A favourite expression of his that I have never forgotten, when talking about someone he disliked, was to pronounce very emphatically, "That man's lower than whale's manure". A turn of phrase I never heard used before or since.

Morris Cohen was born in 1889, the son of a Jewish immigrant from Poland. He had a hard Victorian upbringing in London's East End and never achieved much in the way of formal education. At sixteen he began the rough and tumble of a life that would eventually bring him renown and the rank of general in Canada. In the cattle raising provinces he learned to ride, shoot and gamble. A veteran of the Yukon's Great Gold Rush taught young Cohen the two essential survival skills of those days in the West — card sharping and shooting.

I always found his stories fascinating. Before playing dice you had to check if they were loaded or not. This was simply done by dropping them in a glass of water. If the same side always came up they had been loaded. With cards his undetectable cheating was amazing to watch. He could perform the simplest to the most complicated of tricks, from dealing from the bottom to "bringing in a cooler". This involved switching the whole pack, after it had been shuffled and cut, for another in which the order of cards had been specially arranged. His tutor was a man called Bobby Clark whose most ingenious cheat, Cohen explained, was always to begin a game with an old pipe in his mouth. After a while he would knock it out and place it on the table beside him. Inside was a tiny mirror – he could deal over it and see every card as it left the pack. Cohen claimed his best haul was $27,000 off a professional card sharp in Shanghai.

Although he was an excellent shot with a pistol or revolver, here too he was not above a few tricks to impress his audience. To throw light bulbs in the air and burst them before they hit the ground was a sure way to engender respect for marksmanship. If the watcher knew that the ammunition was not single shot lead bullets but No. 7 buckshot pellets the effect would have been spoiled. His nickname of "Two-gun" came about as a result of his being wounded in the left arm in some skirmish in China. It made him realize that had it been his right arm he would have been defenceless for a while. Thereafter he carried two pistols and by dint of constant practice became ambidextrous in their use.

Cohen had made himself useful with the Chinese community in Canada, and in 1916 had gone to France as a sergeant with the Chinese Labour Corps, where he was wounded in the head shortly before the armistice. Back in Canada he made his first contract with Dr Sun Yat-Sen who became the father of the Chinese Republic and was, most unusually, a Christian. Shortly afterwards Cohen was sent to China to negotiate a contract for the construction of railway lines but decided to stay on and join Dr Sun's service. This he was able to do partly because, as a foreigner his loyalties were first and foremost to Dr Sun, he was not involved in the machinations and cross-currents of Chinese politics. Also he could not speak good Cantonese. He became Dr Sun's bodyguard, was given the rank of colonel, and, with two Chinese, became indispensable as one of Sun's "three musketeers".

He amassed great personal prestige among the Chinese and when Dr Sun died of cancer in 1925 he virtually bequeathed Cohen to the nation in his will. He was made a general and drew a modest govenment pension. The arrival of the Japanese had ultimately forced him to Hong Kong where the British surrender led to his incarceration in the Kempeitai headquarters at the Supreme Court, although not before being involved in organizing Admiral Chan Chak's escape (see Chapter Two). He suffered severely from beatings, and once thought he was to be beheaded when an interrogator jerked his sword from its scabbard and yelled, "Put your head forward". All he got was a violent kick in the ribs. He was sent to Stanley.

Cohen was repatriated with the Canadians in 1943 and after the war returned to Hong Kong, travelling extensively in China, probably on intelligence missions. For many years he could often be seen outside the "Grips" (the old Hong Kong Hotel) swinging his black ebony cane and greeting his friends, although he no longer had to cadge tobacco.

In the last part of this chapter I focus on three Japanese characters who were familiar to us all, particularly after the takeover by the military in August, 1944. The first was the typical warrant officer/ SNCO type, easily recognizable for what he was, no matter the colour of his uniform. The second was an evil individual who abused his power and only narrowly escaped the gallows after the war. The third was his successor as interpreter, a unique man, a Christian priest in Japanese uniform.

Sergeant-Major Matsubishi, stocky, square-headed, bandy-legged, forever bellowing and threatening, forever dashing about gesticulating, was probably the most visible of the Japanese staff in camp. He was responsible for the daily ration issue, he supervised camp working parties, and he was up to his neck in the black market. I can see him now, standing with his legs wide apart, his feet thrust into a pair of slippers instead of the notoriously ill-fitting field boots, yelling and screaming at some minor misdemeanour and waving the weapon he favoured even more than his sword for whacking internees – a baseball bat.

Like his kind the world over in those days he was loud-mouthed, tough, brutal even, certainly not known for his mental agility – but underneath the bluff and the bullshit there was a spark of humour.

Not a man to cross, but equally one knew where one stood with Matsubishi. He would slap faces and lay into you with his bat, but I never knew him to be involved in prolonged cruelty or torture. One day he would belt everybody in reach, the next he would be all smiles in Gimson's office telling him about his new uniform that had just been issued, and asking Gimson how he liked it. The spoilt child personality again perhaps.

All Europeans were "hairy apes" to Matsubishi, and he had the ingrained, old-fashioned quartermaster's attitude of only issuing items from his store with the utmost reluctance. He was also a great believer in eating grass. On 18 September, 1944, I recorded a typical encounter on this subject:

"Last Friday Taylor, the ration officer, went up to the office on 'the hill' to enquire whether vegetables would be coming or not. Sergeant-Major Matsubishi gave his usual long harangue and sent Taylor and Bickerton [the interpreter] packing with these words ringing in their ears, 'No more vegetables for your people. In future you will have to live on grass like the Japanese soldiers did 700 years ago'."

About two weeks later Bickerton got another dose of the same. Matsubishi told him he had been on a grass-eating conference in town, even going to the length of getting Bickerton to follow him round camp while he picked grass and gave it to Bickerton for stewing.

Another memorable occasion was when we were summoned in the middle of the night to unload a large consignment of sacks of rice, beans, salt, drums of peanut oil and wooden cases of peanuts that had arrived at the pier by ferry boat. Two gangs of 100 men each in two shifts were needed. I wrote:

"The man of the moment was Sergeant-Major Matsubishi. . . . [He] was everywhere; he roared and ranted from two [am] to eight o'clock without stop. He took up menacing positions, threatened and pushed. He drove us without stop . . . his vitality is truly amazing; he is a real go-getter. His mouth was without bounds when he discovered a few, small private bags full of rice collected from the ankle-deep rice that was lying around; but fortunately he failed to find the offenders. His favourite position was on the top of the piled bags of rice on the pier, where he stood wielding a baseball bat as we staggered past under our burdens. . . . At one point . . . he picked on Sergeant Brooks and bellowed out a few staccato phrases. Bickerton translated, 'The sergeant-major says you have been working hard, have a rest and a cup of tea'. Brooks, exasperated, shouted back, 'That isn't tea, its fucking piss.' . . . Everybody collapsed with laughter; even the sergeant-major smiled.

"At 8.00 am we knocked off; we had moved over 1000 bags and 900 cases. . . . We were dead tired. . . . We were searched and the Sgt-Maj had his last say. . . . 'The sergeant-major says he saw a few men steal. He is very angry. All day he works for you and then you steal his rice. Men who work for him must be honest.' All this was said with much gesticulation and shouting. One dare not smile. In his hand was his baseball bat with which he tapped Inspector Clark's bald head [we were all sitting down] after at first going through the motions of smashing it."

A bag of rice weighed about 240 lbs. One man was expected to carry it. I shall always remember Matsubishi.

Thankfully one of the worst of the Japanese staff was not with us for long as he had, until 1944, been employed at other POW camps, and was transferred from Stanley before the end of that year. He came to us with an evil reputation. This was Niimori Genichiro, who had been nicknamed "Panama Pete", the senior of the official Japanese interpreters in Hong Kong. He was a small Japanese/American with pointed ears who wore military field boots and a khaki cloak, although he had no Army rank as such. He had lived for years in Ohio, where he owned a sideshow in an amusement park. He coupled the attributes of an American gangster with the cruelty of the worst Japanese. He addressed everybody as "Youse guys".

He had been primarily responsible for the deaths of some 800 British prisoners of war when the *Lisbon Maru* was torpedoed on 1 October, 1942, by an American submarine. A draft of 1816 British prisoners had embarked for Japan in a transfer from Shamshuipo and other camps. Men of the Royal Scots, Royal Artillery and Middlesex Regiments formed the bulk of these men. On board was Niimori, theoretically subordinate to Lieutenant Wada, the camp commandant at Shamshuipo, but in practice the man who wielded most authority on the ship, having executive power over the prisoners.

After the explosion Niimori gave orders that the hatches over the holds containing the prisoners be battened down. Packed like sardines in a crippled ship, with no drinking water and a dwindling supply of air there was fear that all might die. Lieutenant-Colonel Stewart appealed to Niimori to at least pull back part of the tarpaulins to let in fresh air, and to supply fresh water. Niimori's response was to appear at one hatch and lower a bucket full of urine. In No. 3 hold, which held mostly Gunners, the ship was making water and pumps had to be manned by the prisoners. The heat and exhaustion were so acute that the average number of strokes at a pump that a man could manage before he fainted was six. Several men died during that first night; and because the ship was thought to be sinking all the Japanese were taken off by another vessel, which then put the *Lisbon Maru* under tow.

Shortly after this the stricken ship gave a sudden lurch and began to settle down in the water. Stewart organized a party to break out onto the deck. A tiny opening was made enabling Lieutenants Potter and Howell, with a Japanese-speaking prisoner, to clamber out. As they made their way towards the bridge guards opened fire, hitting Howell, who was later to die of his wounds. The party retreated to the hold closely followed by the Japanese who fired down into the prisoners, wounding two officers. Lieutenant G. C. Hamilton of the Royal Scots has described what happened next:

"As soon as the ship settled the men stationed at the hatch cut ropes and the canvas tarpaulin, forced away the baulks of timber, and the prisoners in my hold formed queues and climbed out in perfect order. The men from the other two holds broke out at the same time, but many in the foremost hold were trapped by the onrushing sea and drowned before they could get out.

"When we emerged on to the deck the Japanese opened fire at us and continued firing after the men had jumped over the rails into the sea. . . . Four Japanese ships were standing by. . . . Ropes were dangling from these ships into the water but any prisoners who tried to climb up them were kicked back into the sea."[1]

The Japanese later did pick up survivors; some swam to nearby islands and yet more were rescued by Chinese fishing junks. On 5 October 970 prisoners answered their names at the Shanghai docks where they had been assembled. Niimori addressed them. He told them that their survival was a great disappointment to him. "You should have gone with the others." When a senior officer complained about the battening of the hatches Niimori responded, "You have nothing to worry about; you are bred like rats, and so you can stay like rats." When some of the sick and exhausted prisoners, who had been forced to stand, tried to sit down Niimori beat them unmercifully with his sword and ordered the guards to do the same. Before they re-embarked Niimori forced them to hand over what was left of their clothing. One sergeant-major who refused was kicked in the testicles.[2]

When Niimori came to Stanley his reputation had preceded him and I for one sought to avoid him. One incident involving him had its amusing moments, however. In mid-September, 1944, the Japanese ordered that one of the camp's four pianos be brought up "the hill" to their quarters. This was duly done with a great deal of heaving and sweating, but Niimori suspected the worst one had been sent up, although of course he was told it was the best and that it was the one normally used by one of our expert pianists, one Arthur Hyde-Lay. "Well, send your expert up here at once," said Niimori.

Hyde-Lay hurried up "the hill", sat down at the piano and ran his fingers quickly over the keys. "What do you think?" demanded Niimori rather naively. "It's not bad,' replied Hyde-Lay, perhaps feeling it prudent to veer towards an honest opinion, as it was in fact the worst piano we had. "Take off your glasses," yelled Niimori, as Hyde-Lay's answer had confirmed his suspicions that it was a lousy piano. Hyde-Lay did as he was told and stood calmly to receive the violent slap that bruised his face. Two days later I was told what had really happened and I wrote it down.

"22 September, 1944

Arthur Hyde-Lay was not slapped once over the piano episode but several times. The story why is now out. On being slapped the unfortunate fellow farted and Niimori, hardly believing his own ears, slapped him again and this was followed by another fart. Every time Niimori slapped Hyde-Lay the slap was followed by a fart. After about half a dozen slaps Niimori turned to Davies, who was present and could hardly control his laughter and said, 'Did you hear a noise?' 'No,' said Davies, not knowing what to say. Exasperated, Niimori chased them both out of the house. Incidentally, it was the worst piano that had been sent up the hill. Farting is a nervous complaint of Hyde-Lay's and the man could not control himself."

Niimori was found guilty of eight war crimes by a British Military Court in Hong Kong in October, 1946. All his crimes involved incidents of extreme brutality and, in several cases, the ultimate death of the victim. He was sentenced to 15 years' imprisonment – in my view a ridiculously light sentence. I subsequently read that he had in fact been sentenced to death but that it was commuted by the acting commander-in-chief Far East while his superior was away.

With Niimori's departure in late 1944 there was considerable relief. His replacement as interpreter was as different as black is from white or chalk from cheese. Years after the war this middle-aged Japanese was to appear on British television in the "This is your Life" programme. After the programme this man was dining in a restaurant in London and was recognized by a waitress. She enquired quietly, "Is this the Japanese gentleman who was on television last night?" On being told he was she said, "Up until last night I hated every Japanese that ever lived because my brother was tortured by them and died in Hong Kong. But after seeing you, sir, I can never hate them again, because I know now that there must have been good Japanese too. God bless you."[3]

On 1 December, 1944, I recorded:

"A new face appeared among the Japanese calling the roll this morning. He was in officer's uniform but was not wearing a sword. On his left breast was a large yellow star. His left trouser leg was half hanging out of his field boots. Suzy Potts, who recognised him, said that he is a Roman Catholic the Police call Father John and that he has done good work for our troops in other camps. This may be so."

'Uncle John', as he came to be known to many, was John Kiyoshi Watanabe. He was formerly a Lutheran pastor (not Roman Catholic) now in his mid-fifties who had been called up as an interpreter in 1941. He had a sister married to an American Japanese and had himself studied theology at the Seminary at Gettysburg in the US. Personally, I had little contact with him, but he was certainly a remarkable man whose quiet Christian courage was never fully appreciated until after the war. No book on Stanley would be complete without reference to him.

Watanabe was in a terrible personal predicament. He was an intensely loyal Japanese with a great love of his country but his conscience could never be reconciled to the terrible atrocities and suffering he saw inflicted by his fellow countrymen. He did his utmost to serve his country, but at the same time help the unfortunate victims by carrying messages and bringing medicines into camp at great personal risk. Prior to Dr Selwyn-Clarke's imprisonment Watanabe was of immense help to him when they both worked at the Bowen Road Military Hospital, then run by the dreaded Japanese doctor, Major Saito.

Watanabe arrived in Hong Kong in February, 1942, and was under the direct control of Colonel Tokunaga whose prison camp administrative headquarters was set up in Prince Edward Road. Not long afterwards, at Shamshuipo camp, he was forced to witness the torturing of a British soldier by an evil Japanese called Inouye Kanao nicknamed "Slap Happy" or "Shat in Pants", a swarthy Japanese Canadian interpreter, the seat of whose uniform trousers hung in a heavy, pendulous bag. When the Britisher moaned, as Inouye slashed him across his naked chest with a heavy buckled belt, Watanabe fled the scene to the lavatory in an attempt to escape the horror of what he had seen and heard. The shame and revulsion overcame him – he vomited.

Watanabe, as an interpreter, was at times expected to beat information out of prisoners himself, something he could never bring himself to do. Lieutenant Roger Rothwell, a former patient at Bowen Road Hospital, has written of one such occasion:

"Then he [Watanabe] said, 'The commandant is very angry. He has told me to beat you with this belt until you tell the truth.' He paused, and then he said, 'I think it will be better if we are friends,' and taking my hand, he shook it. I asked him how he would arrange matters with the Commandant. Watty replied, 'I shall tell him you are an honest man and speak the truth.' Then he added, 'Perhaps you can help me and pretend you are in great pain from your beatings.' Poor Watty – how he managed to persuade the commandant I shall never know. . . .

"I kept up the pantomine [of being in great pain] for a few days, and the matter was never referred to again. . . . There is no doubt that Watty saved my life and perhaps those of many others that day, for no one can say how long he can withhold information when under torture."[4]

Nevertheless Watanabe's behaviour infuriated his seniors, including Tokunaga and Saito. After witnessing the latter in one of his rages in a hospital ward, during which he had the patients paraded so that he could dash up and down screaming and striking out indiscriminately, he wrote in a letter to his wife which the latter destroyed:

"He is a doctor, but has never attended a post mortem while I have been here. . . . He is just interested in marching about with a revolver strapped on his hip. All he has time for is swaggering about in that fashion."[5]

Not long after this episode Saito complained yet again to Tokunaga about the attitude of his interpreter. The "Fat Pig" sent for the humble priest. Without preamble he yelled at Watanabe, "I'm not wasting any words on you. Major Saito is dissatisfied with you. He's sick of you. Get your stuff out of the hospital immediately. I'm moving you to Stanley camp."

He arrived shortly before Christmas in 1944 and one of his first requests to Mrs Winifred Penny, who was organizing a children's carol service, was that he might attend. There was much discussion. Should a Japanese in uniform attend? What effect would it have on the children? His attendance was eventually agreed but still with misgivings. As Mrs Penny later recorded:

"We needn't have worried. The children took to him straight away, and Mr Watanabe stood there listening to their little voices. After the children's rendering of 'Away in a Manger' he said he would like to sing for them. First he sang 'Holy Night' in Japanese, and then a Japanese Christmas carol. After that he spoke and brought home to all of us the true meaning of the Christmas message. . . . There was something fantastic about the fact that it was a Japanese, one of our enemies, who, of all people should be standing there telling us of Christmas."[6]

Regrettably Watanabe's stay at Stanley was short-lived. The Japanese authorities had had enough of this snivelling little Christian. When one morning Watanabe was summoned from Stanley to Prince

Edward Road to that fearful man Tokunaga, he was, he admitted, terrified. There was no controlling his emotions. Tokunaga had the power to order unspeakable things and he doubted he could withstand them. He felt himself trembling uncontrollably as he entered Tokunaga's office.

"'Haagh! You make me feel contaminated, Watanabe!' he said as he turned to face Uncle John. 'You make me feel unclean even standing near you. To call you swine would be to insult the pig. But you have reached the end of the road Mister Lutheran minister, because I know all about you. I have all the proof I need. I think I was blinded to your treachery by my own softness and kindness! But no more, no, not any more. So you helped Doctor Selwyn-Clarke did you? And you betrayed Japan? You toadied to the British. I wonder what else you did.'

"'And I'll tell you something else – you are going to die. . . . You're going to die. You are going to bleed and scream with pain, and nobody will pity you. What do you say now Lutheran? It makes you afraid doesn't it? You can't even talk. But it won't be sudden, Watanabe, and it won't be soon, because much as I should like to kill you myself, with my sword, I am leaving it to the hands of the Keenest.'"[7]

For some unfathomable reason Tokunaga did not have Watanabe arrested on the spot. He had worked himself up into a murderous fury only to end with an anti-climax.

"Get out of here now, and get out of Stanley Camp, and leave your uniform so that we can burn it. Scum, leave my office."[8]

Watanabe was never arrested, never tortured, and at the end of the war was well treated by the British and Americans. His entire family was incinerated by the American atomic bomb when it fell on Hiroshima.

CHAPTER ELEVEN

FREEDOM

"Is it a matter of hours or days before we are free? Is the magical, elusive word 'freedom' becoming a reality for us? If what has happened here in the last 24 hours is true then we can safely say freedom, peace, and later comfort as we know it are not far off."
Diary, 16 August, 1945.

As we moved into 1945 it was public knowledge that the war was going well for the Allies in both Europe and the Pacific. The Japanese were unable to censor the news completely. The frequency and ferocity of the American air raids on Hong Kong increased, and we noticed a growing uneasiness amongst the guards. Many were beginning to appreciate that they were on the losing side, and some became openly concerned about their personal future, even to the extent of wearing civilian clothes under their uniform.

By a bit of luck I managed to get a glimpse of the tremendous damage that the bombing had done in town as I was detailed off to join a firewood loading party on 2 February, 1945. The next day I recorded:

"We travelled in an open lorry with four guards, the senior sergeant and the sergeant-major. At Stanley village two Gendarmes joined us. . . . There was no traffic and we travelled at great speed. . . . [At] Repulse Bay there was no sign of life. . . . The Hotel is a hospital but no one was about. . . . The centre of the race course was being hoed up by several hundred men – possibly POWs. . . . Not a cheery face to be seen, everyone was dull and lifeless. Down every side street there were signs of the recent bombing, and looking down Hennessy Road it was quite clear that Wanchai had been heavily damaged. . . . I saw the new passenger vehicle – a 'prairie schooner' – a wooden platform with four wheels and a canvas or tin roof and the whole lot propelled at less than walking speed by one man harnessed in front pulling, and another behind pushing. Eight weary, solemn passengers with the whole day to waste sat inside. It was the funniest thing I have ever seen – even the prehistoric age could produce better transport. . . . Everybody stared at us . . . [but] we got plenty of fun watching the taxi bicycles and the 'lang tsai' [young layabouts] who were still trying to keep up appearances. Our biggest laugh – suppressed – was when a European man rode solemnly past on a bicycle with wheels about a foot in diameter. . . . When we started work we worked damned hard. We emptied a whole junk of wood. . . . The Chinese gathered to watch us work – 'the white coolies'. We ignored them. . . . At 4.30 we returned back to Stanley."

The Japanese were also making obvious preparations to defend Hong Kong, including the vicinity of our camp. These included the positioning of guns on nearby hills and the use of explosives to blast out new positions. Confirmation that things were getting desperate came with the posting of some guards to the Army in Canton or elsewhere. I recall three leaving in March, 1945, to the accompaniment of much singing and celebrating. They left on a lorry, each armed with a Japanese flag which they waved vigorously as they drove off. All the Japanese turned out to see them go, encouraging the festive mood with shouts of "Banzai". A friend turned to me and said, as the truck disappeared, "They never make a fuss like this if they expect to see them again." Later there was talk among the Formosans of not seeing their families again, or of having to turn themselves into human bombs for the great sacrifice in battle. From what I knew of the Formosans this was an exceedingly unlikely way for any of them to die.

At the same time, with the ever-tightening blockade of the Colony, rations became noticeably reduced in quantity and worse in quality. Despite our skinny, gaunt bodies we still lost weight. This in turn boosted the demand for, and prices of, the black market. Dealings "over the wire", involving the internees with the Chinese, Formosans and Indians, were occurring on a nightly basis. The Japanese on "the hill" were all involved, from the commandant downwards. Rival syndicates flourished, and everybody had to watch their backs.

On 11 February, 1945, the sergeant-major made one of his periodic nightly raids on the wire, I suspect not so much to stop the trading but to scare off his rivals for business. He spotted a number of internees doing a deal with an Indian and, with a roar of rage, charged at them. Everybody scattered into the blackness, and the blundering Matsubishi got caught up in the barbed wire. The black marketeers made their escape while the sergeant-major disentangled himself, apparently losing his watch as well as his temper in the process.

Two nights later I recorded:

"At about ten o'clock last night [12 February] a Formosan guard, with Bickerton the interpreter, came to our mess. They wanted Geoffrey and Henry. Old Eurasian Anderson was already with them. . . . On the way up to 'the hill' the guard gave his advice. 'Don't say more than you have to. The raid was a failure. Don't say that you got money from us by selling watches. Say you sold them to Hara [the commandant] and they will drop the case.' When they arrived up there they were told it was too late and to report back at 9.30 this morning.

"It was cold this morning so, expecting a long stand-about both Geoffrey and Henry put on two pairs of trousers and three sweaters. It was just as well considering what happened. When they arrived at the HQ they were all lined up and asked their occupations. The last in the line was old Anderson whose response of 'undertaker' was greeted with suppressed giggles. The sergeant-major took charge and, banging them over the head with a Japanese fighting stick, asked them innumerable questions to which they either lied or evaded. Each answer, being unsatisfactory, was followed by a wallop over the shoulders or back.

'I tell you I have been there three times, maybe four,' said old Anderson, who had been more times than he could remember. Both Geoffrey and Henry said they had been once to buy some food for a birthday party. More wallops.

'Where you get money from?'

'Selling clothes.'

'Selling clothes! I know you lie.' said the sergeant-major. More wallops.

'Why do you buy?' asked the sergeant-major.

'Because I am hungry. We are all hungry,' replied Henry. This really infuriated the sergeant-major, who supplies the rations.

'Hungry! So are we!' Two slaps across the face.

'Tell him the truth. You only make him more angry,' said Watanabe the interpreter. Then three guards were called in and detailed to do some slapping. Anderson's man was not too bad but Hitagyama really laid into Henry, while Geoffrey's old friend 'the Hill Billy' dealt with Geoffrey, punching him flat on the ground."

Sergeant-Major Ito, in charge of the guards, was then called in to provide some new ideas. All were made to stand on tiptoe touching the ground with their fingertips. They had to remain like this for ten minutes. The slightest movement brought heavy blows to their legs and hands. Anderson was the first to collapse. Then Henry decided he had had enough and sat back on his heels. More pounding followed. After more threats to "cut off their hands" they were jammed into a tiny coal shed for several hours before being released, bruised, battered and bloody, back to their quarters.

Another grim example of this behaviour came as late as July, only a month before the Japanese surrender. It illustrates that the hard core of Japanese had no intention of moderating their behaviour to placate internees who might, in a matter of weeks, be free and in a position to give evidence against them. It involved the theft of some 300lbs of sugar from the godown ration store which was being sold on the black market. It was a particularly heinous crime as it meant our ration would be even more miniscule, and the culprits would make yet more money from our desperation.

A youth called Reed was accused and taken to headquarters for a beating. The Formosan guards, watched by the commandant, started to kick and punch Reed all over the place. His yells and screams could be heard throughout the camp. It was not until a heavy shower of rain (it is interesting how getting wet curbs the enthusiasm for so many of mankind's otherwise enjoyable activities) drove the guards indoors, that Reed had some respite. Seizing his chance he dashed off into the night towards Bungalow "C", although it was a futile thing to do as he was bound to be caught eventually.

His flight forced the guards to brave the weather and, with bayonets fixed and rifles cocked, they proceeded to search his quarters. He was not there so they systematically smashed his belongings. Meanwhile Blumenthal, a thoroughly unscrupulous Jew, found him hiding near Bungalow "C" and told him to give himself up. As Blumenthal went to alert the guards Reed bolted again. This time the entire camp had to parade for an emergency roll-call outside our quarters which lasted for an hour and a half.

Reed was finally run to earth in No. 10 Block, sheltering with his mother and five-year-old brother. Needless to say the guards proceeded to pound him to pieces, provoking his wretched mother to shriek hysterically, "If they are going to kill you, Gerald [his brother] and I will die with you." She was dragged 'up the hill' with Reed. In front of her the thrashing continued while gallons of water were forced down his throat. Mrs Reed was asked where and how her son got the sugar. She pleaded pathetically that she did not know. All her son would say was that he got it from some Indians. His head was then thrust in a bucket of water and held there by two Formosans. Despite the awful choking noises and feeble squirming, his mother could still not come up with satisfactory answers as she moaned and pleaded for her son. Within a minute Reed's struggles subsided as he lost consciousness.

Gray Dalziel, who was at the headquarters during this interrogation, was able to confirm events and add a few details. Apparently, after Reed regained consciousness Sergeant-Major Ito (the warrant officer in charge of the guards) took over. He gave Reed at least 200 lashes with a heavy buckled belt before proceeding to practise his jujitsu skills on him. He was thrown over Ito's shoulder, he did somersaults in the air and swallow dives onto the ground. He was a helpless, unresisting sack. At one point, as Reed lay exhausted and panting in a bloodied heap Ito used a lighted cigarette to burn his nostrils. This brought instantaneous results. Reed, summoning some super-human strength leapt to his feet shouting, "Damn you! I will kill you!", and so saying fled yet again into the darkness. This was at about midnight and signalled another frantic search of the camp.

It was several hours before Reed was found crouching in a garden close to the prison walls. The following morning he was to be seen tied to a tree outside the Gendarmarie post in the village. Eventually he ended up in hospital where he tried to kill himself by slashing his wrists with a razor. Incredibly, he survived. Reed was a young man of astonishing physical stamina. We were fairly certain at the time that the theft of so much sugar could not have been accomplished without the cooperation of at least some of the guards; we never really got to the truth of the matter – nor, I believe, did the Japanese.

The events that really heralded the approaching end for the Japanese were the air raids. Starting spasmodically as early as October, 1942, these bombing attacks built up over the next two years to reach a climax at the start of 1945. As an internment camp, known to the Allies, we were theoretically not a legitimate target. International law forbade attacks on prisoner-of-war or internment camps, and at the same time prohibited their use as defensive positions. To avoid confusion such places should have been clearly identified with large white crosses painted on roofs, or marked on the ground. At Stanley no such crosses were made until we had suffered casualties from the bombing. The Japanese resorted to using several of the prison buildings as gun platforms for machine guns, while our camp guards always opened fire on Allied aircraft flying overhead. So, without any identification visible to the pilots, with ground fire coming up at them from our peninsula, plus the fact that we were adjacent to the Fort with its military garrison, it is hardly surprising that we became part of the target on more than one occasion.

The excitement generated in Stanley by the air raids during two days in January, 1945, was unsurpassed. My diary describes what happened.

"15 January 1945.

This morning we had the largest raid since being here. It started at 9.15 am and ended at 11.00 am. Any number between 50–100 planes must have taken part. The noise was terrific with the bombs bursting, the planes diving, and every available gun in the Colony from revolvers to big guns firing. We were waiting for the guards to escort us out to work when we heard the roar of planes and saw fifteen flying in from seawards . . . heading for the harbour. . . . We did not wait but made for No. 10 Block where we knew we would have a good view.

"One's eyes could not be everywhere at once and our view, though a good one, was restricted, but I saw on one occasion six planes falling out of the clouds like stones on their way down to bomb. . . . Smoke rose over the hill that blocks Aberdeen from our view. Out at sea near Waglan Island and over Lamma Island there was also bombing. . . . In the camp the guards, having fixed bayonets, were running around like madmen. . . . Up on 'the hill' the guards had lined the wall. They were highly excited. Every now and then a shot would ring out. They were firing at planes a good 4–5 miles away.

"The 'Schoolmaster' was a guard in the garden. He thought it all a great joke. He fixed his bayonet and loaded a clip of ten rounds. 'I have to fire, and when I get back report how many I have fired,' he explained. He took up a kneeling position and said to the gardeners nearby 'You tell me when you see a plane and I will fire at it.'

"Just then about 30 more were coming in over Lamma Island and these were pointed out to him. He fired ten shots at these planes which must have been five miles away. The gardeners nearly burst with laughter.

"16 January, 1945.

"Hong Kong has had a hell of a hammering this morning. The air raid far surpassed the ferocity of yesterday and lasted for three hours. Our greatest thrill was the attack on the Fort. We have always longed to see this happen. Four planes dived on it firing with their cannons. They did not bother to drop their bombs. When they do bomb the Fort we shall have to keep well under cover. As usual the guards started firing, and so did a machine gun in the village. To our surprise an AA gun hidden among the trees in Stanley village also opened up. . . .

"The planes, 4 or 5 at a time, are diving over the camp and coming straight over our quarters with machine guns blazing. Lying on the verandah we can see them turn and dive with the fire belching from their guns. It is an amazing sight. We are in the front line. The planes appear to be either after our HQ or the guards barracks. I saw one bomb dropping and smoke coming up from near the bungalow. I hope no one was hurt. Another bomb appears to have been dropped near the hospital. A small crater suddenly appeared outside, not fifteen feet away – that was near. . . .

"One of the planes crashed on the hillside to the right of Stanley Mound. The pilot came down by parachute. I just missed the actual crash, others saw it. We hope the parachutist was the only one in it."

I was actually writing up what I saw at the time, in between frantic dashes from one vantage point to another trying not to miss the action. It was not until the following day that I was able to expand on what happened:

"17 January, 1945.

Yesterday was a day I shall long remember. After the bombing in the morning from 8.30 am to 12.30 pm the raid moved nearer and we were in the thick of it . . . saw two planes turn inwards and crash into each other. One of the pilots jumped clear and we saw him coming down by parachute. He landed on the hill . . . the other pilot failed to get clear, his parachute caught on the tail rudder, both planes crashed on the hillside. One wonders what will happen to the pilots who landed."

I will digress briefly here to consider the Japanese attitude to downed aircrews. Generally, if pilots bailed out and were captured quickly they did not live long. If the air attack had caused casualties the ground troops wanted revenge, and this was often achieved by executing captive crew. In the case of this raid the pilot was, I believe, a Lieutenant David Huak who was brought to Stanley jail (we knew nothing of this at the time) "tried" the same day and taken out and shot. We were later told that American airmen were executed or crucified, and that a black pilot was dragged behind a lorry through Kowloon until he died. Another report was that one had his eyes gouged out, although I have no confirmation of this or the crucifixion, which was alleged to have taken place in Statute Square.

In extreme cases, where the unfortunate airman fell into the hands of particularly bestial commanders, he became the victim of cannibalism. A graphic example of this was given by an Indian Army sergeant, Chandgi Ram, who was the horrified witness of an incident in November, 1944, in New Britain:

"I was digging a trench for the Japanese in the Totabil area of New Britain. At about 1600 hours a single-engined US fighter plane made a forced landing.... The Japanese ... rushed to the spot and seized the pilot, who could not have been more than twenty years old.... About half an hour from the time of the forced landing the Kempeitai beheaded the pilot. I saw this from behind a tree and watched some of the Japanese cut flesh from his arms, legs, hips and buttocks and carry it off to their quarters. I was so shocked at the scene and followed the Japanese just to find out what they would do with the flesh. They cut it in small pieces and fried it.

"Later that evening a senior Japanese officer of the rank of major-general addressed a large number of officers. At the conclusion of his speech a piece of fried flesh was given to all present who ate it on the spot."[1]

At the post-war interrogation of one Major Matoba about cannibalism he agreed it took place with the encouragement of his seniors. The text of an order on the subject was captured to substantiate Matoba's claims. It read:

238

"ORDER REGARDING EATING FLESH OF AMERICAN FLYERS

1. The battalion wants to eat the flesh of the American aviator, Lieutenant (Junior Grade) Hall.
2. First Lieutenant Kanamuri will see to the rationing of this flesh.
3. Cadet Sakabe (Medical Corps) will attend the execution and have the liver and gall bladder removed.

Battalion Commander : Major Matoba
Date   9th March 1945
Time   9 am
Place   Mikasuki Hill Headquarters."[2]

On another occasion a Colonel Kato was giving a party for his brigade commander, Major-General Tachibana, but was unable to obtain sufficient food to go with the drinks.

"The General was annoyed, and a discussion took place as to where some meat and more sake could be obtained. The General then asked me [Matoba] about the execution and the possibility of getting some meat in that way. I therefore telephoned my headquarters and ordered them to send over some meat and sugar-cane rum at once to 307 Battalion. The meat arrived and was cooked in Colonel Kato's room. It was human flesh. Everyone ate some but nobody relished the taste!"[3]

To return to Stanley, my diary of 17 January continues:

"We must have run miles between our front and back doors watching what was happening. . . . Suddenly we spotted four planes diving towards us with their machine guns and cannons firing hard, flames belched from the guns. It did not take us long to be lying flat on the floor. They came low over our quarters; later we found out that the leading plane was a Jap. It was shot down and crashed into the hillside above our bathing beach. . . .

"Now quite a few planes started to pay attention to the camp, contrary to international law, [although] there was firing from the camp and prison. The planes decided to put a stop to it and bullets were whizzing everywhere. Three bombs dropped into the jail, one knocking out the gun firing from there; pieces of it . . . landed on the American quarters. Blake was hit in the leg by a machine-gun bullet. . . . A fourth bomb landed outside the prison walls. While all this was going on we had a magnificent view of the planes as they dived over. They carried one long bomb underneath. . . .

"On the road leading to the Fort was a mobile AA gun. This road runs past the wire just below the bungalow [Bungalow 'C']; one barge had been sunk and our planes must have been after the AA gun when, by accident, a bomb hit Bungalow 'C'. From where we were watching we saw the bomb released and the resulting explosion. . . . Two Chinese girls came running with the news that ten had been killed and two wounded."

I was later to learn more accurate details of what happened at the bungalow. In fact twelve persons died and only four of those in the building at the time escaped injury. One of these was Bailey who had been standing talking to Stephane-Thompson on the verandah. He lost a leg and his head instantaneously, while Bailey, protected by a pillar, was not even knocked down.

Poor Peggy Davis was among the dead. She was in the garage when the bomb struck and died when the roof collapsed. Witnesses who arrived on the scene to try to rescue the victims said her left arm was sticking out from the rubble with her gold wedding ring clearly visible. Within a few moments the ring had gone. Another victim we all missed was Penny Guerim who had been a great friend of our "mess".

Unfortunately it is true that the bungalow was looted, even before the bodies had been removed and before the Japanese mounted a guard on it. Blumenthal, the unpopular Jew who lived at the bungalow, had a fortunate escape as he was absent when it was hit. He came dashing up shortly afterwards, not to assist in finding the injured, not because his father-in-law, Jim Dennis, was lying dead in the wreckage, but to salvage his cigarettes and his money which he had made in the black market. He scrabbled around hunting for his ill-gotten gains while others strove to save lives. He also had the gall to express great concern for Hara's hens for whose well-being he was partly responsible. What a miserable man.

The Japanese are an unpredictable people. When the guard arrived at the bungalow and was told that there were still bodies under the wreckage he made all present stand silently while he presented arms. Similarly, at the funeral the next day two guards who happened to be walking nearby came up to the grave and also presented arms. They showed far more respect for the dead than the living. Perhaps this stems from their belief that it is honourable to die in war, but dishonourable to become a prisoner,

After the bombing of the bungalow the Japanese tried to make propaganda capital out of the fact that US planes had killed internees. Gimson was required to submit a report, but his version of events which stressed that the aircraft had been fired on from the camp and prison caused Colonel Tokunaga to fly into a rage and refuse to accept it. Nevertheless, machine-gun positions were dismantled [we were made to construct a large white cross on the ground] and Hara promised that the guards would no longer open fire during a raid.

It was a sad moment when we buried our friends, one of whom was the former commandant of the Police Reserve, Oscar Eager. Poor man, he had suffered terribly when his son had been killed in the MTB attack on the Japanese in the harbour back in December, 1941. I was detailed off to assist in digging the communal grave in the old cemetery. While we were digging news came that two more had died in hospital, so we had to lengthen the grave. Only relatives were allowed at the funeral, and what was left of the bodies, in some cases a few mangled bits and pieces, were sewn up in old rice sacks, there being no coffins. A dreadful tragedy, and so close to the end of the war.

Only the children were unaffected. A week later I recorded:

"25 January, 1945.
The children play no other games but soldiers and air raids. A pit just outside my room serves as a fort; all day long it is being stormed amid high-pitched, piercing screams. Every now and then a yell calls on them to go away, but it is no good. They are as knowledgeable about planes, bombs and all the machinery of war as we are. When they hear planes they know to expect an alarm; when bombs are dropped they too have their guesses as to where they will land.

The following conversation was heard.
'Fourteen were killed,' said one little girl of six.
'Rot, fifteen were killed,' contradicts a boy of the same age.
'Did you see the corpses being taken along the road? I did,' boasts another."

Many small children knew of no other life but internment. Stanley was their world. They could not comprehend life beyond the wire. I will illustrate this by the following conversation overheard between two young boys discussing their future careers.

"When I grow up I'm going to join the ration party."

"Oh no," said his friend, "I'm going to join the kitchen staff."

Air attacks continued with increasing frequency as the months passed, but it was not until July that our camp was hit again. This time Bungalow "A" was the recipient of two bombs through the roof from what appeared to be a twin-engined flying boat. People heard a loud swishing noise but no explosion, only a crashing noise as the bombs tore through the roof. One fell into the lavatory and then exploded with a sharp crack, emitting a sulphurous sort of gas. Another fell into the room in St Stephen's College occupied by Noel Croucher and Kerr. It hit Kerr's bed, from which he had only just got up, rolled on to the floor and lay there without exploding. Croucher, who was bruised by flying debris, was later to claim that it went between his legs without touching him. Several others fell outside near the College but failed to detonate. Two children and five adults were injured in this raid. One of the unexploded bombs had numbers and letters in English written on it.

The following day Croucher was among those questioned by the dreaded Colonel Noma in command of the Gendarmes. The exchange went something like this:

"Was that an American plane that dropped a bomb on your roof?" demanded Noma.

"No," replied Croucher stubbornly.

"What do you mean; why not?" Noma's temper was rising.

"It must have been a Japanese plane because the Japanese have always vowed no American plane could ever reach Hong Kong."

Noma, by now thoroughly enraged, dismissed Croucher but ordered another meeting for the next day in the presence of Gimson. At this meeting Croucher was handed the fragment of the bomb that had English lettering on it and the same questions were asked. When asked to identify the markings Croucher had the nerve to reply to Noma:

"I can't read them as I have broken my glasses. Can you please lend me yours?"

242

Noma was aghast at Croucher's impudence but meekly handed over his glasses and yelled,

"Read! read! read!" Croucher peered at it for several moments and then shrugged.

"I don't know, it must have been captured from the Americans." At this point the exasperated Gimson interjected.

"Of course its an American bomb, Croucher!"⁴

Noel Croucher later became a multi-millionaire and a well known and eccentric figure in Hong Kong.

For our last four months in Stanley we had a number of new Japanese senior officers on "the hill". Towards the end of April, 1945, we were all assembled at roll-call for our first sight of the new commandant, a man by the name of Lieutenant Kadowaki. There was the usual confusion over counting internees, with several different answers to the mathematical problems this procedure posed. When these had been resolved, the inspecting entourage of the commandant, Watanabe and Gimson, with several other hangers-on, walked up and down our lines peering at us. All our eyes were on Kadowaki. He was comparatively tall and lean for a Japanese in a soft job, with piercing eyes. He was dressed in a shabby winter uniform with brown leggings and unpolished field boots. He had an odd walk, an exaggerated thrusting forward of the leg, rather than the expected waddle. He strode along staring at us, keeping the backs of his open hands resting on his hips. I was reminded of a spider.

Although not apparent on this occasion, we were also due for several other changes. Watanabe, as we have seen, was shortly to be dismissed in disgrace to be replaced with another interpreter with a decidedly less endearing personality, called Kushi. Similarly the ugly, if familiar, face and figure of Sergeant-Major Matsubishi disappeared, his responsibility for rations being assumed by a Sergeant-Major Sumo. Ito remained in charge of the guards. This was the final "team" that took us through to the Japanese surrender.

Kadowaki was a stickler for military etiquette. As late as a month before the surrender he had us all attending a demonstration of the correct method of saluting or bowing. Ito was the demonstrator who had to perform in front of the commandant while we all watched with amusement. He marched up to Kadowaki with his cap on and saluted, remaining rigidly at the salute for what to us seemed an age until the commandant acknowledged it. That, apparently, was the whole point. A person must remain at the salute until it was acknowledged. Next came bowing, to be done when no hat was worn. Again the sergeant-major demonstrated. This time he held his body forward at a perfect angle of 45 degrees, with his left arm holding his sword, the right stiffly at his side. Once more he remained immovable until Kadowaki acknowledged with what I thought to be a sloppy salute. We were expected to take all this seriously. Later the same day two internees went to collect parcels from the headquarters office and forgot to bow. The commandant flew into a rage and, with much gesticulating and shouting, sent them packing without their parcels.

Like most new brooms Kadowaki had to have his sweep. He even got the Formosan guards doing field training under Ito. He seemed determined to get them fit to fight and had them put through their paces on a daily basis. It became a common sight to see these scruffy, entirely unmilitary and unenthusiastic men running round camp led by Kadowaki. It was always the guards who tired first. Sometimes the day's session would finish with the commandant taking them on at bayonet fighting practice, with Kadowaki wielding a two-handed bamboo fighting stick. Should the Allies invade the Colony our new commandant did not seem the sort to surrender.

By August we all knew, as I suspect did most of the guards and the Japanese, that the end could come any day. On 6 August the first atomic bomb was dropped on Hiroshima, its awful mushroom cloud concealing the death of tens of thousands in a matter of seconds. In Stanley we knew nothing of this, but on 16 August I wrote in my diary:

"Is it a matter of hours or days before we are free? Is the magical, elusive word 'peace' becoming a reality?.... The first whisper of it was heard last night. Lance came back with a story that peace had been signed at 4.00 pm. He did not believe it and nor did we. The fact that it was attributed to Father Myers made it more unreliable."

Nevertheless it was true. One of the guards came later that night and confirmed that the story was correct. He was worried as to his own fate, and we were able to get the gist of the broadcast that had been heard. The Emperor had told the Japanese people that, in order to stop further slaughter, he had informed the International Security Council that he was prepared to accept peace. The atom bombs dropped on Hiroshima and Nagasaki had convinced him.

When Kadowaki heard the news he started to storm and rage, forbade the guards to listen to the radio and then, as if overcome with despair, slumped over his desk muttering, "This is what it has come to after eight years of war" (he was counting from the Japanese invasion of China). Later that morning a single shot from the direction of "the hill" sparked off the rumour that Kadowaki had done the decent thing. Unfortunately this was not true as he was seen departing for the town with the two sergeant-majors, leaving Kushi in charge. Later a guard was to tell the story that Kadowaki had asked his batman (orderly) to shoot him but had got the response, "I am too humble, perhaps that fat lout Colonel Tokunaga would oblige." I suspect this is apocryphal. The cause of the shot remained a mystery.

That day I recorded:

"As they heard, the guards rushed out to see their various contacts [in the black market]. With them they brought bottles of brandy and other alcohol as peace offerings. . . . They had been drinking all night. Two of them kept saying, 'You don't know, you don't know,' and then giggling stupidly. They closed all black market accounts and even gave away some of their stock. . . . We had a feast from the gardens and were issued with a proper lavatory paper roll each, stamped 'Made in the USA'. . . . Is this the symbol of a normal life to come? We call it the 'Victory Roll'."

On 17 August Gimson issued a statement saying that Kadowaki had told the guards to lay down their arms and that they had been told to treat internees with the utmost civility. He added that he had taken over responsibility for discipline in the camp, and that the commandant had agreed that the Police take over the policing of Stanley as the guards were being withdrawn. Most of them disappeared into town. With the imminent arrival of the Allies they became firm believers in the old adage "out of sight, out of mind".

There was at least one exception to this flight. He was a guard who seized a small Union Jack that a man called Routledge had, perhaps prematurely, produced from its hiding place. He took it triumphantly up "the hill" to Kushi. Routledge was furious and, emboldened by events, stormed up after him demanding that Kushi secure its return. There was a confrontation.

"Give it back", said Kushi.

"No, never", responded the Formosan waving a bamboo stick in Routledge's face,

"The guard says he will hit you," explained Kushi. "What will you do now?"

"Nothing – now, "said Routledge, putting great emphasis on the last word, and smiling knowingly.

Although we could not as yet leave the camp, visitors were allowed in daily. They could bring as much food as they liked but no alcohol. There were many emotional scenes as wives and families came to be reunited. Among those coming into Stanley were Lieutenant-Colonels White, of the Royal Scots, and Field of the Royal Artillery. They explained the situation in the POW camps, which was in fact similar to ours in that the Union Jack was flying and the Japanese staff were being subservient and considerate to their former prisoners. It was these military visitors who told us of the arrest of some five Canadians, plus a British officer, Major Cecil Boon of the Royal Army Service Corps, on charges of collaborating with the enemy. The story going round was that Boon had been given a revolver and told his best option was to shoot himself. He had allegedly been informing for the Japanese, and had given away an escape attempt during which eight prisoners had been caught and subsequently executed. Boon was later tried for his activities but found not guilty, a verdict regarded by many as totally unjust, particularly as he was quoted as telling other prisoners, "We are officers of the Japanese Army now. I don't regard myself as a British officer. I owe no allegiance to the King."

There were plenty of terrible tales emanating from the POW camps. One airman had had barbed wire wrapped around his body in such a way that when he walked it dug into his flesh. He was marched around Kowloon in this manner for the Chinese to see. Afterwards he was strapped to a camp bed and burnt to death. His head was then chopped off – yet further evidence of the Japanese hatred for aviators in particular.

Once liaison between Stanley and Shamshuipo had been established, Gimson discreetly arranged for the notorious Blumenthal to be arrested by the military. I described this in my diary as follows:

"This Polish Jew has been trying to hunt with the hounds and run with the hare. He had the nerve to tell Gimson that the Japanese had appointed him offical interpreter to the camp. Gimson sent him with some despatches to Shamshuipo. He innocently carried the warrant for his own arrest. Gimson had written something to this effect, 'I do not know what to do with this man. He is making a nuisance of himself. Please put him under protective custody'."

On 20 August I, together with two companions, Alton, a missionary and fluent Cantonese speaker, and Finnie, the manager of Tai Koo Dockyard, together with a Chinese contact called Sai Ming, were allowed to walk into town on a fish-buying expedition for the camp. Because it was for me such a momentous day I have quoted my diary account extensively.

"20 August, 1945.
    Today has been a great day for me as I went back to Hong Kong again, and this time not guarded by a dirty little Japanese. . . . My uniform cap and warrant card were to be used to bluff any Japs who dared to try to stop us. . . . The countryside was fresh and green and the undergrowth luxuriant. Such a change from Stanley. This walk through beautiful country and fresh scenes was so refreshing. . . . We strode confidently through Japanese road blocks. They said not a word. Sai Ming showed us the wreckage of the American plane we saw crash last January. . . . He told us that one airman had been captured. 'He was such a young boy,' he said. Across the back of his flying jacket was written the words in Chinese characters, 'American airman who has volunteered to fight in China.' . . . The day was hot and soon our shirts were taken off. . . .
    "At last Hong Kong came in sight and we went down into Saukiwan district. There we went to a fish wholesalers. A crowd gathered outside the shop. They all wanted to see the 'fa kwai', 'foreign devils'. [Some of the smaller children had probably never seen a European before]. We were regally welcomed and taken upstairs where coffee, orangeade and marvellous Chinese dishes were pressed on us. We had four cups of delicious roasted coffee – so sweet. . . .
    "The fish cost MY360 a catty [1.3 lbs] – a fantastic price, but a week

ago it was MY900. We could only get 200 catties. . . . Six coolies pulled it back to camp. . . .

"Before going back to Stanley we walked along to look at the Taikoo Dockyard. . . . Normally it was difficult to drive here as people overflowed onto the road but today I only counted 19 persons over a distance of 200 yards. . . . The people we saw were walking skeletons . . . no happy smiles from these poor creatures. . . . The dockyard was a shambles – the airmen had done their job well. The Chinese say nearly 10,000 people were killed in four raids. The Americans cannot be blamed as they used to come for the docks after they had closed down for the night. On one occasion they [the workers] were kept on for half an hour's overtime and were just leaving when the siren went. The Japanese shut the gates on them so thousands were killed as they were unable to escape. . . .

"Arrived back at 5.30 pm. We had walked about 16 miles – not a bad effort after 3½ years of rotten food!"

In Stanley we were embarrassed and overwhelmed by the generosity of our visitors, mostly Chinese Police and interpreters. The great majority could not afford to give anything and we tried tactfully to decline if we could, or take the minimum possible without causing offence. A good example was Geoffrey's personal clerk/interpreter whose job during the occupation was hawking cigarettes. He was painfully thin but insisted on giving us a carton of cigarettes and a tiny piece of salt pork. He had seven children, one of whom had died of malnutrition. In his case we were able to return his kindness with 18lbs of rice and plenty of biscuits to take home.

The last two weeks of August were a peculiar sort of in-between period. The Japanese had surrendered, we had won the war and yet until Allied troops actually landed the Japanese retained their arms and were still nominally responsible for law and order. We continued to live in the camp and, although food was far more plentiful and nutritious, we still followed by force of habit the routine of internees.

It was not until 30 August that Rear-Admiral Harcourt arrived to accept the formal capitulation of the enemy in Hong Kong. During the period of waiting there was speculation that the Americans were opposed to the British taking over again as a colonial power. They were said to favour handing the Colony back to China. Britain was determined this should not happen.

As early as 13 August, in anticipation of a Japanese collapse, a message was received by Colonel Ride at BAAG headquarters for passing on to Gimson in Stanley. It said, in part, that if the Japanese surrendered without a fight:

"[The] policy of HMG is to restore British sovereignty and administration immediately. . . . It is open to you to assume administration of the Government under the power which you have in absence of Governor under existing letters patent."[5]

This message had to be delivered by hand.

This tricky task was undertaken by the BAAG agent in Macau, Y. C. Leung whose codename was "Phoenix". He delivered the note personally to Gimson in Stanley on 23 August.[6] Three days later Gimson moved out of the camp to take up office in the former French Mission building in town.

The highlights of the last few days in Stanley are best described by the final entries in my diary.

"24 August, 1945.
    I am suffering from beriberi. My legs have swollen and if I press the skin around my ankles the impression remains behind. This is one of the symptoms. Of all the damn silly times to get this nutritional complaint it is now when I have more to eat. . . . My face has also swollen up and I have sores in my mouth. A few days' good eating will soon put me right. . . . They [my eyes] are bad due to lack of proper food and vitamin deficiency.

"25 August, 1945.
    [We have heard that] about 21 August there was supposed to be the big Allied attack on Hong Kong. There is now little doubt that few of us would have survived it. The island was going to be pounded for nine days before the landings. We now know that the Japanese intended to set fire to the whole town and also kill all the Europeans."

Looking back, I am by no means sure that this was true, but it illustrates the type of rumours that were circulating. We had no reason to disbelieve it at the time; in fact it seemed all too credible. The Japanese were quite capable of it. On the 29th we received an air drop of medical supplies and foodstuffs at Stanley.

"29 August, 1945.

On the third run of the plane a package came out and a parachute opened. Everybody was waving, shouting and dancing up and down. There was a great rush to Block 13 to open it. It contained medical supplies. . . . People started to fight over the parachute. . . . 15 parachutes came down, one on the roof of Block 13 and one on Block 16. . . . There were 40 cases. . . .

"30 August, 1945.

The Navy is here. Two aircraft carriers, one battleship, two cruisers, six destroyers, a submarine depot ship, eight submarines, one hospital ship, seven Australian mine-sweepers and a host of transports. We saw them steaming in. All day long planes flew over our camp. . . . Rear-Admiral Harcourt attended the flag-raising ceremony at which all the Allied flags were raised. The Last Post was sounded. It was a moving ceremony. . . . There is so much to write about, but I must stop."

Then came the very last entry in my diary, "We are all celebrating!" In spite of everything I had kept it going for forty-two months.

The next day I was instructed to go to the town with a party of Police to take over Western Police Station (No. 7) and await the arrival of a naval landing force. Similar orders were given to the other police officers. We drove to town in a lorry, and as we pulled up outside the station I did an extremely stupid thing, that could easily have cost me my life at the very moment of victory. There was an armed Japanese sentry at the entrance. Foolishly, and without thinking, I jumped down first and leapt on the startled Japanese sentry, snatching his rifle from his hands. He was completely taken by surprise, but I have often reflected that had he been quicker and shot or bayoneted me it would have been my fault.

Inside was a Japanese colonel who demanded on what authority I was taking over. I had none. It was almost exactly three years and eight months since I had myself surrendered my station to a Japanese colonel. I had a strange feeling of *déja vu*. I was back in my old job. The wheel of fortune had completed an eventful turn.

EPILOGUE

"The Japanese government regrets and sincerely apoligizes for the unbearable pain that these women, regardless of their nationalities, suffered while being forced to work as so-called comfort women. We will seriously consider how to express our views."
Daily Mail, 5 August, 1993.

Almost fifty years on and Japan finally acknowledges one of the appalling atrocities committed by her troops in the name of the Emperor. A few weeks later, at the time of writing these lines, the British press announced that Prime Minister John Major is to take up the issue of financial compensation for the British survivors. Japan's new Prime Minister Morihiro Hosakawa has publicly apologized for all those Service personnel and civilians who died or suffered from torture, execution, inhuman conditions and starvation in countless camps throughout Japanese occupied Asia. Major is expected to ask for £12,000 for each survivor; Hosakawa is expected to refuse payment. This, I am sure, has only been done for commercial reasons.

The Germans have long since confessed to the horrendous crimes perpetrated in the name of Hitler, but the Japanese have, until now, seemingly found it too shameful publicly to accept what their servicemen did with the full authority of the Emperor. Hitler would assuredly have been tried and hanged had he not shot himself, but Hirohito, who failed to commit hara kiri, was never even arrested. Instead he was allowed to continue to rule, albeit stripped of much of his power.

When I arrived in England in December, 1945, after volunteering to stay in Hong Kong for a short while to help in the policing of the Colony, I was met by an official from the Colonial Office. He was there to vouch for me as I had no passport. I had arrived at Portsmouth after a memorable and enjoyable journey on HMS *Odzani*, a river class frigate. The customs officers decently refused to look at my lists of goods to declare – a few items bought on the way – and took me ashore in the customs launch. There was no such thing as a free railway voucher to my home town. There I nearly walked past my brother Peter who was waiting for me at the station. He was in uniform, an officer in the Royal Tank Regiment and well over six foot. I had not seen him, my mother or my sister Daphne for six years. At the local rationing office I was given a few dockets to enable me to buy some sheets and pillow slips and towels which were then on ration. I was also given a few extra food ration tickets above my monthly quota which were meant to make up for being on a starvation diet for nearly four years. The young girl behind the counter looked very embarrassed and slipped me some more. Fortunately, I had managed to eat well before my arrival in England. Then I received my back salary minus about £100 kept for contingencies. What they were was never explained to me. Years later I was paid a small sum of money, somewhere around £100, from the Far Eastern Chattel Scheme. This was paid only on application. It was meant to be compensation for the personal effects which I had lost.

When Emperor Hirohito died in 1989, HRH the Duke of Edinburgh represented HM the Queen at the funeral despite protests from the Far East Prisoners-of-War and Internees Associations. It was disillusioning. Some lesser person could have been sent. More thought had been given to the feelings of the Japanese Royal family and people than to we, the British. The advisers had probably been at school when the war in the Pacific ended. If it was for the sake of business then nothing has been gained. The Japanese must have had a quiet laugh. At least some "face" has been regained.

With some notable exceptions many Japanese guilty of war crimes either disappeared or were given relatively light sentences after conviction. Stanley jail was used to accommodate the Japanese, Formosans and others suspected of serious offences. Among them was the brutal Indian head warder, Rehimat Khan (Redbeard). In total almost 300 were imprisoned initially, including some brought from Formosa and Hainan Island. Their guards were now British troops – a commando unit. The prison régime was relaxed in comparison to the previous four years. There were few complaints when the Japanese in the hospital had to lie at attention and salute when a British soldier entered, or were compelled to walk on the left up and down the corridors and paths. At 'lights out' a commando NCO had them all standing in their cells while he led them in the singing of 'There'll always be an England'. Now, desperately eager to please, these little men did their utmost to raise the roof. The sergeant found it funny – but then he was British.

The first war crimes trials in Hong Kong started in March, 1946. They were military courts. Among those I know to have been hanged in Stanley prison was the sadistic interpreter Inouye Kanoa ('Shat in Pants') who had made Watanabe's life such a misery. He was tried twice, once as a Japanese and then again for treason as a Canadian (the country of his birth). As he mounted the gallows in August, 1947, he had the dubious honour of having had two death sentences.

Colonel Noma, and his successor Colonel Kanagawa, of the Gendarmarie were both hanged. Colonel Tokunaga, the infamous 'Fat Pig', who had been responsible for all the camps in the Colony, escaped the fate he deserved. He was sentenced to death, but this was commuted to life imprisonment. Major Saito, the medical officer who liked carrying a pistol in hospital, and who had sacked Watanabe, was found guilty of inhuman treatment of POWs, causing death to some and needless suffering to many. His sentence of death by hanging was reduced to twenty years' imprisonment.

Major-General Tanaka, the officer whose 229th Regiment had fought for Stanley and whose soldiers had committed so many atrocities, including those at St Stephen's College, escaped with a twenty year sentence. His fellow regimental commander, Shoji (then also a major-general), whose initiative had thrown the Royal Scots out of the linchpin of the Gindrinkers Line, the Shingmun Redoubt, was acquitted outright.

These trials continued for two years. A total of 48 separate cases were heard involving 129 Japanese, many arraigned on the blanket charge of 'violation of the laws and usages of war' – not that Japan had ratified the Geneva Convention anyway. It was a terrible tale of torture, execution and privation. The official figures for Chinese imprisonment by the Japanese was 1816, of whom 181 had been executed. Of those charged with these crimes 21 were sentenced to death, 14 acquitted, nine had the charges dropped and the remainder were imprisoned.

Some 54 European, Indian, Eurasian and Chinese were found guilty of collaboration. Of these five were hanged. It was observed at the time that many escaped punishment, and that of those charged virtually none were prominent citizens. There were complaints that eminent Chinese who had been seen at official Japanese functions were now at similar British gatherings, although that did not necessarily make them guilty of anything.

Our mess members all successfullly resumed our careers after the war, all eventually reached high rank, but only Geoffrey, Henry and I are alive at the time of writing (October, 1993). Geoffrey Wilson, who had really run the mess all those years, went on to be commissioner in Sarawak. He later became commissioner in Tanganyika (now Tanzania). He retired to Portugal where, he tells me, he still practices yoga that he first learnt in Stanley.

Henry Heath, whom I had first met as a small boy in Antigua, eventually became commissioner in Hong Kong. He now lives in Seaford on the south coast of England.

Lance Searle, who joined the Colonial Police after leaving Cambridge, where he was a boxing blue and captained the team, was an extremely brave man. He transferred to the Malayan Police, where he became well known for his Special Branch work against the communist terrorists during the Emergency there. He was one of the first officers successfully to use surrendered terrorists to return to the jungle to persuade other terrorists to surrender. Sad to relate he apparently had a mental aberration and walked into an ambush he had set with Gurkha troops. At the time it was dark and they shot and wounded him. He died later from his wounds.

Colin Luscombe was also shot and killed, but in very different circumstances. He was clever and extremely ambitious, and would surely have ended up as commissioner had he lived. By 1949 he was already the assistant commissioner in charge of Kowloon when he went forward to rescue one of his junior officers whom he thought had been wounded by an armed robber in a gun battle. Colin himself was then shot and killed by the robber and Chief Inspector Clark, who was with him, wounded.

Brian Fay, who was a mess member, although not an original one, transferred to the Singapore Police and was subsequently pensioned off at independence. In Britain he ran a cleaning service for a while and had several security jobs before moving to Spain as a tennis coach. He was a very good tennis player. There he choked to death on a fish bone after lunch at his club.

Fifty years is a long time. As these words are written it is almost precisely fifty years ago to the day that those 32 men and one woman met their awful fate under Hirano's sword. It was such a barbaric tragedy. I particularly remember the first trio to die as I knew them personally. First Ansari, the Indian officer whose calm courage, quiet words of encouragement and magnificent example in the face of a dreadful death won him the posthumous George Cross; next Scott, the acting deputy commissioner and my old room mate kneeling down silently and with dignity to meet his maker; then Fraser, to whose fortitude under torture I, and probably many others, owe our lives and freedom. No memorial has ever been erected where they and the others fell. They should not be forgotten.

NOTES

Prologue

1. Tim Carew, *The Fall of Hong Kong*, Anthony Blond Ltd., London, 1960.
2. Hanlon eventually joined up with another party under a Major Young at Deep Water Bay. They found a leaky motor boat and headed for Stanley, but, when they realized that it had fallen, turned towards Lamma Island. On 28 December they crossed to the mainland only to be spotted and captured.
3. At least three other swimmers made it to Chung Hom Kok but were quickly taken prisoner. One, Private Canivet of the Royal Canadian Ordnance Corps, survived being shot four times while a captive. The Japanese left the four of them for dead. Canivet, however, was alive and made it to the Bowen Road Military Hospital.
4. Oliver Lindsay, *The Lasting Honour*, Sphere Books Ltd., London, 1978, p. 153.
5. Ibid p. 153.
6. Lord Russell of Liverpool, *The Knights of Bushido*, Cassell and Co. Ltd., London, 1958, p. 98.

Chapter One

1. Cantonese is one of many Chinese dialects and is language spoken in Hong Kong and Kwangtung Province. It is not to be confused with Mandarin which originated around Peking and northern China, which is the official language of China.
2. Pennefather-Evans survived captivity in Stanley, although as we shall see he came within a whisker of being executed. He was recalled from semi-retirement in 1948 to become commissioner in Singapore, before finally retiring to South Africa.
3. A gazetted officer was one whose appointment had been "gazetted" or

published in the *London Gazette*. Gazetted officers in the Colonial Police were equated with commissioned officers in the Armed Services.

4. With the Japanese attack Z-Force became operational as a small part of Special Operations Executive (SOE). It went into action in the New Territories and a number of its officers won the Military Cross. Most escaped into China and joined the British Army Aid Group (BAAG).

Chapter Two

1. Gindrinkers Bay has now been filled with more substantial materials than empty bottles and is in use as a container terminal.
2. I later heard that Jones was often to be seen in Shamshuipo POW camp wearing a fur coat belonging to a woman who was interned with us at Stanley. I have no idea how he acquired it.
3. *The Lasting Honour*, p. 48.
4. Ibid p. 48.
5. Ibid p. 50.
6. Woodburn Kirby, *The War Against Japan*, HMSO, London, 1957 p. 122.
7. Taken from Shaftain's unpublished written account.
8. I met S. K. Yee again after the war, by which time he had been promoted general. Later he rose to a prominent position in banking and insurance in Hong Kong.
9. Oliver Lindsay, *At the Going Down of the Sun*, Hamish Hamilton, London, 1981, p. 9.
10. Statement 28/2/46. File 593(D5), National Defence HQ, Directorate of History, Ottawa, Canada.

Chapter Three

1. Li Shu Fan, *Hong Kong Surgeon*, New York, 1964 p. 103.
2. *Daily Telegraph*, 9 December, 1992.
3. The Japanese had collected all their dead and cremated them. The ashes were taken out of the crematorium with long, steel chopsticks and placed in the small white boxes that the soldiers carried on the parade. They were later sent to Japan. No Allied dead or wounded were collected until the Japanese dead had been cremated.

Chapter Four

1. He was unaware that his mistress contrived to send food from Tokunaga's stocks to her friends inside the POW camps.

Chapter Five

1. War crimes affidavit of Vincent Marcus Morrison dated 3 June, 1946. WO311/563 held at the PRO.

2. Ibid.

3. Wallace Kinlock is a colourful character who features several times in this story and a brief résumé of his career is of interest. He started out in the Scots Guards, before joining the Shanghai Municipal Police as a drill and musketry instructor in July, 1938. In 1939 he was on patrol with a section of police in Edinburgh Road in the Shanghai International Settlement when he spotted a large group of Japanese police which had no right to be there. Kinlock dismounted from his armoured car and told the Japanese to move off. As he returned to his vehicle he was shot in the back. He instinctively swung round and sprayed the Japanese with a long burst from his Tommy gun. Four Japanese were killed and five wounded. The Japanese admiral of their fleet offshore put a reward on his head, but after a short stay at the British Military Hospital, guarded by the East Surrey Regiment, he was smuggled out of Shanghai by the Police Special Branch.

   In Hong Kong he joined the Police and, in 1948, after his sojourn in Stanley, was awarded the CPM for gallantry in attacking an armed robber on Castle Peak. Later he was transferred to Malaya as an ASP where he served with considerable distinction during the Emergency, rising to superintendent and being awarded the Sultan of Johore's Diamond Jubilee Decoration for his work. His final post was that of the commander of the Gambian Police Field Force from 1958–66. He then retired to Scotland.

4. The moment one approached a Chinese for help was the most dangerous moment in any escape unless the contact had been arranged beforehand. To do so on the off chance as these escapers did was high risk, particularly near Lei Mun which was a hotbed of Japanese activity.

5. Morrison's affidavit dated 3 June, 1946. WO311/563.

6. Gwen Priestwood, *Through Japanese Barbed Wire*, British Publishers Guild, 1944, p. 55.

7. Ibid p. 59.

8. Ibid p. 63.

9. Ibid p. 72.

10. Ibid p. 76.

11. Ibid p. 77.

12. Edwin Ride, *British Army Aid Group*, Hong Kong University Press, 1981, p. 134.

13. Ibid p. 136.

Chapter Six

1. G. B. Endacott and A. Berick, *Hong Kong Eclipse*, Hong Kong Oxford University Press, p. 204–205.

Chapter Seven

1. Selwyn-Clarke, *Footprints*, Sino-American Publishing Co., Hong Kong, 1975, p. 85. Khorkel survived and was employed in the Health Department after the war.
2. Maurice Collis, *Wayfoong*, Faber and Faber, London, 1965.
3. Howard Tau was still up to his tricks as a Japanese stooge in 1945. Sergeant Roberts records in his later testimony that Tau ended up in prison.
4. *Footprints*, p. 84.
5. Statement of William J. Anderson in Hong Kong dated October, 1945. WO325/42 held at the PRO.
6. Ibid.
7. Ibid.
8. Ibid.
9. Ibid.
10. Ibid.

Chapter Eight

1. Haddock, like all of these prisoners, came in for some horrific tortures, as a result of which he was blinded. He could be seen stumbling around the exercise yard, groping and feeling his way, with the guards tripping him up with their feet or sticks and laughing at his discomfiture. As the months passed what neither guards nor prisoners knew was that his sight had gradually, almost miraculously, returned. He, however, now feigned blindness with the consummate skill of an actor. There is every reason to suppose that he avoided execution in this way, as the Japanese felt he was suffering more by being allowed to live. It must have been an incredible shock when his pretence was ultimately revealed after the final surrender.
2. *British Army Aid Group*, p. 161.
3. W. J. Anderson.
4. Ibid, p. 13.
5. Morrison's affidavit.
6. W. J. Anderson, p. 19.
7. Ibid, p. 19.

8. Statement by Police Sergeant Frank Roberts dated 14 November, 1945, p. 3. WO311/561 held at the PRO.

9. Anderson, p. 24.

10. Ibid p. 25.

11. Ibid p. 30.

12. Ibid p. 29.

13. Ibid p. 30.

14. It is appropriate to record that three of the military prisoners were executed. Their fate is recorded as follows in the statement of Major C. R. Boxer, dated 19 August, 1946:

> "Colonel Newnham, Flight-Lieutenant Gray and Captain Douglas Ford were taken from the prison on the afternoon of December 18th, 1943, and shot by a firing party provided by an unidentified unit of the Japanese garrison, the place of execution being Shek-ko beach, Hong Kong island, and where they were buried and where I personally identified the graves at the end of August, 1945. Information as to the execution was given me by Indian warders who were eye witnesses thereof, and, also, by some Japanese convicts . . . who had obtained this information from members of the firing party and who stated that three shots were taken to kill Colonel Newnham, although the other two were killed by the first rounds fired. Their clothes and effects in the jail were distributed among other British military prisoners. Both Colonel Newnham and Captain Ford expressed to me their hope that their bodies would be exhumed and taken to Britain for reburial after the war was over. Although they were not allowed to communicate with me, they did manage to whisper this to me during a brief moment when allowed out of their cells one morning shortly before execution."

WO311/561 held at the PRO. Each was posthumously awarded the George Cross.

Chapter Ten

1. *The Knights of Bushido*, p. 106.

2. Interestingly, Leo Cooper, the publisher of this book had an uncle on the *Lisbon Maru*. His name was Edmund Jupp who had worked for the HKSB and, as a member of the Hong Kong Volunteers, was involved in the defence of the Repulse Bay Hotel. He was initially imprisoned at Stanley. When the *Lisbon Maru* went down he swam to a nearby island, where he was hidden by the Chinese for two months before being recaptured and sent to Kobi. It is assumed he died there as he was never heard of again. A daughter of his now lives in London.

3. Liam Nolan, *Small Man of Nanataki*, London, 1966, p. viii.

4. Ibid p. 103.

5. Ibid p. 104.
6. Ibid p. 125.
7. Ibid p. 138.
8. Ibid p. 138.

Chapter Eleven

1. *The Knights of Bushido*, p. 235.
2. Ibid, p. 236.
3. Ibid, p. 237.
4. John Luff, *The Hidden Years*, South China Morning Post Ltd., 1967, p. 222.
5. *British Army Aid Group*, p. 286.
6. Y. C. Leung was awarded the King's Medal for Courage in the Cause of Freedom in 1946. The citation states that it was given "for services to the escape and intelligence organisation, Hong Kong". One of his successful schemes included the deliberate flooding of bank vaults in Macau where he knew vital radio valves had been stored. It was his agents who were called to pump out the water, in the course of which they secured the valves. Tragically, he was killed in a fall from the balcony of the Repulse Bay Hotel. It was a strange way to die; the mystery deepened when his son met his death in precisely the same way some years afterwards.

Bibliography

Carew, Tim, *The Fall of Hong Kong*, Anthony Blond Ltd., London, 1960.

Collis, Maurice, *Wayfoong*, Faber and Faber, London, 1965.

Drage, Charles, *Servants of the Dragon Throne*.

Drage, Charles, *Two-Gun Cohen*, Jonathan Cape, London, 1954.

Endacott, G. B. and Berick, A., *Hong Kong Eclipse*, Hong Kong Oxford University Press.

Kemp, Lt-Cdr P. K., *The Middlesex Regiment*, Gale & Polden, Aldershot, 1956.

Lindsay, Oliver, *At the Going Down of the Sun*, Hamish Hamilton, London, 1981.

Lindsay, Oliver, *The Lasting Honour*, Hamish Hamilton, London, 1978.

Li Shu Fan, *Hong Kong Surgeon*, New York, 1964, p. 103.

Luff, John, *The Hidden Years*, South China Morning Post Ltd., Hong Kong, 1967.

Nolan, Liam, *Small Man of Nanataki*, London, 1966.

Priestwood, Gwen, *Through Japanese Barbed Wire*, The British Publishers Guild, London, 1944.

Ride, Edwin, *British Army Aid Group*, Hong Kong Oxford University Press, Oxford, 1981.

Russell, Lord, of Liverpool, *The Knights of Bushido*, Cassell & Co. Ltd., London, 1958.

Selwyn-Clarke, Sir Selwyn, *Footprints*, Sino-American Publishing Co., Hong Kong, 1975.

Stericker, John, *A Tear for the Dragon*, Arthur Barker Ltd., London, 1958.

INDEX